Working at Inglis

The Life and Death of a Canadian Factory

David Sobel and Susan Meurer

James Lorimer & Company, Publishers
Toronto, 1994

James Lorimer & Company Ltd. acknowledges with thanks the support of the Canada Council, the Ontario Arts Council and the Ontario Publishing Centre in the development of writing and publishing in Canada.

Every effort has been made to trace the ownership of all copyrighted illustrations reproduced in this book. We regret any errors and will be pleased to make any necessary corrections in future editions.

Cover photograph: Inglis History Project, David Smiley, photographer. The worker is Cliff Bent.

James Lorimer & Company Ltd., Publishers
35 Britain Street, Toronto M5A 1R7

Canadian Cataloguing in Publication Data
Meurer, Susan
Working at Inglis: The Life and Death of a Canadian Factory

Inglis Limited - Employees - History. 2. Electric household appliances industry - Ontario Toronto - Employees - History. 3. United Steelworkers of America. Local 2900 (Toronto, Ont.) - History. 4. Trade-unions - Electric household appliances industry - Ontario Toronto - History. I. Sobel, David (David Malcolm). II. Title.

HD8039.E542 C37 1994 331.7'68388'09713541
C94-930433-6

Printed and bound in Canada

Contents

This book is dedicated to the memory of Frank McCuaig and Mary Spratt

who made the union and the world of work at Inglis a little bit better.

Foreword

bour history is most frequently, and not inap-
opriately, presented in terms of significant
uggles, victories and defeats, the initiatives
d reactions of the workers' movement to the
es of history and the challenges of economic
wer. Much less frequently it is expressed in
ms of the lives of its grass roots institutions
d their members, the day-by-day activities and
ses, the events both grand and commonplace
ich comprise the reality of our movement and
ich, cumulatively, de-
mine its impact.

This magnificent sto-
of the trials and
umphs of Local 2900 of
e United Steelworkers
America presents exact-
that reality. It does so
h an eye for detail, with
ple use of resource ma-
ials, both written and
l, from those who were
re and with a profound
derstanding of what it
s meant to be a worker
the industrial belt of
uthern Ontario during
e middle and later
cades of this century.

I was privileged, briefly, early in the
st–World War II period, to be a worker at In-
s and from then on, for the most part of my
in the Steelworkers, to have continued to be
ues-paying member of the local union. I had
ight out John Inglis and Local 2900 because I
nted to become involved in the labour move-
nt, to become a member of the Steelworkers
t all possible, and John Inglis was one of the
re likely places at which employment could
found.

Two experiences stand out from my very
t days at Inglis: the first was the hiring process
lf; the second was being sworn into member-
p at my first local union meeting.

What was very different about being hired
John Inglis from most establishments in 1947
s that the last person you saw, or, more accu-
ely, the first person you saw after you were
mally hired and on your way to work, was the

Local Union President, Jock Brodie. Jock interviewed each new employee in a little office he
had at the plant. He told you about the Union,
he presented you with a copy of the contract and
described a few key provisions, and then he
asked you to sign a dues check-off card.

This process was a substitute for not having
a closed union shop and, so far as I know, was
given up when, in the ensuing years, we negotiated such a provision. In recent times we
have established a modern
counterpart in many con-
tracts, usually identified as
an orientation program.
Some are quite elaborate,
with videos and overheads
and professional-looking
brochures, but I am not
sure they are any more effective than Jock's rather
focused efforts which had
a signed check-off card
and a new local union
member as the very specific objectives!

It was also expected
that the new employee
would not only sign the
check-off and an application for membership
card but would be present at the next general
membership meeting to be sworn in. Obviously,
that was a singularly important event for me,
which has not lessened in its significance over
the years.

Membership meetings were held at the
west end office of the Steelworkers, located in a
Methodist church on Shaw Street. Meetings were
quite well attended despite the fact that Jock's
brogue did not make him the easiest person to
understand. New members were called to the
front of the hall early in the agenda of every
meeting and sworn to be loyal to their fellow
workers and to the Union. I was most impressed!

Much that is happening in the current
economy is reminiscent of elements from that
postwar period. The John Inglis factory had
been a war plant and was in the process of conversion to peacetime products, a process of
much greater relative magnitude but not dissim-

ilar to what is now required by the substantial impact of the end of the cold war on today's North American economy. My job was on a line on which the final assembly of insulated glass water-heaters occurred. The number of jobs in the plant, while still substantial, was much reduced from the peak of wartime munitions production. Public concern was widespread about how the future of the economy might develop, with little expectation that economic growth would continue on the path which had been established during the war-induced recovery from the Great Depression.

The fact is, of course, that economic growth did continue for a generation and more for a variety of reasons, such as pent-up demand and vastly improved social legislation and wealth distribution by means of unemployment

insurance and workers' compensation a health care. Not the least important eleme however, both in distributing the wealth and improving purchasing power as well as achieving progressive social legislation, was t growth of the labour movement led by the ene gy, commitment, and example of pioneeri locals such as Local 2900.

Local unions are the bedrock upon whi the entire structure of the labour movement c pends for strength and support. One cannot re this book without being profoundly impress by the continuous vitality of this local union a the broad range of its activities.

More than any labour movement in t world, the North American model as develop in the United States and Canada, concentra with painstaking detail on day-by-day life in t plant, on the conditions of work and on t treatment which individual workers receive. T story of Local 2900 is replete with examples this aspect of the union's work. It's this whi impacts so directly on the lives of workers, th security, their right to live free from prejudi and discrimination, their hopes and opportu ties. These elements of the story alone make more than worth the telling, but the reach of I cal 2900 goes far beyond the lives of individual members, however compelling th struggles and accomplishments may be.

Local 2900's history is also the history the growth of our Union, of the occasional te sion, usually creative, between the rank and f base and the leadership imperatives of the ce tre; of strength and solidarity in times struggle; of the democracy of meetings, conf ences and elections, and of individual rights a group decisions, as a way of life; of political a tivism and the never-ending search for soc and economic justice.

If you are truly interested in knowing w working people and their labour movement a most fundamentally about, you will be richly warded by every page of this book.

Lynn Willia
former International Preside
United Steelworkers of Amer

Introduction

This book is about the life and death of a Toronto factory. It is about the people who made the products and lived many years of their lives inside the factory walls. It is about the complex weave of history, economics, culture, labour, industry, production, and ideology that represents 100 years and more of Inglis. Finally, it is about workers' history, that invisible contribution to the collective biography usually reserved for kings, millionaires, and generals.

In telling the Inglis story, we make no claim to completeness. This book presents only a small portion of what we discovered and learned. It is a history of one factory and its industrial work force only; we excluded other Inglis manufacturing facilities, all their office and technical staff, and their respective unions. Their story is worth telling, but it is a different story. We were interested in the continuity of production in one location during more than a century.

For 108 years, the John Inglis factory operated almost continuously on Strachan Avenue in downtown Toronto. Few plants in Canada ever manufactured the range of products that Inglis did. Few plants have seen as many generations of workers pass through the same factory gates or have played as important a role in equipping other industries as this factory did. It was one of the small number to have witnessed the changes that manufacturing underwent over the course of their existence. When the plant opened in Toronto in 1881, skilled metalworkers custom made steam engines, milling equipment, gear wheels, and other heavy metal parts. But when Inglis closed in 1989, the plant churned out just one product — washing machines.

Although this is the story of one plant, Inglis serves as a symbol for the rest of the Canadian economy. This company, like the country itself, emerged as a small but powerful player in the 1890s, full of potential and ideas. For a time it performed well, but by the 1960s it was weakening, a victim of mismanagement, growing foreign ownership, and too much short-term thinking. The plant began to be fitted into a global production strategy that was controlled increasingly by Whirlpool Corporation from the United States.

When the plant closed, "free trade" was blamed by those who mourned the factory's end. Yet this claim, we believe, is too simple an explanation for the closure. The agreement signed between the Canadian government and the United States in 1988 may have been the death knell for the Strachan Avenue factory, but the Inglis plant had been sick for a long time. Canada's manufacturing economy was weak long before 1988, and so we have tried to connect the events at this plant to the broader discussion of an economic policy that is decades old.

Public discussion of economic independence in the 1960s and 1970s was taking place while events on the shopfloor reflected what the economic nationalists were saying. We have tried to link Canadian economic policy to the lives of factory workers and to the decisions of their bosses, and we hope this book contributes to the long-standing discussion about the threat

This ad appeared in the Globe's *Christmas supplement of 1908.*

Inglis workers found their own way to personalize a sign on the side of one company building.

Once surrounded by other operations, the Inglis plant in 1989 stands alone in a neighbourhood empty of factory life.

that foreign ownership represents, not just Canada's survival, but to working-class empl ment in this country.

The factory's past also reflects broac social history, and so, by tracing the transforr tion of production on the shopfloor, we want open a window on other changes that to place both inside and outside the plant. T Strachan Avenue factory was intimately c nected to its immediate neighbourhood, a pla of vibrant working-class experience. Tl neighbourhood today presents a picture physical desolation.

When a plant like Inglis closes, more tl the means of production is lost. No matter h many new factories are subsequently built, a no matter how many new jobs are found, culture in the plant cannot be recreated. T wrecker's ball eventually destroys more than bricks; it wipes out the mortar as well. Work culture is the mortar between the bricks, material that cements workers together, a makes the hardness and roughness of daily w in a factory bearable. Such a loss is profou and irredeemable.

We make no claim to a neutral perspective. For almost two years, we observed production, roamed the cavernous factory, and spoke to many workers. As our work progressed, photographs and historical documents were shown to interested workers. Local union members responded with cartoons, drawings, names of interview subjects, and other suggestions. This sharing of materials and information continued as the book went to press. Our vision includes an ongoing process of living history, as former Inglis workers discover themselves and add to the body of knowledge. That's why we saw our efforts as a project and not just as a single volume. As writers, historians, and trade unionists, we established and maintained a relationship with both the factory and its workers. We never assigned to ourselves the role of objective observers.

Our interest in the Inglis story has roots in an earlier work collaboration. That study included interviews with industrial workers facing new technology in their factories. We met them in century-old buildings, operating out-of-date equipment. When we crisscrossed the once highly industrialized centre of Toronto along the Gardiner Expressway, the large Inglis billboard with its fleeting daily advice was often in view. As one after another of the companies we studied closed down, we realized that the recorded interviews were often all that remained of a huge factory. That loss disturbed us and prompted us to make sure that in the case of the Inglis workers, more substantial documentation would be left behind.

We had heard that Inglis could claim a long, colourful history for both working people and the greater national economy. Inglis was a quintessential Canadian company, its name known in Canada's kitchens and laundry rooms. Thousands of industrial establishments and public works owe their machinery and production structure to Inglis. Heavy engineering projects from boilers to engines to pumps were basic products at Inglis for decades. Throughout the country and in some overseas locations, Inglis machinery, equipment, and expertise beat at the heart of industrial operations.

We had also heard that the Inglis workers belonged to an activist local of the United Steelworkers of America. Inglis workers demonstrated their skill on the shopfloor, and their collective power, in the many union and worker organizations they formed. Some type of

union was present during nearly all of the company's years of operation. Talking about Inglis meant talking union and the associated shopfloor traditions and workplace folklore. USWA Local 2900, we were told, had fought some bitter strikes over the years and had been a presence at the Strachan Avenue plant since the 1940s. Moulders and machinists from the late nineteenth century would have understood the pride and independence of Local 2900. That pride, which we have experienced and admired ourselves, is perhaps the most enduring quality of the workplace.

Our method of exploring Canadian labour history has little tradition behind it. At the beginning of our project we were telling the story

Drawn by Inglis worker Jack Blake.

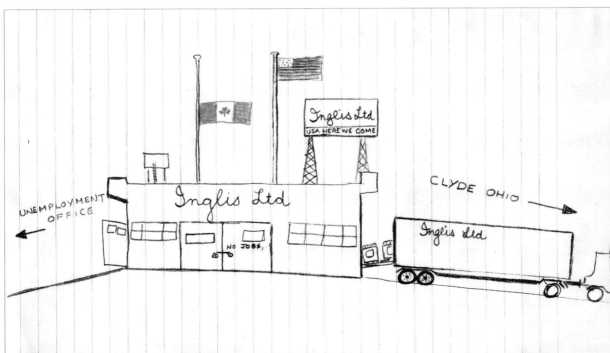

of a living, functioning workplace, which we were able to study directly. Our research methods were varied: we interviewed former and working Strachan Avenue employees and union officials; we listened to hundreds of stories, both on the line and at the in-plant union office; we systematically sought out former employees and were welcomed into their homes. Much of this book is based on the memories of those people. This study later became a project of cultural documentation and recovery, and a recognition of a way of life that centered around a union and the workplace.

To keep a visual record of the fascinating factory doings, we collaborated with a professional photographer who had extensive experience and interest in working-class and trade union issues. David Smiley took more than 1,000 photographs in his several visits to the plant, and his images document the entire production process. Peter MacCallum, another photographer, created further documentation of production. All of this in-plant research was possible because, at the urging of the union, the company allowed those of us involved in the project access to the plant on a regular basis. Security at the plant gate kept permanent visitor passes for two persistent writers.

Finally, archival research added to our knowledge of the Inglis factory — in particular, of its earliest history, which is no longer accessible through oral history. Considerable time and energy went into digging for this information. Our interest was hardly academic. We believe that early patterns of behaviour were maintained with tremendous force at this factory for over a century. Worker militancy, which began during the early life of the factory, reinforced a radical tradition and provided a remarkable continuity in plant culture. Together with the continuity in location and a diversity of production techniques, it allowed a remarkable workers' community to thrive for over a century.

We examined records in collections at the National Archives of Canada in Ottawa, the Archives of Ontario, and the City of Toronto Archives, among others. Former Inglis workers entrusted us with their documents, photographs, and keepsakes. The deep trust of the union was demonstrated when the records of Local 2900 were opened to us. Eventually, through the efforts of this project, local government officials, and the union, some of the Inglis company

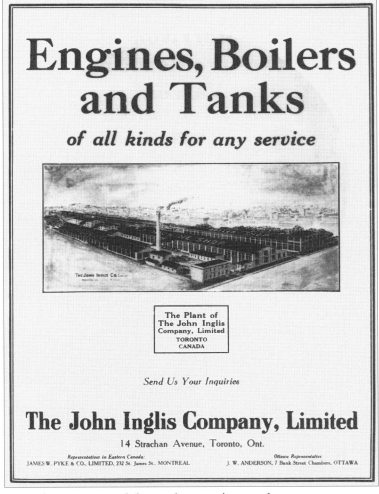

Engines, Boilers and Tanks

of all kinds for any service

The Plant of
The John Inglis
Company, Limited
TORONTO
CANADA

Send Us Your Inquiries

The John Inglis Company, Limited

14 Strachan Avenue, Toronto, Ont.

Representatives in Eastern Canada:
JAMES W. PYKE & CO., LIMITED, 232 St. James St., MONTREAL

Ottawa Representative
J. W. ANDERSON, 7 Bank Street Chambers, OTTAWA

records were saved from destruction and are now deposited with the City of Toronto Archives. But much was destroyed over the years, some of it even after we came on the scene.

Three groups of records form the basis of this book. The oral histories we collected are especially precious; they are deposited in the City of Toronto Archives in the awareness that few respect the kind of oral tradition that was once so alive on the shopfloor of Inglis. The union records and the company records were also utilized and compared. Out of this complex triangle of stories and events, we attempt to fill in the picture of what may have been Canada's most important factory.

This book, then, is a call for action to those interested in the past. We must recognize that social and economic change is contributing to the destruction of the very sources that will help us understand the past. Labour historians, in particular, cannot wait for collections to be de-

Berto Blaskowic, Art Cormier, and Ed Kalyshov shortly before the plant closed.

posited into archives. Both trained historians and workers with an interest in the past must become activists and save these sources.

Labour history is not a new field of study in Canada. The past two decades have witnessed a virtual explosion of knowledge with the release of new and exciting studies. Few labour histories, however, focus on one factory and concentrate on production itself. This study reaches beyond the physical structure of the buildings and presents a living culture, a working community. The character of a local union, the factory folklore, the personalities of its members and the values they shared — all of this is endangered in our postindustrial economy. We feel connected in this respect to the "Dig Where You Stand" movement in many parts of Europe. Sven Lindqvist, a Swedish historian, is responsible for the formation of hundreds of grass roots history clubs that enable workers to appreciate and value the link between their present and past.

In writing the history of Inglis, we wanted workers to speak for themselves whenever possible. While we never added to any oral history, we did from time to time rearrange and edit for better understanding. We wanted to avoid creating paper cut-out figures of workers as victims of economic conditions and forever on strike. In reality, the workers and the union exercised control over the plant as much as management did. We also wanted to show that much of what happened at the level of the union local was independent from, even contradictory to, its broader union affiliation, the United Steelworkers of America. Without the rich sources of workplace, labour, and personal records, we could never have painted the full picture in which labour disputes play a less significant role than people think. In this respect we see our work as part of a greater popular history movement. We hope this book moves more workers to do historical research. The workers themselves determined much of the content and form of this book. Their memories are equally valid historical sources, though they are rarely found in books, libraries, or archives.

We also hope that this book will point labour history in a new direction by speaking to an audience rarely considered in history writing. We believe working people have an interest in the past, both as readers and subjects. We fervently believe that academic and popular history meet somewhere and hope that such an encounter takes place on these pages. References are included for those readers who wish to pursue the original source material. These notes are found at the back of the book, where they may also be ignored.

By 1989, the Strachan Avenue Inglis factory had become a relic. During its closure, the media portrayed the plant as antiquated, obsolete, and unprofitable. Our aim was to add depth and contours to such a flat image. Making this "intelligent scrapbook" of factory life was both a challenge and a pleasure for us. In doing so, we had the privilege of getting to know something that is now gone. We hope this book does justice to the memories of all those who worked at Inglis.

We wish to acknowledge the help and support of many people and organizations. Our list

Bev Brown (second from left), vice-president of USWA Local 2900, and Mike Hersh (second from right), president, talk to authors Susan Meurer and David Sobel on the day the plant closure was announced.

is considerable because this book took five years to complete, and because we encountered so much generosity along the way. From the past to the present of the project's history: Ken Signoretti, who opened the door; Leo Gerard, who trusted two unknown but enthusiastic writers; Michael Lewis, who never wavered and always returned phone calls; Harry Hynds and USWA staff at District 6; staff at the Toronto Area Council and the National Office.

We benefited from the historical and archival expertise of many along the way: Karen Teeple, who always found a way to assist us and was a good friend throughout; Craig Heron, whose knowledge guided us and who bravely made his way through an early version of the book.

As well, many people in many organizations helped: staff at the City of Toronto Archives; staff at the National Archives of Canada, especially Larry McNally; and staff at the Archives of Ontario. Research assistance was provided by Helen Harrison, Gene Long, Luc Laporte, Mark Rosenfeld, and Rob Kristofferson. Greg Kealey generously shared his newspaper files with us. Technical help came from various transcribers, and external readers; Leon Kaplan, Vince Pietropaolo and David Hartman assisted us with illustrations and graphics; Marian Hebb, whose legal advice and knowledge of publishing in Canada helped put this book in print.

We were fortunate to receive financial support from: United Steelworkers of America, International, District 6, and Toronto Area Council; USWA Local 2900; Ontario Federation of Labour; City of Toronto; Metro Toronto; Ontario Ministry of Culture, Tourism and Recreation; Ontario Heritage Foundation; Ontario Arts Council; and Labour Canada.

Finally, thanks to members of Local 2900, who treated us like family.

Chapter One
From Craft to Corporation

Nearly a century after his death, the name of one man, factory owner John Inglis, burns brightly on a sign that thousands in Toronto read daily. The thousands who have toiled for the company over its years remain nameless. Learning the early history of Inglis meant discovering more about the many workers who had come and gone through the Strachan Avenue factory gates. This research was a political act as much as it was part of learning labour's long history at this one plant. We wanted to discover the deep roots of worker militancy at this factory to learn more about what those early Inglis workers did and thought.

The history of Inglis, prior to World War II when the USWA came to organize the plant, had been all but forgotten. As we recovered the workers' history, our understanding of the factory and union tradition deepened. Some details remained hidden in the factory's foundations, but the ideas and attitudes that had persisted for over a century were alive, even at the end.

The Early Years

The founder of the Strachan Avenue factory, John Inglis, was a metalworker, a skilled patternmaker, and a travelling metal craftsman before he opened his own shop in Guelph in

In the summer of 1859, John Inglis moved to Guelph, into an existing factory known as the Wellington Foundry. He and two other partners, Thomas Mair and Francis Evatt, leased water rights on the Speed River for their two-storey shop which employed about 25 workers. By 1868, the original partners had left the business and Daniel Hunter became the junior partner in the firm Inglis & Hunter. The Guelph Herald *of 22 May 1878 reported that $1,600 a month was paid in wages by the company.*

*Portrait of
Daniel Hunter*

*Portrait of
John Inglis*

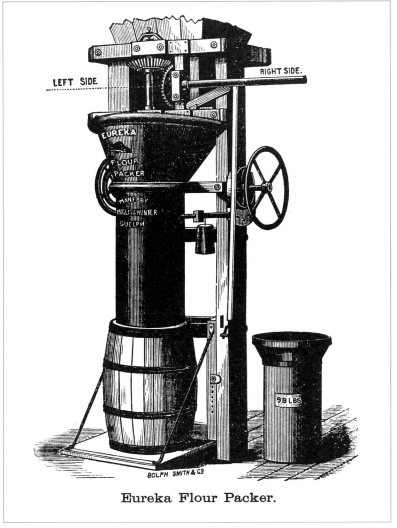

Eureka Flour Packer.

Above right: This Eureka flour packer was featured on page 55 in Inglis & Hunter's 1881 catalogue of patterns, also the year the company moved from Guelph to Toronto. Other products included pulleys, fly wheels, steam engines, water wheels, and mills — the basic technology of Canada's industrial revolution.

1859. Most cities in the nineteenth century were involved in a cut-throat game of self-promotion and salesmanship. Railway development had by-passed the town of Guelph. John Inglis's company, then known as Inglis & Hunter, was located on the Speed River, formerly a major attraction for both transport and power generation. By the 1860s, the river had become too slow and shallow for further industrial use. With the conversion to steam power in 1864, John Inglis and his partner Daniel Hunter had shifted the company away from complete dependence on the river.

Originally the firm served rural customers, like country millers and village shops, throughout Wellington County. But by the 1870s Inglis & Hunter enjoyed a strong reputation for quality that extended beyond the local area. Engines and mill machinery were shipped "from Quebec to Sarnia." The management of the firm decided therefore to move and take advantage of the changing nature of business. The increasing concentration of population and economic activity in cities like Toronto, Hamilton, and Montreal was transforming the young country. Industrial capitalism was being built in Canada, and the Inglis company was on the ground floor.

In its early days the shop produced just about anything that had a manufacturing application. Steam engines and boilers were its speciality, but the firm produced a range of standard metal products such as chains, grates for windows, manhole covers, iron plates, replacement parts, and doors and covers required for forging equipment.

THE LADIES WHO PRESENTED THE BANNER.

| Miss McDonald. | Mrs. T. A. White. | Mrs. A. Farquhar. | Miss M. Adamson. |
Mrs. Wm. Hill. Mrs. A. W. Holmes. Mrs. E. Parker. Mrs. H. Bedell. Mrs. W. Singer. Miss Quinn.
Mrs. C. A. Crawford. Mrs. S. W. Graham. Mrs. W. Boland.

Lodge 235 of the International Association of Machinists represented metal workers in many early Toronto factories. These women, who were not members, supported the union struggle and presented the banner shown.

In 1881 the company moved from Guelph. Having outgrown its premises and the town of Guelph itself, it located in Toronto, a city with a rapidly growing manufacturing sector. Toronto's opportunities for the Inglis shop were evident even before it moved. Among the company's major contracts in 1879 were the manufacture of a large engine for the *Toronto Mail*'s newspaper printing plant and of four large boilers for the Toronto Reformatory.

The size of the Inglis & Hunter factory increased dramatically within a year of its opening in Toronto. Eighty men were employed by 1882, a number roughly double the size of the Guelph operation. The value of goods produced increased to $100,000 — five times the industrial output of the Guelph enter-

prise in the 1870s. The Toronto factory was not only much busier, taking advantage of the larger Toronto market, but machines were used more extensively and intensively than in the past. Well connected to railway lines, Inglis assured prompt and efficient delivery to its customers. The new factory was part of the growing age of mechanization that had swept Toronto.

In the fall of 1881 the debate within Canada with the United States over free trade, then called "Reciprocity," continued to interest the public and to affect companies like Inglis. The three-year-old, tariff-based industrial strategy had been a central plank of Conservative John A. Macdonald's election campaign in 1878. The policy sought to protect and nurture Canadian

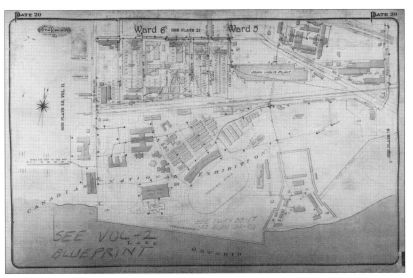

This plate from Goad's Fire Atlas *of 1912 shows the location of the Inglis factory in Toronto's west end.*

The Factory's Neighbourhood

The city's west end, the Inglis neighbourhood, was the site of an unprecedented boom. The Massey Manufacturing Company, the largest agricultural implement company in the country, employed about 350 workers and a few years earlier had located just to the north of the Inglis site, on King Street. The Toronto Wheel and Wagon Works had recently opened on a property adjoining the Inglis & Hunter shop and employed about forty men. The Toronto Silver Plate Company, the first factory of its kind in Canada, had also recently opened nearby. The area became a solid working-class district, a good place to find industrial jobs, affordable housing and food — and to organize unions.

The Iron Moulders' International Union (IMIU) was especially active in the area. Its members' confidence and power were evident at a large union meeting at Dufferin Hall in October 1881. Just months after the Inglis company arrived in Toronto, the moulders discussed the Massey Company, which did not recognize their union. It was decided "to withdraw the seven union men from their employ and put them to work elsewhere."

Such decisions were increasingly typical of relations between workers and their bosses. The following year the Great Western Railway locked out its moulders. The old bonds between employers like the Inglis family and the skilled men in their factory slowly transformed into a more rigid and increasingly hostile relationship. In 1883, foundries in Hamilton and Toronto cut wages by 20 percent in response to a recession. Those at the Inglis shop foundry may also have found less money in their pay packets.

When it first arrived in Toronto, the Inglis company operated out of the Canada Car Foundry. By 1885 that structure was torn down, and the factory that would come to operate for over a century began to take shape. The new grounds included three one-storey buildings, only one of which was brick. A small stable, sixteen by twenty feet in size, housed the Inglis wagons and horses that delivered the products. For the first two decades, the offices were housed in the main production building, which was almost 400 feet long. The factory operated its own forge, located in the centre of the complex. A gate with a small guard house, which fronted on Strachan Avenue, appeared sometime in the 1890s. It kept people from wandering into the factory unannounced and made it diffi-

industry by creating protective tariffs so that American and British goods were more expensive than domestically made products. Contemporaries commented on the impact this policy had on Inglis even before it had moved to Toronto. One reporter remarked indirectly that the Canadian-made gears from the Inglis shop were "more satisfactory in every way" than those from New York, which "were poorly made and almost useless."

Toronto's industrial base flourished under this protection, and manufacturing became one of the fastest growing sectors of the economy. The national policy indirectly helped the Inglis & Hunter shop grow quickly. It not only enjoyed tariff protection, but the burgeoning number of new foreign factories locating over the tariff wall in Canada were ordering Inglis products, because such heavy and cumbersome machines defied easy and inexpensive transport.

Toronto's press made much of the city's industrial expansion, which was a source of pride. The growth of industry was an exciting development, transforming the landscape and the city's people. In 1878, just footsteps from the future location of Inglis, industrial products were displayed to the public at the Toronto Industrial Exhibition. This small industrial fair would later become the Canadian National Exhibition. The transformation of the city by manufacturing, as showcased at the industrial fair, was particularly noticeable in the western district where Inglis & Hunter would locate.

cult for workers to leave unnoticed. The structures were immense by nineteenth-century standards. The power of industry was increasingly evident by the size of its activity, dwarfing everything in the neighbourhood but the churches.

Once erected, the Strachan Avenue factory buildings themselves changed little in the 1880s. More machinery and power were slowly added to specific departments and the partnership was restructured in 1887. Daniel Hunter, who had joined John Inglis in his earliest days in Guelph, moved on and entered municipal politics, and the company would win its share of municipal contracts and enjoy close relations with the civic authorities for years to come. With the departure of Daniel Hunter, the company became John Inglis & Sons. William Inglis, John's eldest son, played a larger role in the operations than he had before.

An especially distinctive feature of the pre-World War I factory was the presence of Toronto's Central Prison next to the Inglis & Hunter shops. More than once, public hangings and lashings were conducted during factory hours. Prison labour was widely discussed in the labour movement in those years. Inglis workers were reminded daily of the issue, because prisoners made brooms next door.

The manufacture of waterwheels, flour and grist mill machinery, engines, and gears took many, many hours of direct hand labour by highly skilled metalworkers. They stood on a dirt floor, were cold during the winter, and depended on natural light in order to do their work. Products reached customers in two ways: horse-drawn Inglis wagons delivered small products and most goods within the city, while convenient rail access at the Strachan Avenue factory allowed rail-car flatbeds to move large products to distant customers. On large jobs the task of installing the machinery was often bigger than that of making it in the factory.

Strachan Avenue was a dirt road that ran in

Boilers ready for installation at sites outside of Toronto sit on railway flatbed cars. Behind the train can be seen the brick wall of the old central prison which was in the rear of the Inglis complex.

front of the early factory. It was named after John Strachan, the city's Anglican Bishop and educational activist. Though the factory was always in the same location, the area looked substantially different in this early period. Ninety-four-year-old Clifford Lindsey, who delivered newspapers in the neighbourhood as a boy at the turn of the century, remembered the factory area as it was around 1906:

> The prison grounds had a steel picket fence on Strachan Avenue. The high brick prison wall was about the end of the 14 Strachan Avenue building, west of the yard. It had an arch gate, heavy wooden doors and a nice driveway from the gate. I delivered papers to the watchman at the railway crossing on Strachan Avenue. His cabin was on the grounds, elevated for better vision of the street and tracks. John Inglis had a building down near the bridge that crossed the lower railway tracks. Between the two railway tracks, on the west side of the bridge was a squatter living [in] his cottage. They chased him out when they built a new bridge. The road running over the bridge ran through the Exhibition Grounds to the Stanley Barracks, called Garrison Common before my time. It was closed when the fair was on. There was no Lakeshore road at that time. The edge of the shore line was where the streetcars enter the Exhibition Grounds today. There was a little bay east of Strachan Avenue.

Inglis products were delivered within the city by horse and carriage. The wagon driver also tended the horses and lived in a cottage on the company's grounds.

Across the road, now the police garage, was a cattle yard, the Strachan Avenue Stock Yards. Harris Packing House had a slaughter house, away in the rear.

For a time, some housing was provided for men on the factory grounds. For others, it was hastily constructed in the blocks surrounding the plant. A large proportion of the early Inglis workers lived nearby for both convenience and economy. The surrounding blocks were filled with moulders, labourers, blacksmiths, boilermakers, and other workers, and their families.

Up the street, less than ten years after John Inglis had moved to the plant on Strachan Avenue, Mary Ann White, widow and hotelkeeper, hired F.H. Herbert, architect, to replace a vacant house at what is today 950 King Street West. The Palace Hotel, with an addition built in 1897, still stands on the northeast corner of King and Strachan. In many ways, its history mirrors that of its industrial neighbours, Massey and Inglis, and the people who worked there.

This new Palace Hotel and Tavern was a relative latecomer to Toronto, a city with no shortage of public houses in the nineteenth century. In a time before cars and suburbs lessened their importance, local pubs played a significant role in working-class life. For the many factory workers in Toronto, home away from home was a boarding house. As lodgers, they shared meals with the host family. Others, living in rooming houses, would have to eat in taverns. Since many of these workers spent up to half of their income on housing and food, entertainment had to be affordable.

The Spadina, Wheatsheaf, Gladstone, Selby, and Winchester Taverns still stand in Toronto today. Many of them were established in the early- and mid-nineteenth century. It was not uncommon for women, often widows of hotelkeepers, to continue the family business. Mary Ann White might have known Susanna Robinson, who owned the Gladstone Hotel on Queen Street West.

During the course of the following eighty years, some Palace residents were, on occasion, Inglis employees. Its nineteenth-century residents held occupations that reflected those of the rest of the neighbourhood: carpenter, machinist, labourer, and teamster. We know that each generation of Inglis workers included many who were frequent visitors to the tavern, and that many stopped in after work on the way home.

Clifford Lindsey in 1989, age 94.

Such taverns were central to the working-class culture, and the Palace was an important part of this neighbourhood. Within the tavern, and the Palace was no exception, all patrons were equals, treated like kings. Innkeepers were known for their independence, so taverns became centres for socializing and political discussion. Without doubt, the Palace was a working-class tavern. Since the Inglis factory remained in the neighbourhood for so long, a local culture grew in and around it. The Palace, as one of the area's important institutions, was more than just a drinking establishment; its atmosphere was formed by a fierce independence that was typical of the Inglis work force.

Labour and the Union Shop at Inglis

It is not clear whether the Inglis factory was a union shop from its beginnings in Guelph. The Iron Moulders' International Union Journal mentions a large lodge in Guelph that had to surrender its charter in the early 1880s because so many factories had closed. The Inglis & Hunter shop may well have been one of the closures that made this necessary. Inglis's move to Toronto, however, placed it in the middle of a trade union renaissance that swept much of the continent in the 1880s.

The generally strong economy in the second half of the 1880s buoyed this new, exciting workers' movement. Labour was in demand. Workers in Ontario and across the continent were joining

Factory production of engineering machinery was just part of the job at Inglis. These pipes had to be delivered and installed on sites throughout Canada.

the Noble and Holy Order of the Knights of Labor. The Knights arrived in Toronto in 1882 and proceeded to organize with unprecedented success. By 1886 the Knights had over 5,000 members organized into over fifty local assemblies throughout the city. Many of these assemblies were industrial locals and included both skilled and unskilled workers, which was a radical departure from the somewhat aristocratic craft unions. The Knights' vision of the labour movement and society included equal rights for women workers, people of colour, and immigrants, groups typically ignored by the otherwise traditional labour movement.

Despite the Knights' presence, most workers at the Inglis factory in the 1880s remained members of the Iron Moulders' International Union, Lodge 28. The lodge had been a powerful one in Toronto's metal industries for more than a decade. In 1871 the union's international president, Saffin, declared the lodge to be "one of the most flourishing organizations in the IMIU, comprising as it does nearly all the moulders in Toronto, in fact all who they are willing to take in." The moulders' organization was also among the most progressive of craft unions. Many activists in the lodges were political radicals, questioning the impact of industrial capitalism on their workplaces, neighbourhoods and beyond. Though different in orientation, the Knights and the Moulders' Union initially reinforced each other, contributing to the working-class political movement that was growing in the 1880s. All Massey's factory workers, skilled and unskilled, were organized into a

"Maple Leaf" assembly by the Knights. Organizing breakthroughs like these were surely noted by the iron moulders at the Inglis factory down the street.

The IMIU appeared to be solidly in control at the Inglis factory until the turn of the century. The nature of production at Inglis gave the moulders' lodge considerable leverage. The absence of regimentation in the shop stood in contrast to the Massey works, where limited product types made standardization easier. At Inglis most of the work was customized. Despite the growing expansion of steam-powered production, there was little standardization in shop methods at Inglis. This reinforced the power of the unions, because much was left to the judgment of the iron moulders and blacksmiths themselves. Each work order involved considerable problem-solving by the craftsmen.

Complex, customized contracts placed limits on how fast the work could proceed, the extent to which methods could be reorganized, and the degree to which machinery could substitute for skilled worker know-how. Having manufactured and installed a good many initial industrial power systems, Inglis enjoyed a steady return of repair and upgrading business. Previous knowledge of these systems was essential, so the company needed loyalty, skill, and commitment from a large portion of its workers.

The nature of such work allowed the workers to maintain a maximum degree of control over the manufacturing process. Hence the deskilling effects of technology were minimized compared to other metalworking shops, like implement and stove factories. These features of production, control and diversity, attracted the most skilled metalworkers and allowed an especially strong union presence to develop. The most skilled moulders and blacksmiths in the factory were indispensable.

The company's growth, in addition to adding more workers to its payroll, led to visible differences between owner and worker. In the 1880s, junior partner Daniel Hunter was still intimately involved in the making of the machinery, and especially in its installation, while John Inglis became more of an administrator. Then in his sixties, Inglis took his place among Canada's industrial elite. By 1886 he was a prominent member of the Canadian Manufacturers' Association, appointed to voice business's concerns over the first-ever health and safety factory legislation in Canada. As the Act was about to be

An unidentified worker stands beside machinery that he helped build.

"Fitting up derrick at temporary shop" shows unidentified Inglis workers at an installation site away from the factory. The picture was probably taken in the early years of the twentieth century.

Trades and Labour Council, to which the Moulders' Union belonged. For years the labour movement had lobbied for factory legislation, insisting that a qualified inspectorate be unconnected to the businesses visited. Inglis and his colleagues saw inspectors as meddlesome people, dangerously interfering in their private business affairs. The legislation passed, but the business lobby prevailed on the issue of enforcement. A total of three inspectors were appointed for all of Ontario, only one of whom had any real interest in or sympathy for the workers they were protecting.

The union's position grew out of experience on the shopfloor, and Inglis's position developed due to his growing distance from it. Dangers and accidents at Inglis had been experienced directly and tragically by many employees for years. Details about these conditions are scarce, but we know several workers were seriously injured or killed at the Strachan Avenue factory before World War I.

The reporting of such incidents is sadly incomplete, a comment on how little the industrial carnage concerned the elite. An employee lost a finger to a planing machine that severed it in 1891. Three employees suffered broken bones in separate incidents within weeks of each other at the turn of the century. A sixty-three-year-old worker was crushed to death between two boilers in 1912. Only the union offered compensation to injured workers or to the families of those who were killed.

Tensions over the enforcement of factory safety revealed differences between workers and management that foreshadowed more open hostility in the future. The following year the moulders' union moved to counter the growing clout of organizations like the Canadian Manufacturers' Association. In 1887 thirteen of Ontario's largest moulders' lodges formed a district union, which allowed better control of labour supply and coordination of strikes against specific employers. For example in 1890, Lodge 28 waged lengthy strikes against both Gurney's Stoves and Massey's by communicating with unions across the province. The Inglis factory appears not to have been affected directly, perhaps because skilled workmen were absolutely essential to the company's success.

In the 1890s the firm grew and diversified. Each metalworker was responsible for specific products and materials. These craftsmen owned many of the tools they used and understood the

passed, Inglis was part of an influential trio that met with the premier of Ontario, Oliver Mowat. Inglis, Hart Massey, owner of the Massey Works, and Frederick Nicholls, an especially antilabour industrialist with many interests, sought to weaken the power that the Act intended to give to factory inspectors.

The position taken by Inglis and his colleagues opposed the wishes of the Toronto

IAM Lodge 235 issued a circular to their employers on 11 April 1900. The Canadian column of the IAM *Journal*, "From the Land of the Maples," listed the demands of the machinists:

FROM THE LAND OF THE MAPLES

1st. That after April 23rd, the wages of machinists, die and toolmakers be increased 12 1/2 percent.

2nd. Minimum rates Machinists, 20 cents per hour; die and toolmakers, 25 per hour.

3rd. All overtime till midnight, time and one-half.

4th. After 12 midnight, legal holidays and Sundays, doubletime.

5th. All employees laid off through slackness of work to be given the first opportunity for employment, seniority and proficiency to govern.

6th. In case of a grievance arising the company agrees to receive a committee of employees, and adjust the same if possible.

7th. All time, after 12 (noon) Saturday, governed by clause 3.

8th. Agreement to be in force till April 23, 1901.

9th. Thirty days' notice on either side in case of change of agreement or renewal.

complexities of the machinery that was part of the Inglis shop. The small shop was transformed into a relatively impersonal and rigid environment. The union became a central focus for the socializing relations between workers in the plant. Separate departments were formed within the plant. Moulders were responsible for cast-iron products, blacksmiths worked on wrought iron, and boilers were constructed by boilermakers. Near the turn of the century, more machinists were hired as the complexity of industrial machines and technology changed. Each of these trades depended on less-skilled labourers and helpers who had no union and worked for far lower wages than the skilled metalworkers. Such was the working-class hierarchy in all metal shops of the day. At the end of the decade John Inglis, himself a metal craftsman and Scottish immigrant, died. His death in April 1899 ended the apparent harmony in the company.

Employees attended the funeral and presented a "funereal pillow," a common custom at the time. The workers who paid their respects quickly learned that a new managerial style would now prevail. The eldest Inglis son, William, was more of a businessman and less of a metalworker than was his father. His approach to the union would become typical of most owners in the industry.

Early Militancy and Management

Within months of John Inglis's death, William faced a strike by his machinists, members of the International Association of Machinists (IAM), Lodge 235. The IAM was not as old a union as the IMIU, but quickly grew as the machine age created much work for this new class of craftsman. The machinists were unhappy with their wage rates and hours of work, and requested a grievance procedure for disputes. Initially all the companies under agreement with the lodge refused to enter into a contract for any definite period. A five percent increase was offered, but owners wanted to give it to whom they chose. The company offered straight time for Saturday, not the overtime the machinists wanted.

Several negotiating sessions were held between the workers and employers before the 23 April strike deadline. The employers' offer was sweetened to eight percent, but as an "old charter member" of the IAM reported in his column, "Our boys would not stand for it." With negotiations deadlocked, the machinists struck against the following firms: Bertram Engine Works, Polson Iron Works, Inglis and Sons Engine Works, the St. Lawrence Foundry Co., and the Northy Manufacturing Co.

"We put up a good, square orderly fight," wrote the columnist, applauding Brother Holmes, who supervised "his forces like a skilled general." The effectiveness of the

Toronto strike depended in part on "our brothers in sister lodges" for keeping others away from Toronto. Keeping away the itinerant craftsmen was an essential part of metalcraft strike strategy. The lodge's business agent met trains and steamboats and intercepted potential scabs in the strike effort. Two lodge members from Quebec, Brothers Bogart and Fournier, "rendered us most valuable service through their knowledge of the French language, or we would have been swamped with French-Canadians from Montreal."

The men went back to work on 11 June, after the bosses offered arbitration. On 29 June a settlement was reached. An increase of ten percent was the compromise and some improvement in overtime rates was agreed to. While workers were short of a complete victory, the employers had moved significantly from their original offer of five percent. The partial victory established the practice of increased pay for night and weekend work. The original demand that seniority rights be established appears to have been conceded in exchange for a better wage increase.

Owners like William Inglis probably saw this partial union victory as interference in his shop. Factory owners were determined to fight the power of militant metal unions like those at Inglis. The divergent interests of workers and owners like Inglis had burst into the open. Influenced by the growing open-shop movement in the United States, Inglis was well placed to learn about this powerful corporate movement, whose mandate was to reduce the power of unions — especially in the metal trades. The Inglis company had been doing business with many American firms where the open-shop movement was spreading. At a meeting in October 1902, 200 Toronto employers gathered to discuss "their rights to manage their respective businesses in such lawful manner as they deem proper."

As a result, the IMIU faced a more determined and better organized group of employers when it called a massive strike of its Toronto shops in 1903. The new anti-union leadership introduced other changes at the company. The production of mill machinery was discontinued and the business in waterworks pumping and engine equipment was expanded. This shift in organization likely led to the hiring of more machinists, which would have changed not just the structure of departments, but the labour process in the factory. Such growth, directed and controlled by management, may have challenged the traditional methods and techniques that the workers sought to maintain.

The battle lines had been drawn. The largest metalwork companies, Inglis among them, set out to destroy the power of the IMIU once and for all. The factory owners appeared less inclined to talk than they had been with the machinists three years earlier. The firms declared war by hiring a famous professional strikebreaker, D.C. Graeme-Hunter, who was reputed to have broken "more than 7,000 strikes."

The strike was initially sparked by the Canada Foundry's insistence on an open shop in July 1903. A demand for the nine-hour day saw it quickly spread to other factories, including Inglis. The strike dragged on into the late fall. Employers were determined to break the union through the common front of the Toronto Employers' Association. Yet the moulders of Lodge 28 never capitulated. Some firms, like Inglis, unable to conduct business without them, eventually hired back their union workers. The secretary of the lodge reported, "Just after adjourning the meeting this afternoon the foreman of the Inglis shop, R. Goods, came to the hall and informed us that he had discharged all the scabs in his shop and that he wanted the union men in on Monday, that the firm was tired of the scabs and was willing to give the nine hours."

The moulders' strike at Inglis was more successful than at some other manufacturers. Piecework, the introduction of less-skilled workers called "bucks," and the general degradation of the moulders' work were minimized at Inglis. The breaking down of the job into simpler or repetitive parts, known as "cutting up" in moulders' language of the time, worked well at plants like Massey's because agricultural implements were mass produced. At Inglis, the opportunities for deskilling were much more limited. Skilled moulders could drive the hardest bargain. Like all good union men, they were keenly aware of their power.

Alterations a year after the strike included moving the Inglis company's offices away from the production buildings. Managers were physically separate, even distant, from the shopfloor they directed. The move had daily consequences and symbolic significance. An architecturally rendered façade graced the "head office." These changes reflected the desired separation between planning and decision making and the execution of the work.

This boiler was transported uphill on logs. Such work was typical on hundreds of engineering projects for which the Inglis company became famous. The name of the workman is not known.

Three years later, the machinists' attempt to win the nine-hour day brought two rival labour organizations together. The Machinists of Lodge 235, part of the American Federation of Labor (AFL), and the members of the Amalgamated Society of Engineers, a British-based union, struck for the nine-hour day with no cut in pay in 1907. The work stoppage took place in June, after two failed attempts were made to meet with employers. The Toronto Employers' Association coordinated a virulent anti-union campaign in the press.

Three large firms were affected initially: the Canada Shipbuilding Company, Polson Iron Works, and the Canada Foundry. Within two days the machinists at Inglis and the Abell Agricultural Company had walked out too. The dispute involved some sixty firms and roughly 1,000 machinists within a week.

Under the coordination of the secretary for the Toronto Employers' Association, James G. Merrick, the manufacturers "refused to entertain the demands of the machinists union and insisted on the open shop." Smaller shops agreed to the terms in the weeks that followed.

Larger companies, Inglis among them, continued to resist the call of the remaining 400 machinists for the shorter day.

The Labour Temple at 137 Church Street was "a very busy place" during the strike. Every morning at 10 a.m. the men met for roll call and the regulating of pickets. This was a very serious affair, as one IAM official noted, "when you have a city to watch and all the different avenues of ingress to the shops." Strike pay strained the organization. After the men in the small shops returned to work, they paid two dollars a week to help the brothers who had yet to return. The remaining machinists still on strike and their families wouldn't be starved into returning to work.

Picketers risked physical attacks and police intimidation. One picketing apprentice was beaten and then jailed on the trumped-up charge of "intimidation." The incident was sparked by his asking someone heading into a struck shop if he was a machinist. The poor apprentice was beaten by the scab and carried down to the City Hall police station. As IAM organizer L.H. Gibbons noted, "Well if you had

D.C. Graeme-Hunter, a strikebreaker with an international reputation, was depicted in the Toronto World of 23 July 1903, during the moulders strike at Inglis and several other companies in Toronto.

Remembering Harry Goudy

Harry Goudy was one of the longest serving workers in the factory's early history. He started there in 1908 and did not retire until 1943. Over the course of his five decades at Inglis as an expert blacksmith and forgeman, Goudy watched the metal craftsman's control of production decline. The shop already had been undergoing profound change when he began at the factory. In the first two decades Goudy and his union brothers fought the company over wages, hours, and skills.

In 1919, Goudy and his union brothers at Inglis took their final stand. The dominant union at the plant at that time, the International Association of Machinists, led a militant, citywide metal industries strike that paralyzed manufacturing in the city. The action soon spread to become a general strike in Toronto. While the workers' revolt was inspired in part by the events surrounding the Winnipeg General Strike, it was grounded in the gradual erosion of wages and working conditions that had taken place over the two previous decades.

Hired at Inglis at a time of worker militancy, Goudy was a proud, highly skilled tradesman who loved practical jokes both in the shop and after work. He was one of six brothers, all trained as blacksmiths. They came from Galt, a small town in southwestern Ontario. In the previous year Goudy may have attended a Machinists' Union rally. Such rallies were held across the province while the union was on strike against Inglis and several other firms in Toronto.

As a young man, Goudy sported a red handlebar mustache, not uncommon among metalworkers of his day. His arms bulged from years of working the metal. Like the majority of his fellow workers, Goudy lived near the plant. He walked to work from his Parkdale residence every morning, arriving early to banter with his coworkers before the paid time actually started. During his years at Inglis, Goudy saw the factory grow from a handful of dirt-floored shops to a complex of nearly thirty buildings.

He and his union brothers thought Inglis was a good place to work. Goudy was a loyal union man, making sure the union rules weren't broken in the forge shop. Wages and conditions were among the best in the city, in part because the union was active there. Some of the best metalwork in Canada came out of the Strachan Avenue shops. The most challenging and interesting orders for forgework came to Goudy's shop because of its reputation for quality. Some men in the shop with Goudy had known John Inglis personally, as the company founder had died less than a decade before Goudy arrived.

This brief outline of Goudy's five decades at Inglis is just about all that we will ever know about his career there.

Little can be discovered about the many others who worked at Inglis when it first moved to Toronto from Guelph. The handful of names we traced through the records lived in the neighbourhood and were members of the Iron Moulders International Union, Lodge 28. In the 1880s, men like Charles Pierce, William Osborne, and Edward Curtis, all moulders working for the company, controlled much of the production process of metalcasting. They established the Inglis name across the country. Boilermakers like Thomas Higgins, who lived north on Strachan Avenue just up the street from the factory, determined the pace of his own production and the manner in which he built the machines that provided power to thousands of factories and institutions. We know little about these specific Inglis workers and their union lodges, but their collective identity helped us to learn about them.

seen that boy and the galoot that claimed to have been intimidated, you would have laughed if you had been standing at a funeral." The police kept the apprentice in jail until the end of the day and then, since no one appeared to lay a charge, released him.

The Toronto Employers' Association also hired "private constables" for intimidation. Special organizer Broland made a sharp distinction between the police and those "Pinkerton thugs" who, "not having the courage to dress in the uniform of a policeman, sneaks and crawls around in their uncle's old private duds with a sneaking, crawling look which is only suitable to the thing that wears it and which every honest man will despise." Over the course of the strike, the union complained to the police numerous times about the "overzealous" constables and their treatment of the strikers.

By November, the strike had all but collapsed. Lodge 235 had waged a valiant struggle, but the larger establishments like Inglis refused to settle. Inglis undertook an extensive expansion of the Strachan Avenue facility during the dispute. The company may well have taken advantage of the work disruption. The long and bitter strike of the machinists touched every metal manufacturer in the city. Its impact was lasting. The power relationship at Inglis began to change. By 1908, the number of foremen employed had nearly tripled. The atmosphere was increasingly impersonal and the ratio of watchers to workers was growing.

In the years that followed the 1907 machinists' strike, boilers became a central part of the Inglis product line. Steam heat was being introduced in a wide range of buildings and became the basis for the production of power in industry. The Brotherhood of Boilermakers, Iron Ship Builders, and Helpers may have recognized their importance to the business and believed they were in a strong bargaining position. In April 1913, the members of "Maple Leaf Local 1," echoing the name of the Knights of Labor assembly that was formed in the neighbourhood some thirty years earlier, presented six different employers with a contract requesting, like the machinists, the nine-hour day and a wage increase. After negotiations became deadlocked, the boilermakers and helpers in these firms called a strike.

By this time the John Inglis Company employed by far the largest number of boilermakers in the city. All 140 at the Inglis shop went on strike. William Inglis's opposition to the nine-hour day was clear in a letter sent to the Ontario deputy minister of labour, F.A. Acland:

> I am enclosing you [sic] a copy of letter received from them with their demands, which you will readily see is all out of reason. The great difference between us practically is the nine hour question. As their [sic] are no other boilermakers in this country working nine hours, or in any other city or town in Eastern Canada paying the rate of wages we are paying, and as we have to compete with all different concerns, we cannot compete and give them any concessions such as they ask.

But financial statements from that year suggest the company had little difficulty competing, since it generated a profit of roughly $60,000, half of which was put in "reserves."

Three hundred boilermakers struck against a total of five companies across the city. After a five-week strike, William Inglis conceded the nine-hour day. A slight increase in wages for both boilermakers and helpers was also gained. Only those at the Canada Foundry company gained nothing through the strike.

The strike was well organized. At the outset, strikers were supported by about 100 additional men who came from the surrounding areas to assist in the picketing. The union paid the fares of these men, who received no strike pay and clearly sacrificed their wages in a show of solidarity for their Toronto brothers. Solidarity between the various metal trades in Toronto was formalized that year, as the Metal Trades Council, an umbrella body of the metalcrafts, endorsed industrial unionism.

The Great War

World War I began within a year of the boilermakers' strike. The first large scale "modern" war would transform Canadian society and industry, especially metal manufacturing. The metal trades became a crucible for the social upheaval that the Great War triggered.

War contracts were awarded through the Imperial Munitions Board, headed by Joseph Flavelle, president of a large meatpacking firm in Toronto. Inglis received many contracts. The company made eighteen-pounder shrapnel, 4-1/2 inch howitzers, and miscellaneous machine-shop and foundry equipment. This work transformed the shopfloor profoundly. The company's size, pace, and product mix were all affected by the demands of wartime production. Company owners like William Inglis, in contrast to his employees, benefited from the war in many ways. Much of the retooling that was necessary for war production was factored into the final price, so manufacturers risked little financially. But higher profits were just one of the benefits to companies like Inglis.

Shell production at Inglis created new possibilities in both the organization of production and the deployment of new technology. With every shell being manufactured to strict specifications and government inspection, Inglis workers experienced their first exposure to repetitive, machine-driven production. When traditional machinists were faced with this work, there was strong resistance on the shopfloor. Eventually large numbers of lesser-skilled, nonunion workers were introduced into various aspects of production.

The possibilities for scientific management were far more extensive in war production than in the traditional departments of the Inglis company. New technologies emerging from the war were introduced with more invasive and intensive management systems.

World War I did increase the demand for metalworkers, but they were prevented from fully exploiting their position. Unions agitated for higher wages and better working conditions, but they were under strict controls and brutal suppression from employers, police, and government. It was wartime, and the patriotic call allowed nothing to get in the way of maximum production. Government censors suppressed news of any union activity that challenged factory working conditions. Trade union activists were harassed and jailed if they advocated struggling for higher wages; those who did were labeled traitors and criminals. Metalworkers experienced deteriorating working conditions, speed-ups, and deskilling technologies. During the war, unions fought against these difficult conditions to secure small gains.

Like other employers, Inglis sought to establish lower rates of pay for many classes of work related to war production. War workers were paid rates far below those of traditional machinists. By early 1915, at the beginning of wartime production, William Inglis employed nearly thirty regular machinists in various categories of shell work. Almost all of them were making 25 cents an hour compared to the average of 32 cents formerly paid to machinists. In a letter to Prime Minister Borden, IAM representative James Somerville complained that Inglis was among the firms "that made the reduction in wages ... an effort to break in unskilled labour at low wages to perform the operation universally recognized as skilled machinists' work, and skilled machinists to obtain employment are compelled to accept a lesser wage rate than is paid a common labourer in the City of Toronto."

The practice of wage shaving on war work was widespread in the metal industry, where relatively good wages had existed before the war. James Somerville urged Prime Minister Borden to insert necessary restrictions in contracts, "to curb those who would snatch a profit during these unhappy times, under the guise of 'Patriotism'." The Toronto Trades and Labour Congress urged that a Wage Board be created to correct and prevent abuses that were taking place in a wide range of war-related production. The Congress understood that "the demands for patriotic service at this time makes [sic] it almost impossible for the workers to protest against unfair conditions without being charged with unpatriotic action."

The IAM remained critical of companies engaging in such practices. The feelings were reciprocated by business. The Inglis company complained bitterly about its war workers in a memo the following year:

> Almost impossible to co-operate with present class of help as they appear to be getting too much money and don't want to work. Nurse them along, and applicants not very particular whether they get work or not. Have taken 250 men in the last two weeks and do not believe have 25 of them now. Always shifting, not trying to help, but seeking highest wages. Something should be done to stop hiring other companies [sic] men and causing unrest.

The high turnover rate suggests that workers simply refused to accept the conditions and wages that Inglis was offering. The intervention of the Department of Labour averted a strike in February 1916 when the company attempted to use semiskilled machine operators or "specialists" in the place of machinists. The union ultimately agreed to allow management to de-

The first two decades of the twentieth century were good to the John Inglis Company. Numerous expansions and enlargements of the factory turned the once-small shop into a large complex of specialized buildings. The most significant growth early in the century occurred during the First World War. In 1916, there were two extensions to existing buildings. The following year a new power station and time office were completed and a new machine shop was added in the summer. Finally, a tunnel which ran northward under the tracks was begun in November 1917.

termine pay rates and classifications on the basis of proficiency tests.

While William Inglis lowered wage rates, he was appointed to a Royal Commission on the troublesome munitions industry. Unrest was rampant in munitions plants in both Toronto and Hamilton. In the spring of 1916, Inglis joined John McClelland, the IAM official who was labour's representative, and an "impartial government appointee," Judge Colin Snyder, to "make inquiries and investigations concerning the relations between employers and employees ..."

Inglis was now an active and outspoken member of the industrial elite. His anti-union position altered the investigation's outcome. While the two other appointees favoured granting the nine-hour day, his intransigent minority position both prevented the acceptance of the report and further inflamed industrial relations.

In 1917, a large but short-lived strike affected the war-related Inglis forge shop. In March of that year, 500 forgemen and labourers struck for four days, demanding higher wages and overtime rates. The size of the work stoppage indicated the extent to which war-related production allowed nonunion labour to be hired at the factory. The plant's unions did not represent the workers in the shell-forging department initially, but slowly saw the forgers' struggle as their own. The skills of the machinist in other departments were also under attack.

Discipline of workers was swift and decisive. William Inglis wrote to F.A. Acland, the deputy minister of labour, shortly after the strike:

We might say that this matter is all straightened out now, and we got rid of the agitators and everything is going along in better order than it has for some time. We regret to advise that several agitators got in among our men and stirred up the trouble and when we got rid of these the trouble seemed to be over …

The strike did secure some improvements. An increase was granted but the request for double-time for Sunday work was flatly refused. From the perspective of William Inglis, the problem didn't stem from the inherent working conditions in the shell-forging department but was the result of a minority of "problem" employees.

Inglis's failure to agree to the nine-hour day

in his own factory left management and labour there in even greater opposition. Workers resented the treatment they had received during the war years. Large numbers of working-class men had served overseas with the promise of a better world when the war was over. But when the war was won, it seemed to have little connection to their welfare and advancement. This angered and further politicized trade unionists across the country. Yet for an industrialist like William Inglis, the war was a positive, watershed experience. With the war barely over, he wrote to Joseph Flavelle, the chairman of the Imperial Munitions Board, summarizing what industry and government had together accomplished:

Looking out east through the company gates onto Strachan Avenue, 16 July 1915.

… We wish to extend to you and all connected with the Imperial Munitions Board our sincere appreciation of the treatment that we have had and the help that you have so gladly given us at all times to assist us in carrying out our contracts. We wish the same could be carried out into our everyday mercantile life, as it has been the greatest education the manufacturers in this country have ever had or hope to have, and hope we will all benefit by the experience we have had in the last four years through your good offices.

While we regret exceedingly the thought of having to discontinue our dealings with the Imperial Munitions Board, I am sure Canada should be justly proud of the great part she has had in the great victory …

The windfall of war production had allowed Inglis to finance its most dramatic expansion to date. Seven extensions and alterations were undertaken during the years of World War I, including a large extension of the main building and a new machine shop, power station, time office, and tunnels on the property. More than the buildings grew. Profits also increased in size. Wartime profits exceeded any other in the history of the company. Total sales in 1918 were $3,498,833, compared to $604,679 in 1913.

The Inglis company also took the lead in transforming the wartime production facility into a modern factory with increasingly standardized production. In fact, it began changing over from war work to civilian production before the armistice was signed. Ever-bigger and -faster machines were introduced in the factory and were, in turn, produced by the Inglis workers for other factories.

The General Strike of 1919

From the perspective of trade unionists the World War I era was one of social disruption, excess profits, repression, and increasingly inhuman work. People worked harder and faster but had less at the end of the day in an era of rampant inflation. These realities turned many workers towards direct political action. Patience in talking with employers and government had resulted in disappointment and betrayal. With the war over, a large proportion of soldiers returned home to the prospect of unemployment. This further inflamed the situation, especially in cities like Toronto. There was a growing recog-

nition that if workers were to enjoy a better world, they would have to fight for it.

Planning for an industry-wide strike took place at two provincewide conventions, organized by the machinists' union in July and November of 1918. On 1 April 1919 the Metal Trades Council, which included the Inglis workers, presented the Toronto Employers' Association with a list of demands. The metal trades sought a uniform wage schedule, an eight-hour day, and the closed shop, among other improvements. Their employers refused all demands. The industry-wide strike began on 1 May 1919. Strikers at Inglis shut down production more quickly and effectively than workers at other plants. Newspapers commented indirectly on this level of militancy. One noted, "The only large firm to admit that practically all the men had failed to report for work was the John Inglis Company."

There were 5,000 metalworkers on strike across the city. To be fully appreciated, the conflict must be seen in its broader context. The strike's beginning on 1 May 1919 suggested a growing number of the metalworkers were embracing what their employers would define as dangerous, subversive, foreign ideology.

The citywide industry strike quickly moved beyond specific points of dispute and harnessed the anger that wartime production had fostered. Metal craftsmen had watched their factories change in ways that fundamentally challenged their trades and skills. Other workers, both union and nonunion, had similar complaints. Towards the end of the war, the only effective avenue left open to them in combatting employers — the strike — was deemed illegal.

Events in Toronto were part of a broader wave of strikes and uprisings that swept the country in 1919. The most famous was in Winnipeg, but nearly every industrialized centre in Canada witnessed a widescale workers' revolt. The depth of worker unrest indicated the extent to which workers had become politicized. The struggle at Inglis was reminiscent of the moulders' challenge of management in 1903. Yet this time, the issues of the war and the growing presence of socialist ideologies increasingly put the struggles between labour and management in class terms.

Several Inglis executives, including William and another key man, Campbell Reeves, claimed, "They couldn't stay in business and give into the strikers' demands." After nearly

Originally named The Shamrock, *this ferry was renamed* William Inglis *after his sudden death in 1935. The ship's boiler was manufactured at the Strachan Avenue factory. As of 1994, the boat continued to carry passengers to Toronto Island.*

two weeks, the striking metalworkers called for their employers to negotiate. They also called for a general strike convention, to take place a week later. The vote at the Toronto Trades and Labour Council received the support of forty-four unions representing 12,000 workers in the city. The endorsement was overwhelming and, on 30 May, approximately 10,000 workers went on strike across Toronto.

The strike was strongest in the metal trades, the building trades (especially among carpenters), the shipyards (which used many of the same trades found in metal industry), and the garment industry. Nine metal trades workers dominated the fifteen-member Central Strike Committee. On 4 June the Committee called off the strike by request of the Metal Trades Council. The effectiveness of the general strike had been lessened by the decision of civic workers,

including those who operated the streetcars, to remain at work until expiration of their contract on 16 June.

Progressive trade unions had suffered a major defeat. The end of the strike was filled with intrigue and corruption. It was revealed that right-wingers on the Toronto Trades Council executive had accepted $5,000 from the Toronto Employers' Association to publish a right-wing paper that divided the metal trades workers during the strike. A detailed investigation spearheaded by the left wing on the Council confirmed the charges, and the ugly affair helped the left to take control of the Council in elections held later that summer.

The massive but ultimately ineffectual show of strength, in which Inglis workers played a significant role, was the last instance of overt worker action at Inglis or in the Toronto metal trades for many years. The unions that represented the metal trades at Inglis were largely silent and seemed weak after this period.

The 1920s were quiet years at Inglis. To the north on King Street, a new alternative to industrial conflict, the Massey Industrial Councils, were instituted. Rather than accepting the power of trade unions, this experiment sought to "democratize" the plant by instituting internal joint committees. The council system met with some success at a number of large plants across the country. Corporate welfarism, as practised by Massey, Goodyear, and Dominion Textile, did create the illusion of democracy, offering some of the financial supports that only unions and workers' "friendly societies" had had in the past.

In 1922, the Inglis company was consolidated and reorganized. The Inglis family took a million dollars in profit out of the company. The transformation of the production process continued. A professional, university-trained engineer, George Fax, was hired as a manager. Workers' control and shop knowledge at the Inglis plant faced a more powerful enemy. The market for some of what were once customized products expanded, allowing efficiency in their manufacture. These more standardized products created areas of the factory where the metal craftsmen no longer maintained much control. However, complete industrial installations, high-speed machinery, and complex repair work meant that Inglis continued to depend on some highly skilled workers.

These were good years for business at the John Inglis Company. Profits remained strong throughout the decade, especially in the latter years. They were not good years for the unions, though. Work was relatively steady, but the trades controlled less and less of the shop production and seemed politically impotent. As institutions, the unions were pushed to the margins of daily operation. Reflecting this decline in union power, little was recorded of the work force's activities during this period. What remain are reports of the fruit of their labour: gigantic projects that secured the ever-prosperous company even greater profits. Inglis became a key manufacturer of equipment for other manufacturers and large institutions as it took its place among the industrial pillars of Canada. Over the next decade, thousands of factories would be powered by machinery made at Inglis.

The company was able to retool quickly after

William Inglis reads a speech at the Canadian National Exhibition, 1932. He was director of the CNE in 1925.

the war, which put it in an excellent position and said much about William Inglis's growing prominence as an industrialist. The experience of war production had changed management's thinking and planning fundamentally. New emphasis on marketing was visible throughout the 1920s. Sophisticated advertisements were published in a number of Canadian magazines. William Inglis rose to the top of Toronto's business community, serving on many civic and industrial committees and as president of the Canadian National Exhibition in 1925.

In an age of rampant consumption for some, the Inglis company was portrayed as a firm of managers and marketers, not workers skilled in machinery production. There were images of the engineer and businessman — not the crafts-man of old. In magazine and newspaper articles, technologies were portrayed as the achievements of planning and managerial excellence, not workers' skills. The power of the engineer eclipsed the control of the craftsman.

As William Inglis vacationed at his large Muskoka cottage in the late 1920s, he, like other successful industrialists, couldn't conceive of the incredible economic disaster that was about to unfold. The economic system that had put William Inglis on top and overshadowed worker organizations was approaching collapse. It would have been hard to imagine that the busy shops, the marvel of industrial machine technology, the growth of automobile transportation, and the explosion of consumerism would all collapse for most of the next decade.

With nearly ten years of strong business on its books, the depression hit the John Inglis Company and the workers in the shop a little later than the actual stock market crash of October 1929. Orders had been placed well in advance, and government itself had become an important client. Complex projects took several months to complete.

Profits for 1930 were still healthy, but by 1932 the situation was more serious. The company lost nearly $67,000 and total sales were only a little over $460,000. William Inglis's letters soliciting business in the early 1930s had a desperate tone. He looked to government for new work because private business investment in factories was practically nonexistent. In this climate, men like Inglis watched their near-dormant machines with rising anxiety.

Under these hardships, a number of senior company officials died suddenly in 1935–36. In February, Clarence Fierheller, secretary-treasurer of the company with which he had been for more than thirty-five years, died. Later that November, William Inglis himself died. His passing came as an additional blow to an already suffering company. For the first time in nearly seventy-five years, the company did not have an Inglis at the helm. Obituaries reflected the prominence William Inglis had attained, citing his positions in the Canadian Manufacturers' Association and the Board of Trade, and his activism as director of the Canadian National Exhibition in 1925. The mayor of Toronto himself announced, "The city has lost a fine citizen with a personality which earned him a host of friends."

As was to be expected for such a man, the actions that made William Inglis many enemies were not publicly remembered. While a company tender on a piece of civic business that included a fair-wage clause was recalled by Mayor Simpson, this former trade union leader would have had difficulty convincing Inglis workers, like the blacksmith Harry Goudy, that their employer was a man of any benevolence.

In his thirty-five years as head of the company, William Inglis had overseen tremendous expansion and, in a few short years, a complete collapse. More than once, he seemed to be at the forefront of management initiatives that made the lives of his employees more difficult. He refused the nine-hour day publicly when it appeared that consensus for the standard was growing. He was known, like many other businessmen of his time, to dismiss union activists as agitators.

After Inglis's death, there was an attempt to reorganize the company. Long-time company and family associate Campbell Reeves tried to save Inglis from collapse. But the death of another Inglis official was the final blow for a company crippled by financial losses. Alexander Inglis, William's brother, head of the company's Montreal sales office, died in July 1936.

While Inglis workers had been laid off before, especially during winter months, there were hardly any people left in the factory when the company went into receivership in April 1936. In the once-bustling neighbourhood of factories, there was no work for the hundreds of Inglis employees or for the thousands of other factory workers unemployed in the 1930s. Most of the thriving manufacturing neighbourhood was quiet, and the workers in the area were hungry and suffering.

Chapter Two
World War II: Bren Girls and Guns

The Strachan Avenue factory hadn't been closed long when another businessman took an interest in the attractive property. This man would lead the company on an unprecedented path of growth. Out of the grave of the depression came a factory that employed more people than ever before, presented the workers with new challenges, and created new directions for their unions.

There were millions of victims in the depression years of the 1930s. In 1936, the average yearly income of Canadians was still only slightly above what it had been immediately following the economic crisis of 1929. The John Inglis Company was just one of many industrial establishments that had been unable to survive. A player on this reduced business field was Major James Hahn, forty-five years old, an American-born industrialist and entrepreneur, big game hunter, Canadian army intelligence veteran, lawyer, and member of the old boys' network. Hahn was a visionary with big plans.

At the age of only thirty-two, Hahn had become the head of the DeForest Radio Corporation in 1923. For the following ten years, his company made radios and expanded into producing other domestic appliances. Although Hahn had secured rights to manufacture several U.S. appliances, the tariff situation at the time permitted U.S.-made goods to flood the Canadian market. In 1934 Hahn sold his interest in the company to his main competitor, the Rogers Company, and proceeded to combine a personal hobby of guns — his home contained a pistol range — with a new undertaking. Hahn intended to secure a contract to manufacture the Czech-designed Bren gun in Canada. The Bren was a light machine gun invented and patented in Czechoslovakia. It weighed twenty-one pounds and fired at 450 rounds per minute. Easy to assemble, the Bren was air cooled and gas operated. It was to become a standard weapon in the Allied arsenal. By the end of World War II, Inglis would manufacture a total of 186,000 Bren guns.

The necessary pieces for Hahn's operation began to come together in 1936. Hahn learned about the Inglis site, then in the hands of receivers, from his Toronto Island neighbour,

Herbert Plaxton. Plaxton's brother, Hugh, was the Liberal member of parliament for Trinity-Toronto, the riding in which the Inglis plant was located. The facility in April 1936 had only a skeleton maintenance staff of three. Hugh Plaxton was concerned about the high rate of unemployment in his riding and the great number of former Inglis employees on relief. He arranged for Hahn to meet the deputy minister of national defence in Ottawa, Colonel Leo LaFleche. The minister, it was said, wanted 7,000 Bren guns for Canada.

Major James Hahn and his guide, Oliva "Papa" Dionne, father of the famous quintuplets, pose next to an elk Hahn shot while hunting.

In Britain a secret demonstration of the Bren gun was arranged for Hahn, who also carried a letter of introduction from the Canadian high commissioner, Vincent Massey. Perhaps Hahn also exploited old army intelligence connections on both sides of the Atlantic to achieve his ends. It is also unclear just whom Hahn may have outfoxed while attempting to secure the Bren gun contract. Hahn's ability to secure the contract before other competitors even knew of the military's plans was based on a number of complicated circumstances.

Hahn had served in Canadian military intelligence during World War I. This shadowy network of officers kept in touch and may have occasionally broken the rules for a friend. It is likely that Hahn was privileged to information that would not have been shared with just any civilian businessman. The Strachan Avenue factory's availability was also an important factor. Developments in Europe in 1937–38 disturbed military insiders and some politicians. Arms could be needed quickly, efficiently, and in large numbers. A confidential military report authored in 1936 had concluded that most of Canada's arsenal was dangerously obsolete. The military leadership in both Britain and Canada may have wished to avoid a complex tendering process. In their minds, the time it would take to retool an operating factory could also have been costly, if not harmful, to the Allied effort.

Quietly, in November 1936, Hahn purchased the property and the Inglis name and incorporated the resurrected company first as the Anglo-Canadian Engineering Company and then as British Canadian Engineering Ltd. The company was renamed Inglis in June 1937. The undertaking involved Herbert Plaxton through his stock brokerage firm. Hahn met the following year with various officials in Britain. It was decided that the Bren gun could be produced in Canada, but there was a stipulation that production be carried out in a government-owned factory. However, as production began, the distinction between ordnance, or military, and commercial, or engineering, work was to become blurred.

Hahn pointed out that he not only had an ideal factory site, but also a skilled work force that could return to Inglis immediately. The situation at the Inglis factory in 1938 was that without the Bren gun contract there would be little commercial activity. The company didn't resume full operations until early April 1938, precisely the time that the Bren contract was finalized. After 1940, Bren gun production was housed in a separate, government-financed building that extended all the way to Hanna Avenue. Much of the company's initial revitalization was related to building and installing of the production tools and equipment for the Bren gun.

This unnamed man is involved in the production of a Colt, one of the guns manufactured at the Strachan Avenue Inglis plant during the war.

Most of the senior management team would come from contacts at Hahn's earlier business. Despite the fact that the Inglis plant had been closed for almost two years, in 1938 Hahn was able to get most of the department heads, foremen, and long-time employees from the original John Inglis company to return. Reports that celebrated the reopening of the Strachan Avenue factory made much of the continuity of the John Inglis Company. Men like Herbert Carkiff, who headed the machine shop, Fred Kalbfleisch, who oversaw the plate shop, and Harry Goudy, who was in charge of the Forge and Flange shop, had all been with the company prior to World War I.

The terms of the Bren gun agreement reached by Hahn and the Department of National Defence on 31 March 1938 were generous. There was a ten percent allowable profit above cost, hardly an incentive to contain expenditures. Machinery and necessary gauges were provided by the Department of National Defence, and the cost of the preliminary feasibility study was to be reimbursed up to $20,000. Parliament approved the agreement in June 1938. The issue of profit was a touchy one from the beginning, and Hahn addressed it in a letter to Leo LaFleche:

A SALUTE TO THE WOMEN OF INGLIS

A new industry is being pioneered and established by the John Inglis Company. This will involve, in common with pioneering any industry, all the difficulties to be met and overcome in the installation of the plant and the production of the gun. In view of this, it is most unlikely that the maximum profits, as set out under this contract, will be attained by the Company.

But the generosity of the terms for the new Inglis company and the manner in which the contract was secured began to attract attention. In Parliament, J.S. Woodsworth of the Co-operative Commonwealth Federation, the forerunner of the New Democratic Party, and a number of Conservative members grilled the government on the arrangements that had been made so quietly. The curious way Major Hahn secured the Bren gun contract became a full-fledged national scandal after a sensational article by George Drew appeared in the 1 September edition of *Maclean's* magazine. The piece, entitled "Canada's Armament Mystery," alleged that there had been improprieties in the

"Do not touch this machine" is printed clearly but this unnamed woman war worker had to break the rules to do her job. While much of the traditional machining skills were removed from Bren gun work, women war workers lived with the realities of war time production.

awarding of the contract. Drew, who was also a Conservative politician, suggested that certain Liberal politicians may have benefited from its award. Just days after the publication of the article, the federal government launched an investigation into the means by which the Bren gun contract had been secured. The investigation kept the Strachan Avenue factory in the headlines for months.

The Royal Commission on the Bren gun contract was headed by Henry Hague Davis, a supreme court justice. And while irregularities were uncovered, by the time the investigation was completed Canada was at war, and it was too late to stop production. The John Inglis Company became the largest munitions manufacturer in the Dominion. In a summary of its findings, the Royal Commission concluded:

> Notwithstanding that the contract involves the expenditure of several millions of dollars by the Canadian Government, no industrial producer (other than Major Hahn) was consulted by the Department of National Defence as to the proposed manufacture of Bren guns for the Canadian Government or invited to give competitive bids or terms of manufacture. Nor did anyone, so far as the evidence shows, ever visit any industrial plant (except Inglis) to consider the possibility of production of Bren guns in Canada.

The investigation nonetheless led to a new contract being signed with Inglis. The company would operate the Ordnance Division of the plant on a management-fee basis instead of the former cost-plus agreement. The government also indicated that it would take a more active and visible role in the management of the operations. These changes were not made public for nine months, during which time the John Inglis Company was given new, lucrative orders for more weapons.

The issue of profiteering was an especially sensitive one as the country prepared for war. Allegations and investigations of corruption during World War I were remembered by many involved in government. In the previous war, millions in profits were made by factory owners while thousands of Canada's working class died in Europe. The government moved quickly to prevent any perceived parallels, wishing to avoid the social unrest and protest that took place both during and after the 1914–1918 conflict.

George Drew, whose *Maclean's* article instigated the entire investigation, believed that the country would save millions of dollars as a result of the rewritten Inglis contracts. He also went on to win the Ontario Conservative Party leadership, partly on the basis of his allegations. Hahn, he pointed out, had been making profits as though the undertaking were a private company. "The operating agreement under which Hahn is left in charge is nothing but camouflage to save the face of the Government and make it appear that they still rely upon him for the production of these weapons," Drew was quoted at the time.

The disruption in the plant caused by the Bren Commission's investigation affected the operation of the business and the tight delivery schedule that the Bren contract demanded. Robert Bruce was a twenty-five-year-old engineer at the time, hired to write specifications for Bren gun production. The Royal Commission investigation of his employer caused more than a little uneasiness for Bruce.

In November 1938 all hell broke loose at the Royal Commission. MPs from right across Canada came to Toronto, to the Inglis plant, and we were each given so many people to take through the operation. The MPs had no idea what they were looking at, what they were looking for. They were farmers, most of them, from out west. It was pathetic. To have an investigation is one thing, but how these people could ever come up with any kind of an answer is something I would never know.

When that Commission came along, nobody wanted to talk to me, nobody wanted to accept any orders, because there was already machinery delivered to the plant that hadn't been paid for. Nobody knew how they were going to get paid or if they were going to get paid. There were a few weeks in that period of time when nobody knew what was going to happen. Major Hahn didn't tell us anything about the Royal Commission. We read about it in the paper. I was upset. A lot of people were concerned. And a lot of people in the business world were concerned too.

Preparing for production was an overwhelmingly difficult task. Bren gun machinery would eventually consist of 2,600 manufacturing operations that would produce almost 400 parts. And Bruce was forced to start from scratch.

Everything was to be built in that plant. When they took me into the factory, I just about had a fit. There wasn't anything in that factory at all. It had been empty since they went bankrupt. There wasn't concrete floors in the biggest part of the building, just mud, dirt floors. All the windows were broken, the place was full of pigeon dirt — I never saw such a mess in my life.

When I went [to Inglis] I was number seven. Major Hahn was the chairman. Bill West was the comptroller. Miss Steward was Major Hahn's secretary but she carried the title of secretary-treasurer. Lee Ainsworth, general manager, was a General Motors dealer and the only one who didn't come out of the radio company. Walter McLachlan was factory manager. P.J. Percy Baldwin was the administrator. He was involved in establishing standard practice. They put a manual out to everybody: this is how you do your job, your job description.

The whole thing was unlike anything that had ever been done before in Canada. I never believed I could see the things that happened, and the way they happened. People would say, 'It can't be done,' and it was done, and it was done damn well, and it was done very, very fast. When money is no object, a lot of things can be done. There was no cap on what you spent. We got the

The vast machine shop during the war years. Women worked primarily in the assembly of guns. The Commercial Division and areas like the machine shop were still male-dominated. In March 1943, there were only 47 women among 1,101 men in the Commercial Division.

As the Second World War became a reality, the staff hired to organize the factory began a huge undertaking. Machinery was purchased from both Canada and the United States and installed in a facility that had been cleared of its pre-war equipment. Some buildings still had dirt floors when James Hahn purchased Inglis.

finest machinery and the finest tooling; but we were building the finest gun.

Despite the political turmoil and the magnitude of the task, Bruce knew he was involved in unprecedented industrial development. There would be less dependence on older forms of work organization and industrial processes. The job of manufacturing the Bren gun would be taken from the hands of traditional craftsmen and given to less-experienced workers for assembly-type production. Since men would presumably be away fighting a war, work on the Bren gun would have to be reorganized to become "women's work," or at least what suited the image of appropriate work for "girls." Robert Bruce had not anticipated who would operate the machines he purchased. No one

could have anticipated the transformation of manufacturing that the war would bring about, least of all Bruce, who was working long hours getting the plant ready for production.

When I was putting together the specs and buying the machinery for it, I had no idea who would be working on those machines. The only problem, is the fact that at that point in time, women had not been integrated in industry to the degree that they are now, or were by the end of the war. So they really had to have training for a lot of these specific operators. There are some very intricate operations, like rifling a barrel. That's a very sophisticated job and it can't be done by just anybody. It was a piston-activated firing mechanism. There was a gas that physically moved the piston. That's like building a small engine. There were a lot of highly technical, close-tolerance operations to be done. But these people were taken and trained to do that job.

When you look at the fact that there weren't too many men available, then [hiring women] was the obvious alternative. It was a natural thing to happen. When you think about it, it was much better to have them. They were much more sensitive with the feel of their fingers. They could do things that a man with clumsy fingers couldn't get at, and in many cases, we were probably better off having the ladies doing the job.

In reality, women had worked in factories for decades. Women's participation in industry did not begin in World War II, despite the high profile of Rosie the Riveter. Between 1891 and 1921 women in Ontario represented more than 25 percent of the total manufacturing work force. The establishments where women worked were concentrated in certain sectors. The garment, textile, food, and bookbinding industries had been ghettoized. There was the precedent of some women being used in large scale munitions work during the First World War, though this did not take place at Inglis. Metalworking plants like Inglis were traditionally male domains.

Despite the imagery and rhetoric surrounding the entry of women into production during World War II, the arrival of women at Inglis occurred for complex reasons that involved more than a labour shortage. Women who worked at Inglis during the war never filled jobs that men had filled. Large portions of the plant remained male dominated, controlled by metal craftsmen. Female employment was confined to war work and was centred in specific departments structured for women doing jobs designed specifically for them. On the whole, women were still shut out of opportunities that required extensive training and experience. Not surprisingly, women's denied access to craft and trades positions meant they would have little right to industrial jobs when war production was no longer required. For a brief time only, women were paid well, though less than men, for jobs that were created specifically for female labour; these jobs required a minimum of training and offered little opportunity for advancement.

Where are you Dorothy Stone?

OUR ONLY GIRL TOOL DESIGNER

Dorothy Stone, of Ordnance Tool Design, was one of those little girls who was always getting into hot water by drawing not too complimentary likenesses of the teacher on the edges of their textbooks. And every time she had the chance she went swimming. She still enjoys doing those same things more than anything else. She says that painting is her hobby. In the past six years she has painted a hundred and fifty portraits, and illustrated a book—sounds like work to me! Dr. E. F. Burton, head of the McLennan "Lab" at Toronto University asked her to illustrate "The Electron Microscope," his book on that famous new invention. It was that old habit of school days that landed her the job; Dr. Burton remembered a certain cartoon of him that she had done at one time! She was the first girl in Tool Design to take a job formerly done by a man; in fact, the first girl in the plant—for the rest of the girls here at that time were stenographers and clerks. She started back in October, '39, in the old Bren Building, helping with the first sheets on the Browning Gun. She worked as a tracer till December, 1940, when she got her rating as Tool Designer.

She is an excellent swimmer—has her silver Life Saving Medal and her Instructor's Degree in life saving. In 1927 she was president of the Women's Swimming Club at Varsity. She is a graduate of the Ontario College of Art, class of '31. She likes detective stories and flees from soap operas on the radio and the smell of cigars.

Wartime in Canadian industry brought concerns about national security. Each munitions factory was closely watched by representatives from the armed forces. Controlling a large work force over several shifts was not an easy task, and personnel work was developed with the aid of the University of Toronto. The 1940 Conditions of Employment were a complete set of rules for guiding worker conduct in the plant. A few of the rules were:

> Employees ringing in late will be paid from the nearest quarter hour following time rung in, and must begin work at once on entering shop.
>
> Everyone must keep his machine, tools and working place as clean as possible. Paper, rags and other refuse must be kept from shop and washroom floors and placed in the receptacles provided. It is the duty of all employees to see that the shop is kept scrupulously clean at all times.
>
> All employees are bound by the "Secrets Act" which is prominently displayed throughout the Company's property and it is pointed out that ignorance of the conditions of this "Act" does not constitute an excuse for violation.
>
> No employee of the Company shall take any part, drawing, specification or other information out of the Company's premises for any reason whatsoever, unless specific permission is first obtained from the Superintendent.

The War Effort, the Home Front, and the Canadian Economy

The war altered the world of manufacturing as much as it did the map of Europe. The boom spawned by the arrival of hostilities came on the heels of eight years of the Great Depression. New prospects for employment were created by arms production and the industrial build-up that began in the late 1930s. When the war started in 1939, a great many Canadians were still unemployed. As Wilf Finch, who started his apprenticeship at Inglis during the war, recalled, "Remember we had nothing. Canada had nothing. Nobody had nothing in this country. We were just a bunch of bums, that's all we were. We had a Depression, and it was basically still on."

Bert Bowler also gained his first work experience at Inglis, along with thousands of other young men.

> *I was about 18 when I went to Inglis. I tried to get in the army and they wouldn't take me. In those days I weighed about 90 pounds. None of the kids were really heavy in those days because it was coming out of the Depression. People worked very hard, they were conscientious. They'd just come through a period when there was no work, so they were extremely anxious to produce and to have a good record.*
>
> *They were trying to improve production and improve the way things were done. They put up buildings in half the time they do today. They used to turn around and move the machinery in one day, and have it running the next morning. I'd come in to find my cart and there's nothing there. I'd have to search for where to go to work. I was working three shifts, rotating.*

Inglis was just one of thousands of Canadian companies involved in war production, but it eventually became the Commonwealth's largest arms manufacturer and played an important role in supplying weapons and equipment to the war effort. Activity at Inglis increased earlier than it did at other companies because the Bren gun contract was signed a full eighteen months before the war formally started. With the arrival of the war, not only did industry change its products for the war effort, but the scale and structure of manufacturing was altered forever.

As Inglis began Bren gun production, the old, privately-owned company now called the Commercial Division, was reactivated. Unlike the Ordnance Division, Commercial was a private company owned by Major Hahn and his partner interests. All work not directly ordered by the Crown was done by this division of the company. Turbines and boilers were manufactured for Canadian-made warships. Inglis produced equipment for steel mills. Blast furnaces were manufactured on Strachan Avenue. Pumps for the oil and gas industry were assembled, while other arms facilities purchased presses and forging hammers from Inglis. "There has hardly been an industrial war expansion in Canada that the company has not participated in in some way," Hahn told the *Globe and Mail* in 1941, and he wasn't exaggerating.

The demands of war production required unprecedented numbers of workers. In the early war years, there were no labour shortages as Hahn had easily reunited much of the old work force in 1938–39. The company's slow, but ultimately widescale, introduction of women into the work force might have been based on an assumption of future shortages, but for the first half of the war there were financial benefits to employing women that were just too good to resist.

During the First World War there had been serious and widespread unrest in munitions factories like Inglis. Government had learned that the skill and supply of munitions workers were important considerations when it came to maintaining peace on the home front. The idea of using women in war work was first raised by Hahn with the federal deputy minister of labour when the war was just a few days old:

> Mr. Hahn told me that the Inglis Company was being pressed to expedite delivery of the Bren gun and that to this end the company had requested permission to extend their working hours from 44 to 54 per week, also to employ girls and to increase the present wages scale as circumstances may require.
>
> With respect to the employment of female labour I gathered that his desire was that sanction should be given for a payment of a lower scale of wages to girls than would apply under present arrangements to male help.

A few weeks after this request, the acting deputy

Building 10, Ordnance Division, housed these unnamed workers at bench lathes. They produced tools and gauges which in turn were integrated into the Bren gun production.

Two pages from Wilf Finch's apprenticeship book. He started at Inglis in 1939 and was a proud member of the IAM.

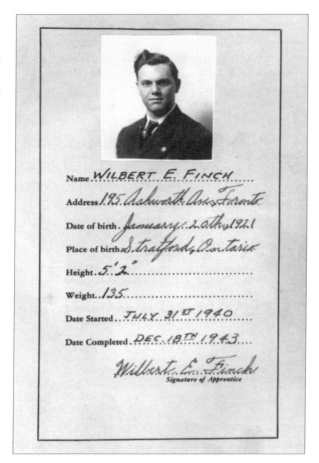

Name *WILBERT E. FINCH*

Address *195 Ashworth Ave, Toronto*

Date of birth *January 20th, 1921*

Place of birth *Stratford, Ontario*

Height *5'2"*

Weight *135*

Date Started *JULY 31ST 1940*

Date Completed *DEC 18TH 1943*

Wilbert E. Finch
Signature of Apprentice

To whom it may concern:—
Wilbert Finch has at all times taken a very keen and intelligent attitude towards his work. His work and conduct during his apprenticeship were highly satisfactory

J H Fearncombe
Wks Manager
April 1944

minister of militia endorsed the request by noting, "If there is likely to be a shortage of male labour in future, it would appear to be of some advantage to start female labour at the beginning of production rather than to train male labour and then have them subsequently replaced by female labour."

The introduction of women into Bren gun production was not without controversy. Within days of the request, the Machinists' Union representative, James Somerville, who had had an association with the John Inglis Company for over thirty years, objected to the idea of women being introduced to any job classifications at Inglis. The government's initial response to the company request was lukewarm, at best. The federal minister of labour noted that the Bren gun plant at Enfield, England, employed no female labour. More importantly, he wrote, "There are still many thousands of workmen registered in the public employment offices throughout Eastern Canada for whom employment is not at present available, and in these circumstances the proposal of the John Inglis Company to engage female labour should not be entertained at present."

One month later, in November 1939, the government determined:

> The Company may engage and train five female employees at a wage rate of thirty cents per hour. The training period to be limited to three months, after which the wage rate will be subject to further consideration. Male employees are not to be laid off or their services otherwise dispensed with for the purpose of engaging female labour.

The determination was made on the advice of the War Supply Board. Important questions raised by the Ministry of Labour, which went to the heart of early labour market policy with regard to women, were ignored. Deputy Minister Lacelle, in raising objections to the War Supply Board's decision, remarked that at the end of October 1939, "There were approximately 40,000 male workers registered in the Employment Offices of Toronto alone as seeking work."

Three stokers first class attend a special course on ship boilers at Inglis in 1943. At left is Gordon Sides, behind him, John Swietanski. Jack Haddow, from Sudbury, crouches inside this huge freighter boiler.

Canada's prime minister, William Lyon Mackenzie King, visits Gladys Morton on the job at Inglis. Morton wears the signature head gear of female war workers, a bandanna. The liquid pouring into the process was coolant for metalworking.

Politicians, soldiers and celebrities often called on the Inglis plant and throughout the war the factory became an important propaganda source and morale booster for the media. Here Prime Minister Mackenzie King addresses an unnamed older woman war worker. To King's left stands Lee Ainsworth, Inglis company vice-president. Slightly behind to his right, with his hand on his chin, is Burford Trestrail, head of personnel.

The potential sensitivity of the issue required that the decision be carefully crafted to avoid disagreement among the several parties. The number that could be hired was small and unthreatening to the union. The wage rate of thirty cents an hour, far below all other classifications in the Bren Division, likely pleased both the union and the company, because it conformed to their slightly different yet compatible visions of how women might fit into the growing war plant. Finally, the ruling gave the impression that this might be a temporary situation and would in no way endanger the employment prospects of men.

Kay Drybrough Bradley was one of these first five women hired to work in the Ordnance Division in 1940. She too had worked previously at Hahn's radio factory. The demands of production, especially on women for whom manufacturing was foreign, necessitated a strong commitment to the war effort that would overcome any initial hesitation and strangeness that many women may have felt. Kay Bradley's memories of her first days on the job reveal what were clearly powerful experiences for the thousands of women who came to work at Inglis:

Oh, all these machines in the Bren building — beautiful gray machines. They had a coolant running on them, like white milk, to cool the cutters off. We had to stand for two days and watch the set-up man. I was so nervous. We had micrometers for gauging. What I was working on was a little component in the barrel. I'd be running the machines and thinking about all these young lives, killing people, and what a terrible thing war is.

The pace and nature of the female classifications, while limiting from the standpoint of skilled industrial jobs, allowed women new independence and experiences. Bradley recalled:

It was busy. You'd work and have your supper, if that was your shift. You were always trying to do your amount. I found it very pleasurable — watching to see that we gauged it properly. The foremen would go around, and the inspectors — they'd take a piece and inspect it with their instruments. You had to watch the machines — there was no time for fooling around. On our breaks we'd talk about our boyfriends, and where we'd go on our day off. We'd go to the

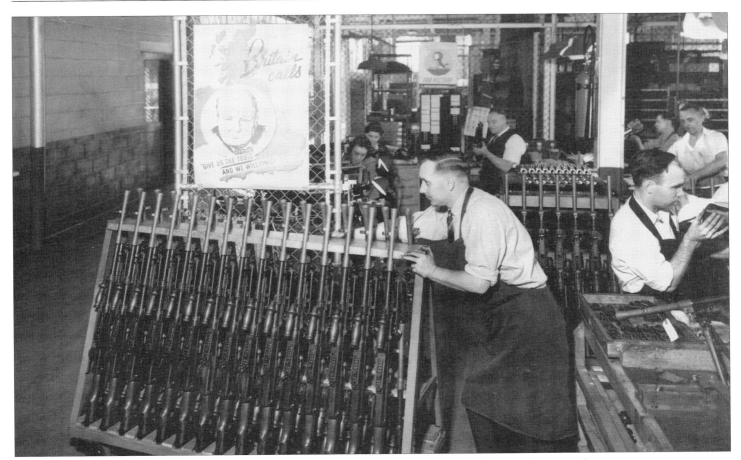

The face of Winston Churchill encourages workers on the main floor of Building 19, the Bren Annex, to keep the guns coming. Many Inglis workers had family ties to Britain and the war effort of an individual was often a very personal matter.

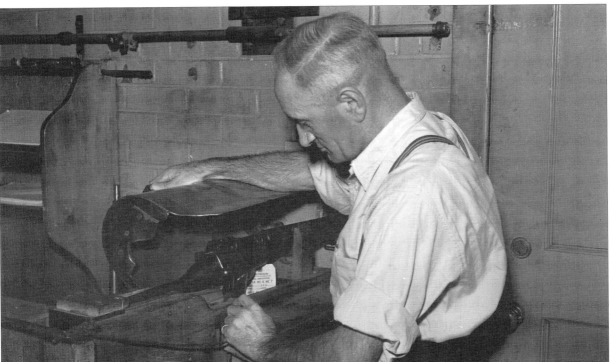

Some of the older war workers at Inglis were tradesmen who had worked metal before the plant was sold in 1936 to Major James Hahn.

This picture of the main floor in the Bren building gives a sense of the size and scope of the operation. In this area there was a mix of men and women working side by side

Palais Royale. We'd often go out to Long Branch Park and dance there. Or go in the boat sometimes, to Port Dalhousie. Going out to work gave me experience. I became aware of what war was. It made me more independent money-wise. It helped me a lot, that way.

The request for five women soon led to new and larger questions and concerns. In May 1940 the company requested that an additional twenty women be permitted to work on the Bren with the knowledge "that they may not be needed right away." By the summer, the company requested permission to hire additional women "up to maximum of 100 women." This was granted on 16 July 1940, with "the understanding that these females are to be employed on light machine operations and as inspectors, pro-vided, however, that the employment of the additional female workers will not have the effect of displacing male workers who are presently employed by this company."

At the same time, Gerald Brown, the federal assistant deputy minister of labour, cautioned, "No definite policy has been adopted as yet in respect of the employment of female labour on war work." Brown suggested that the Inglis company's request be treated "with reserve for the time being, pending determination of the broader aspects of labour policy which are involved." As memos were exchanged between the various levels of an ever-growing wartime bureaucracy, a process began by which Inglis became the largest employer ever of women industrial workers.

Mary Spratt was one of many Toronto schoolgirls who received technical training to be

On the top floor of Building 19.

This 1940 display at the CNE for the Bren gun must have been very impressive. Canadians were interested in details of the gun which was used by their sons, brothers, fathers and friends serving in Europe. By 1943, Inglis workers had produced over 100,000 Bren guns.

part of the war effort. Youth training programs had been a government strategy to help combat the effects of the depression. Home Service Training Schools for young women were organized to encourage domestic skills. But the War Emergency Training Program from 1940 began to prepare women for work that was previously reserved for men.

At first only Ontario women participated, and in very small numbers. Programs were quite specialized and lasted only two or three weeks. By the end of 1942, women in these preemployment programs made up forty-eight percent of participants. Coursework covered subjects such as machine shop, ammunition filling, fine instrument mechanics, power machine operation,

welding, sheet metal, bench fitting and assembly, industrial chemistry, aircraft-related subjects, electric wiring, radio and electric assembly, drafting, mechanical drawing, and laboratory technician work.

Spratt's father, Fred, who was plant chairman of the Machinists' Union at Inglis, suggested she apply there after completing high school. She couldn't yet join the armed forces, so Spratt enlisted in Canada's industrial army instead.

There weren't many girls working [at Inglis]. They were mostly men, older men. The girls were allowed to punch out five minutes ahead of the men, so we wouldn't

The Inglis Girls' Club on Cowan Avenue offered a range of activities for women war workers. The company hoped that establishing a club would help alleviate loneliness in those women living away from home. The building was an old roller skating rink and the wooden floors were perfect for dancing and for badminton.

be pushed and hustled on our way out of the plant. We could go out and wash up five minutes early, and we got paid for it. It didn't last long, maybe four months. There were more and more people being hired, and it became too unwieldy. Shifts were being put on. It became very crowded.

A significant number of both men and especially women who worked in the Ordnance Division, or "Crown," were considered unskilled labour. Fred Spratt, Mary's father, was a journeyman machinist in the "real," unionized John Inglis plant. The division between Bren production and the original John Inglis factory went beyond their housing in separate build-

ings. Throughout the war, women would comprise a large proportion of many departments, but these were always in the government-owned Ordnance Division. The rest of the company, which also grew during the war, remained a male world. The traditions of the original John Inglis Company continued in these departments, although they witnessed unparalleled growth and technical development.

The introduction of women into Inglis, then, did not represent a shattering of all shopfloor traditions. Confining women to the Ordnance Division created distinctions in the minds of both the workers and management. New jobs were created that simplified tasks and, by design, involved repetitious, semi-

These Inglis "Chauffeurettes" transported people and papers from building to building on the vast Inglis complex. From time to time they were called on to drive sick workers home.

skilled operations. This simplification imposed limits on what women war workers could achieve. While Mary Spratt achieved much at Inglis, she didn't receive pay equal to that of men.

As late as May 1941, nearly two years into the war, there were still objections about Inglis's practice of using cut-rate female labour to build Bren guns. The company had by then revealed (or formulated; it is unclear which) its plans to use large numbers of women to make arms. The provincial deputy minister of labour, James Marsh, objected in a letter to his federal counterpart:

It has been brought to my attention that a representative of the John Inglis Company, Toronto, had indicated that in the process of adding to their production staff to the end that it would be increased from 5,500 to at least 10,000, the intention was to employ a far larger number of female workers than males so that at the completion of their full complement of employees there would be in round figures something better than 5,000 females and under 5,000 males.

One of the number of reasons given was that they are required to pay on an average of $32.00 per week for the male employees

Wilbert Finch started his apprenticeship at Inglis in 1939. In the group photo, he is seen kneeling at the far right. The names of the other apprentices are unknown.

where as they were able to employ females at an average of $20.00, thus saving for the company a considerable amount of money in the matter of wage costs ...

Marsh went on to state that he had "no objection" to the idea of large numbers of female war workers, but that this had to be in keeping with a decision reached by provincial labour ministers. They supported the idea that "women should be paid wages equal to those paid men for equal work." Marsh further noted, "There are still large numbers of male labour available for industrial work which should be absorbed by industry rather than deliberately ignored as seems to be the case at the John Inglis plant."

For at least two years, then, the company had slowly and quietly developed a policy of hiring women, although men were available. This was not a declaration of gender equality because the company paid the women significantly less. With the company collecting a flat fee for each gun produced, it had developed a sophisticated, though invisible, system of profiteering. In addition to being cheaper, women workers

For safety reasons, women war workers covered their hair, usually with a colourful bandanna, and left long sleeves and jewellery at home. Pants or overalls were also required instead of skirts and dresses.

Cafeterias, tuck shops, lunchrooms — all were necessary to feed the Inglis work force. One cafeteria was run by the Canadian National Institute for the Blind. Nutrition was an important concern, as war workers often spent several weeks in the factory without a day off. The Strachan Avenue plant had its own staff of nutritionists.

may also have been perceived as potentially more docile than men, less apt to cause trouble, and less familiar with trade unions.

Shortages of male workers did eventually become a more important factor in the hiring of women. A memo dated 18 May 1942 listed all the Ordnance Division departments and the proportion of women in them.

The pattern of hiring women had created departmental ghettos, following those historical patterns that had long existed in other industries. The light assembly employees in both the Bren and Browning departments included large majorities of women. However, there was not a single woman in the tool room. An earlier memo noted with concern that the proportion of girls was dropping and "drastic steps should be taken at once to correct it."

With the enormous growth of the factory and orders to match, more and more workers were required. The local labour market was very competitive, the work force, very mobile, until the creation of the National Selective Service in 1944. The Inglis Company began to develop a personnel department to look after its hundreds of employees and to recruit hundreds more. The war was a formative period for Canadian "personnel strategies" and industrial relations systems. Kay Bradley was soon transferred from production to this new department. Bradley recalled that the company required so many women that it had to recruit actively across the country. The local labour market, with hundreds, if not thousands, of other companies hiring women, led Inglis to create a sophisticated recruitment and screening process:

Production had to get up and girls were needed. So I was to be one of the first girls in personnel, in war work. We were going to put 21 girls, every two weeks, in a training school to learn machines, and when they came out, we'd place them. We couldn't get girls, so we decided we'd go out west for girls, and all over. We went to North Bay and Sudbury, even out east a little bit. And then we went to Winnipeg, and Saskatchewan, Calgary, Edmonton, and Red Deer.

We had to have the Mounties okay them. We had to have medical tests, and they were told all about what their privileges were here. We got them rooms in boarding houses in a proper district.

For the most part, Inglis war workers came for their shift, and went home to sleep. Some brought a meal from home, some purchased snacks at the in-plant tuck shops, and still others ate at the cafeteria run by the Canadian National Institute for the Blind. By 1941 there were three cafeterias, two canteens, twelve mess rooms and eleven mobile canteens. Prices ranged from three cents for a glass of milk, to twenty-five cents for an entree. The nearly 7,000 employees in 1941 favoured roast beef, apple pie, steamed pudding and ice cream, of which thirty gallons were served every day.

Recruitment was not an easy task. Young women were lured to Toronto with the promise of good wages. This, in turn, put great pressure on the service sector, where women had previously been employed in larger numbers. Restaurants and retail stores were forced to increase wages to maintain staff. "Servants" were virtually unavailable for many wealthy families.

As the company reached its peak employment levels in mid-1943 and as war production shifted into high gear, the character of women's employment at Inglis was established on a larger scale. Despite restrictions to employment mobility and despite endless recruiting, the numbers of employees fluctuated month to month. Not all of those women recruited proved suitable for the job. In January 1943, the company recorded 215 terminations for that month alone.

Bert Bowler recalled the experience of working with so many women:

One of the most astounding things is that for every man in Inglis, I think you had about 30 women. These women were exceptional. There were mothers, there were wives, there were the daughters of soldiers, and there were the lovers. They were all doing what they thought was best to help out to get the war over. A lot of times there were a lot of tears. A lot of times there was a lot of fun and laughs too.

Workers leave the factory by the back gate at shift change.

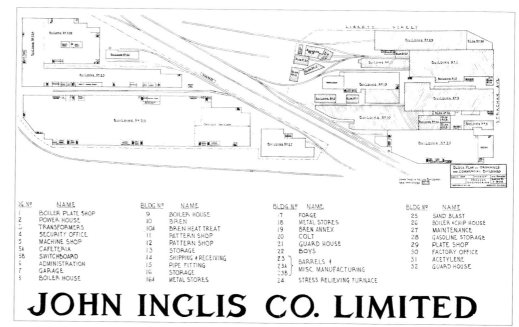

BLDG Nº	NAME	BLDG Nº	NAME	BLDG Nº	NAME	BLDG Nº	NAME
1	BOILER PLATE SHOP	9	BOILER HOUSE	17	FORGE	25	SAND BLAST
2	POWER HOUSE	10	BREN	18	METAL STORES	26	BOILER & CHIP HOUSE
3	TRANSFORMERS	10A	BREN HEAT TREAT	19	BREN ANNEX	27	MAINTENANCE
4	SECURITY OFFICE	11	PATTERN SHOP	20	COLT	28	GASOLINE STORAGE
5	MACHINE SHOP	12	PATTERN SHOP	21	GUARD HOUSE	29	PLATE SHOP
5A	CAFETERIA	13	STORAGE	22	BOYS	30	FACTORY OFFICE
5B	SWITCHBOARD	14	SHIPPING & RECEIVING	23	BARRELS &	31	ACETYLENE
6	ADMINISTRATION	15	PIPE FITTING	23A	MISC. MANUFACTURING	32	GUARD HOUSE
7	GARAGE	16	STORAGE	23B			
8	BOILER HOUSE	16A	METAL STORES	24	STRESS RELIEVING FURNACE		

JOHN INGLIS CO. LIMITED

$

"Thar's Gold in Them Hills"

WE PAY FOR $IDEAS$

The

Suggestion Award Plan

For Employees of the
JOHN INGLIS CO., LIMITED, TORONTO

INGLIS

These are the first and last pages of a company booklet on the Suggestion Award Plan. The three unnamed workers appear less "happy" than the text would suggest. Maybe the amount of the award cheque was less than expected. Some awards were as little as $2.00.

Opposite page: This map of the Strachan Avenue plant was drawn during World War II. The shaded areas are buildings which belonged to the John Inglis Company. The buildings in white were so-called Crown property and were erected during the war. Many of the publicly owned buildings were sold after the war to private industry.

ORGANIZATION CHART
JOHN INGLIS SUGGESTION AWARD PLAN

CENTRAL COMMITTEES
ORDNANCE & COMMERCIAL
APPOINTED BY THE MANAGEMENT AND INCLUDES REPRE-SENTATIVES OF ADMINISTRATION, PRODUCTION, RESEARCH AND ENGINEERING, INSPECTION, EFFICIENCY, PERSONNEL AND LABOR

AND THE

SUGGESTION SUPERVISOR
WHOSE DUTIES ARE TO COLLECT, ANALYZE AND DISTRIBUTE SUGGESTIONS FOR INVESTIGATION, ACT AS CHAIRMAN OF THE MAIN COMMITTEES, PREPARE PROGRESS REPORTS, SUPERVISE CLERICAL ROUTINE AND MAINTAIN RECORDS, CONTACT SUGGESTORS WHEN ADVISABLE, ARRANGE FOR DISTRIBUTION OF AWARDS

SUB-COMMITTEES
ORDNANCE & COMMERCIAL
DUTIES ARE TO ANALYZE SUGGESTIONS, DETERMINE PRACTICABILITY AND MAKE RECOMMENDATIONS AS TO USE

OTHER CONTACTS

| DEPT. HEADS | LEGAL DEPT. | STORES DEPT. | TIME STUDY | PURCHASING DEPT. | COST ACCOUNTING | SPECIAL INVESTIGATORS |

Three happy winners looking at their Award Checks and comparing notes.

WAR-WORKERS NIGHT AT SUNNYSIDE

Kay Bradley

Women were well represented in Bren, Colt, and Browning, the three Ordnance Departments, but even within these, departmental ghettos were created. Women consistently found themselves in the jobs with the lowest rates. In the Commercial Division, which included the original heavy engineering work for which the company had become so famous, 1,200 workers, including Harry Goudy, toiled away. This division of the most highly skilled, well-paid, entirely unionized metal craftsmen built marine boilers, steam turbines, and other sophisticated equipment directly related to the war effort. In this entire department there were forty-seven women, only four percent of the total.

In 1943 Inglis's vice president, Lee Ainsworth, requested that the average departmental wage rates be calculated in relation to the proportion of women workers in each. The results were surprising to the employee doing the calculations. They couldn't have been a surprise to company management, given the report of Ontario's deputy minister, James Marsh. The

Bert Bowler

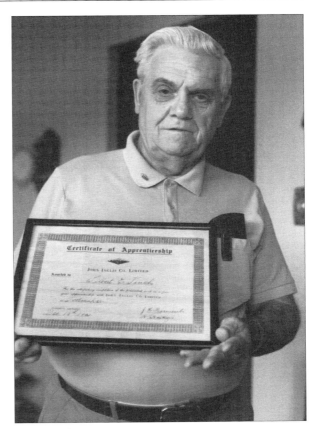

Wilf Finch

results revealed that the higher the proportion of female employees in a department, the lower the average wage rate paid. Ten years after the war ended, Hahn wrote that employing women in production work was more than just a question of labour supply: "By the 1930s weapons were so designed that up to seventy-five per cent of female, semi-skilled or unskilled labour could be employed in their manufacture in the event of an emergency." While no "emergency" ever threatened domestic production, for the duration of the war there were significant differences between the wage rates of men and women at Inglis.

The Strachan Avenue plant became an enormous complex of the old buildings and those that were altered or constructed for the production of guns. The largest war production plant in Canada, Inglis became the largest single employer of women in the country. Inglis also reflected the national economy. Women's participation in the paid labour force increased from about 638,000 in 1939 to approximately 1,077,000 by October 1944. This dramatic change was supported by a sophisticated ideology and considerable propaganda, much of it in

women's magazines. Doing factory work was compared to using a vacuum cleaner or other familiar but feminine household equipment; filling a shell was as easy as baking a cake. Women were encouraged to stay women by using make-up even when wearing overalls. Women, it was thought, were well suited for repetitive tasks, as they were used to the monotony of housework.

The year Mary Spratt started at Inglis — 1940 — Erma Wilson Hughes was still living on her family's farm in Tolston, Manitoba, but big-city wages were beginning to entice young people. In 1943 she started work at Inglis.

I operated machines. That was what I was taught to do, milling machines and other machines. I don't remember what the first machine was that I worked on at Inglis, but it was war work. The lead hand was mostly always men, but it was mostly women working on the machines.

I don't know of any women that were a lead hand. I think there were some women could have done it. Some of the jobs were not that complicated. A lot of the men had

Robert Bruce

June Lake

The three unnamed women in this photograph are inspecting gun barrels. Tolerances were very fine for these weapons.

These workers gathered in the Boiler Plate Shop for Victory Bond rally. Inglis employees contributed millions of dollars.

very simple jobs. Women were not as aggressive then as they are now. If it was now, I'm sure there would be women lead hands.

Women at first had a hard time being accepted by the older male workers. Plant propaganda, while celebrating the contributions of the women, also singled them out as "girls." Such material gave recognition to the thousands of women in the plant, but it could not substitute for true equality.

Nowhere was this more clear than on the issue of skill. Women, untrained in the skilled trades, were not found in the departments needing the higher skills or in the Commercial Division as a whole. Members of the craft unions that had been at Inglis for decades anticipated that their control in the skilled trades could be undermined when companies began to hire women. The Metal Polishers' Union wrote

to an official at the Ministry of Labour, expressing these craft union concerns. Speaking for the union, R.A. Gerard was upset that his members were expected to train unskilled workers while there were still "competent" mechanics unemployed. Particularly upsetting was an accident involving one of the untrained women:

Directly following this accident the Superintendent was notified by two of our Members that they would not act as instructors.

As this work has to be very accurate and a slowing down of production is taking place in this department owing to the fact that the work produced by these Girls will not stand inspection and therefore some of our Members have to refinish it. We are hoping that your department will immediately intercede on behalf of the

Above: During the shooting of a National Film Board movie, Inglis workers are shown on the job. In the foreground a Bren gun hangs from the ceiling. The banner in the background refers to the "Lost-Time Campaign." The text says, "Help them do their stuff. They're shooting for 6." The film lights make the faces of some of the workers unrecognizable.

One of the oldest sections of the Strachan Avenue factory was the forge. It was located in a building attached to the boiler shop.

Government before this organization is forced to take direct action against this firm.

When the situation was investigated, the company, represented by Vice President Ainsworth, made it clear that there was no intention to operate without female labour:

Mr. Ainsworth informed me that there are about 12 males and 6 females in the polishing department, and that the females are engaged in polishing that part of the Gun, known as the "platform magazine." He claims that for this particular part, females are faster and more competent, then [sic] the regular male polishers and it is the intention to employ more females on these operations. Mr. Ainsworth claims, it is not necessary to have polisher mechanics in the polishing and buffing departments of the plant as it is a simple matter to give unskilled help sufficient training in a short period, to enable them to become efficient enough to perform the work required.

I was also informed by Mr. Ainsworth, that the female mentioned in Mr. Gerard's letter, was not injured because of her lack of experience, but because she was wearing a dress, which became caught in a spindle. Instructions are to be issued that overalls will have to be worn by females in the factory.

These overalls and bandannas would become the signature apparel for women war workers. The company sold them with and without the Inglis logo. Clothing alone did nothing to ensure that the women would be taken seriously on the shopfloor. Many of them probably sensed the limitations that had been imposed on them. They were called, after all, war workers, a label that implied theirs was a temporary position.

In 1942, the company, perhaps to improve its recruiting, compiled information about "the best female workers" in each department. The names were submitted by the foremen. Of the 192 women interviewed, thirty-one percent had attended technical school for training. The average age was 22.5, with a range of 18 to 37. More interestingly, of the 192, only fifteen, or less than one percent, had no previous work experience. The variety of their previous jobs crossed all levels of education. Women clearly were limited in their work and career options, despite formal education. The most frequently mentioned occupations were waitress, farm and domestic worker, sales clerk, office worker and industrial worker. This last category comprised a range of jobs: shoe factory worker, machine operator, brushmaker, radium painter, bookbinding, dipping chocolates, and printing.

The Girls' Club

The rapid increase in women workers in 1942–43 led to explicitly paternalistic concerns on the part of the company. In the summer and winter of 1942, the company began to explore seriously the need for some kind of "girls club." It was thought that, "Through the club, we build up the correct mental attitude of the women," "discover personal grievances," and "the employee improves her coordination control which in turn should prove itself in her work."

Thousands of women working at Inglis, especially those from outside Toronto, were living in boarding houses. The company sought to create an institution that could provide basic hygiene and recreation facilities for the 10,000 women working at Inglis. Following much discussion and consultation, the new John Inglis Girls' Recreation Club opened on 30 November 1942.

The Club was located at 212 Cowan Avenue in Parkdale, previously the site of a popular skating rink, the Pawlowa. The business manager of the Girls' club was Bill Currie, a man. While the experience that many women gained working at Inglis was liberating, power sharing was not part of their war experience. Even the colour scheme for painting the club walls was decided by the man who headed up personnel. In a memo to Currie, it was suggested that silver gray with powder blue trim would be nice, "along the lines of the interior decoration of places like Honey Dew, Murray's, etc. … In any event, don't let them proceed with this until we have the opportunity of passing on it."

The club served many practical and ideological purposes: hygiene facility, dance lessons, friendship clubs, socials, dances, and cabaret and theatre. Some of the women were involved in community work through the club, visiting patients in hospital and arranging mutual events. Bazaars and raffles were held to fund these activities. Showers were available for weary war workers, and a snack bar was open. The club library offered a wide selection of books, including *Women in Industry, Women at War,*

Bandannas were one way that women avoided getting their hair caught in the machines they operated. Mary Spratt noted: "We used to have to wear bandannas to cover our hair. It started with hair nets, but the girls, being girls and liking to look nice, would put a hole in the hair nets, so they didn't last very long. We had to keep our hair completely covered."

Anne Saegert

These Bren guns were packed and ready for shipment to the Forces overseas. In this picture, the guns were stored in Building 22, the Boys Building, named after the Boys rifle which Inglis workers also produced. The Bren received its name by combining the name of the Moravian town, Brno, and the place where production began, Enfield, England, the same city where the Enfield Rifle was produced. The gun could be fired from a tripod, bipod or from the hip. It had an effective range of 1,000 yards and a maximum range of 2,000 yards.

More Zest for Life and *Germany's Master Plan.*

The Girls' Club sought to prevent bouts of loneliness in young women who were far from home and working long hours. A wide range of recreational and social activities was organized. The club also channeled the energies of these thousands of women into safe, wholesome pastimes. Recreational activities, the company reasoned, could help reduce absenteeism and prevent workers from returning home. Professional instructors were hired to teach dance, "from ballet and folk to jitterbug," swimming, handicrafts, and "beauty" exercises. Membership in the club cost fifteen cents per week; the club was open weekdays from 8 a.m. to 11:30 p.m. and on weekends. Tickets for live radio broadcasts were always available. Little was left to chance at these events, and appearance mattered. For a 1942 broadcast of "Truth or Consequences," the company's director of personnel asked that some tickets be given to "some regular girl war-workers including a few who are particularly attractive."

Despite its plans, the club never achieved the expected level of membership. Perhaps the women who worked at Inglis found it paternalistic. With so much of their energies directed to the production process, they may have found the club excessively regimented if they simply wanted to have fun.

Rituals of Morale

Keeping up the morale of war workers was often difficult. Although wages were relatively high, there was little opportunity to spend the money earned. The government even extended restrictions to fashion. A dress could have no more than nine buttons, and a hem had to be less than two inches deep. Clothing with cuffs, double-breasted jackets, and flap pockets were forbidden. And women wishing for lounging pyjamas, bloomers, teddys, or shadow-panelled slips were out of luck for the duration of the war.

The Inglis Company published a biweekly newsletter, the *Shotgun*, with the motto "They Shall Not Die Because We Faltered." The paper was full of in-house news and gossip, medical advice, inspirational messages for war workers, jokes, cartoons, and news and pictures of "Inglisans" in the armed forces.

The schedules of the many sports leagues were printed: men's and "girls'" softball, hockey, basketball, bowling. Baseball was played at fields across the city like Stanley Park and Christie Pits. The basketball teams met at Parkdale Collegiate on Close Avenue, while hockey players shinnied on the Humber or Don River and tournaments were held at Varsity Arena.

After work, there were movies, dances, trips to Toronto Island and Port Dalhousie, and lots of clubs to visit: Tophat, Arcadian, Palais Royale. Sunnyside on the Lakeshore was a popular destination for both the live orchestras and the amusement park. Loew's Theatre in downtown Toronto was open throughout the day and into the night. There, war workers could see Claudette Colbert, Paulette Goddard, and Veronica Lake in "So Proudly We Hail," or Olivia de Havilland in "Government Girl," or one of many soldier films, like "Captains of the Clouds" with James Cagney and Dennis Morgan, which was filmed in Canada with the assistance of the Royal Canadian Air Force.

Those war workers with a radio probably listened to "The Army Show" starring Johnny Wayne and Frank Shuster. In addition to popular U.S. shows — Jack Benny, "The Lone Ranger," "Fibber McGee and Molly" — Canadians listened to homegrown programs: "Carry on Canada," "Theatre of Freedom," the Happy Gang, and soap operas such as "Soldier's Wife" and "John and Judy." At 10 p.m., Lorne Greene would bring the news of the day into Canadian homes.

Lorne Greene also participated in morale-boosting events sponsored by the Department of National Defence, one of which was the celebration of the building of the 100,000th Bren gun at the Inglis plant in the summer of 1943. Representatives from the Chinese military were on hand to accept the presentation, and over 9,000 Inglis employees attended the event. The *Globe and Mail* of 31 August 1943 reported:

> Slim as a rattlesnake and a thousand times more deadly, a Bren machine gun was yesterday presented in a symbolical ceremony to the Chinese army. It was Bren Gun No. 100,000 … The company had an original contract for 32,000 Brens — a contract which, it was expected, would have taken five years to fill. Actually, the plant can now turn out that number in five weeks.
>
> All traffic in the plant, considered one of the largest machine gun factories in the world, was stopped briefly yesterday while dignitaries spoke from a flag-draped stand over a frise [sic] of Bren guns … surrounding the enclosure in which the ceremonies were held were thousands of employees, men in their working togs and gay bandannaed girls. They climbed on railway cranes and cars near by, lined every window and were on all available roofs … Miss Kay Dryborough [sic] pledged all the employees to keep turning out Brens at record speed.

The ceremony was planned to the second, leaving no room for surprises. No hourly workers were involved in the planning, and many must have felt the entire ceremony was a simple morale booster. This wartime pep rally would help shape workers' attitudes, and company and government had every intention of getting as much ideological mileage as possible out of the presentation. Inglis's vice president, A.L. Ainsworth later received a "thank you" letter from Gordon Garbut, of the Department of National Defence's Publicity Branch, who pointed out the propaganda value of the day's events:

> I look back upon the 100,000th Bren Gun ceremony with much satisfaction. I feel that it more than achieved its purpose both as a morale medium, and as a vehicle for Munitions and Supply publicity. Our Clipping Bureau reports excellent coverage in

This photograph appeared on the cover of The Monetary Times *in April 1943 with the description "Womanpower goes a long way in the manufacture of the Colt-Browning machine gun at the John Inglis Co. Ltd. One woman handles four milling machines, processing the right hand cam of the all important Breech block."*

all parts of Canada. The radio program struck me as being ideal and it lost nothing in the compression to a fifteen minute period. I believe the newsreel shots will be included in the releases to first run theaters beginning this Friday, but it is possible they will be carried over for one week. You may be interested to know that a five minute resume of the proceedings was beamed to London late Friday night and was carried in all programs to all parts of the Empire for the full twenty-four hour transmission on Saturday.

In 1942, there was even some discussion of using music in the Inglis plant to improve worker morale. There was debate over whether military marches or "salon-type" music would be most suitable and effective. Workers, during the trial period, requested popular music. The company, on the other hand, employed one of its staff, "a former organist and choir master, who made a considerable study of music and [was] particularly interested in music in war plants," to plan the programme. The original plan to allocate programming decisions to a labour/management committee was discarded, because "the music is designed to accomplish a specific purpose and to attain maximum effectiveness."

When the sound equipment was finally installed in March 1943, the former choir master played four types of music: "Opening Selections, Fatigue Selections, Lunch Period Selections and Closing Selections," despite the fact that "there are some of the younger employees of the Company who would prefer more the `boogie-Woogie' type of music of today, and a surprising number have asked for a much heavier type." But, he concluded, "It has been proven that these types rather frustrate the purpose of these programmes."

Women's Place at Inglis

For the duration of the war, craft unions would have to accept the reality of a vastly changed labour market. It was, Assistant Deputy Minister of Labour Brown wrote, the government's intention to ensure a constant supply of variously skilled help for the munitions industry — but only during wartime:

> It is not the intention that the skilled mechanics should be kept out of employment by the use of unskilled labour but at the same time it is vital to our war effort that

every step should be taken to relieve the pressure on the highly skilled trades by having some of their work, which is of a nature requiring less skill, done by others specially trained for the purpose.

Industry generally has been invited to co-operate by establishing training plans which would insure an adequate supply of trained personnel. You, of course, will appreciate that in carrying out a policy designed to insure a maximum war effort, it would not be possible to wait until every available skilled mechanic is actually in employment before commencing to train those who must be used temporarily during the war ... I know it is very definitely the wish that any such temporary help that is taken on in this wartime emergency, will be

---

The Girls' Club hosted countless dances. But the events were highly structured, which might explain in part why the Club never became as popular as planned. From a company memo:

> Servicemen will be welcomed by a committee of two senior hostesses and Miss Larson, who will turn the bos [sic] over to the two girls on the Register to sign their names. These girls will then call two Junior Hostesses who are close by to direct the boys to the check room. After checking, the two Junior Hostesses will suggest some games for the boys or a tour of the club.
>
> Dancing will commence after the first twenty boys have arrived. It has been suggested that only half of the gym floor be used for dancing and that this space be divided with the partitions provided for same.
>
> It has been suggested that the surplus girls can retire to the powder room and casually drift into the lounges as the boys begin to fill the club
>
> Refreshments will be served at 10:50 and to close the evening there will be sing-song which we hope, as said before, will be lead [sic] by Mr. Currie, THE KING
>
> After the boys have left the girls would like to take on the responsibility of seeing that all the dishes are cleaned up and that the club is left in ship-shape order.

Page Eight — The Shotgun — January 22, 194

GIRLS' CLUB ACTIVITIES REVIEWED

Groups Being Organized to Bring Cheer to the Boys at Christie

It all started down in 51 (now Dept. 50) when a group of five girls, Miriam Nadon, Agnes Turner, Leola Frost, Lillian Marler and Euphemia Hopkinson decided that a real need among the boys at Christie Street Hospital—wounded veterans of both this war and the last—for cheer and companionship and cigarettes could be satisfied by just a few hours of effort on their part and a small sum of money.

For the past two months they have been distributing boxes of fruit, cakes and candies, cigarettes and magazines among the patients in Ward 317, and stopping to chat with the boys for a while. The letters of thanks they have received testify just how much happiness the girls of 51 have handed out.

These girls are now hoping to broaden their organization, to be known as the "Friendship Club For Christie Street", to include girls from every shift of every department. Their aim is to reach as many of the patients as possible with gifts and a word of cheer and eventually to organize groups of girls for entertaining these boys who have given so much for their country, with songs, dance routines, etc.

There will be a meeting in the near future at the Girls' Club to carry out organization plans. **Would any girls interested in helping in this splendid work give their names, shift and clock No. to Foreladies, and they will be notified as to date of meeting, etc.**

A collection box will be placed in the Girls' Club for contributions to the fund of the "Friendship Club For Christie Street".

IN A HAPPY MOOD AT THE TAP CLASS

They look as if they're having a good time. And they really are. Ask anyone who attends Adele's dancing classes.

Sunday Night Canteen at the Club

Our Sunday Night Canteen is fast becoming known among servicemen as the "best canteen in Canada", at least so say the boys who spend Sunday evenings there. In any case it is definitely a success and certainly very popular.

Two hundred servicemen and a hundred and fifty Club members crowded the Club Lounges and Gym for the Canteen of January 9th when Judy Richards was guest hostess for the evening.

The boys were entertained with various impromptu games. Four boys competed in an hilarious "baby bottle race". The one to down the milk first, received a large milk bottle, complete with nipple, plus a flat fifty of cigarettes. This was followed by a "Daisy May" race with four girls chasing four Airmen madly around the floor. A Musical Quiz rounded off the "games period", and each of the winners for these games also gained a flat fifty.

During the evening, "sit-down" games in the lounges were a rest from dancing now and then, and the program was topped off as usual with refreshments.

At the Canteen of the Sunday before, Frank Bogart and his band with Bonnie Surrey were down for the evening.

The organization for the Canteen is gradually being built up to accommodate more girls and servicemen each time and to improve the whole set-up as much as possible.

Notice:

Lists of the canteen hostesses for the following Sunday will be posted on the bulletin boards each week.

Please notify Irma Larson in writing of any change in the shifts.

First "Book Chat" A Great Success

The girls who gathered in the Upper Lounge of the Club on Monday evening, January 10th, for the first "Book Chat" by Miss Elspeth Lehman of the Toronto Public Libraries, found it so interesting that they have been requesting that a book review night be held once a week.

Miss Lehman reviewed briefly several of the new books—Daylight on Saturday, by J. B. Priestly; Roughly Speaking, by Louise Pearson; Winter Harbour, by Bernice Richmond, and Tomorrow is Forever, by Gwen Birstow. She introduced them so well that there has been a long waiting list for them at the Club Library, since that evening.

An open forum followed, conducted by Miss Lehman, Miss Waugh and Miss McSweeney, all of the Public Library, and the girls greatly enjoyed the lively discussion and the questions asked and answered.

The next "Book Chat" will be held February 3rd, at 9:30 p.m. in the Upper Lounge of the Club. All Club members are welcome.

Open House

Saturday, February 5th, at 7:30, will be "Open House" at the Club when any girl at the plant may come to see "what goes on at the Girls' Club".

There will be an informal program to show non-members the activities that take place in a usual evening at the Club, followed by refreshments in the lounge for which there will be a charge of fifteen cents per person.

Handcrafts will be on exhibition in the balcony, and on the gym floor regular classes in dancing, gymnastics, apparatus, etc., will go on, followed by periods of games—basketball, volleyball, badminton, etc. And sometime during the evening the dramatic class will put on a skit.

So, come on out to classes, girls, so you'll be in top form for "Open House".

The Future Revealed

Looking After Your Curls

On Thursday, January 27th, at 9:30 p.m., Miss B. Robitaille, scalp and hair specialist from New York, will give a talk and demonstration on the care of the hair. She will also give a personal hair analysis to any girl interested.

Open House

Saturday evening, February 5th, will be Open House Night, the time to bring your friends and let them see "what's cookin'" at the Club.

Valentine Party

Really super plans are under way for a gala Valentine Box Social to be held at the Club, on Saturday evening, February 12th.

**CLUB ADDRESS—212 COWAN AVE.
BUSINESS MANAGER
BILL CURRIE
PHONE NUMBERS—PLANT LOCAL
492 OR LAKESIDE 7165**

Lifebuoy Follies Play To a Large Audience At the Clu

On Saturday evening, January 8th, with a gay, fast-moving program, the Lifebuoy Follies played to a tightly packed audience of approximately 1,000, in the Girls' Club Gym.

The smart dance numbers, catchy tunes, and numerous laughs make it a show that will long be remembered by all who saw it.

Irene Hughes and Jimmy Devoe won many a gasp from the audience with a snappy and intricate tap number.

Joan Elaine delighted everyone with her accordian-playing, songs and dances. And Pat Rafferty had the entire audience roaring during the times he was on the stage.

Helen Bruce, Norman Evans and Daphne McFarlane proved to be a superb line-up of singing stars. Jack Ayre, aside from doing a very able job at the piano, produced plenty of laughs with his talk on birds.

It was indeed a well-balanced and delightful show and we look forward to another visit of the "Lifebuoy Follies" in the near future.

The members and staff of the Girls' Club wish to express their thanks to Lever Bros., the sponsors of the show.

Make These for Your Cupboard

Skeletons vanish as soon as these colorful closet accessories make their appearance! They'll dress up your cupboard, keep your clothes free from dust and your hats free from wrinkles. No more stumbling over a pile of shoes in the dark! Directions for making these closet accessories may be obtained from "The Shotgun" office, free of charge.

taken on definitely on a temporary basis with a view to discontinuing their employment after the emergency is over ...

Elizabeth and Roy Bragg worked and met in the ordnance tool room at Inglis. They shared a mixed feeling that employment conditions were only temporary and their contribution never quite equalled that of the original Inglis employees, let alone the military personnel. Roy described the situation:

There was a kind of a division at John Inglis between the war workers and those who were there prior. They were there: they were the originals, they were John Inglis. We were just the johnny-come-latelies. The old-type worker there was more loyal to John Inglis than maybe the war workers were. We all knew it was temporary. We were only there until the war ended. But the other boys — *they were certainly hoping they would stay on after the war, because they had worked there before the war. I don't think they ever really accepted us 100 percent as being true John Inglis employees.*

The participation of women in the wartime production was accompanied by considerable attention and propaganda. Many companies celebrated their female workers, while at the same time prescribing limits to what their role would be. At Inglis, the role of women workers in the war effort was recognized and prescribed in the biweekly *Shotgun*. The 24 June 1944 edition was "A Salute to the Women of Inglis." In July of the same year, the "girls" in the press room were highlighted: "Our hats are doffed to the girls of the Press Room — they're one of the toughest jobs in the Plant," read the issue, "yet they still manage to have an excellent safety and absentee record. Nice going, girls!"

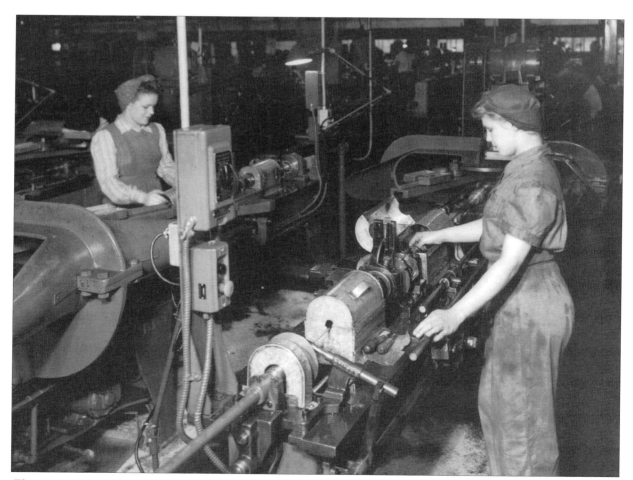

These two unnamed Inglis workers probably had an opportunity to exchange a few words during the work day. Arranging machinery face-to-face like this became unpopular as efficiency experts came to dominate management decisions.

In the regular column "Pot Shots at Style & Beauty" from the same edition, fashion advice was dispensed:

Two ways to use hankies for a suntan top with shorts: Buy a large one and fasten one end to a cord to tie around your neck. Tie the other two ends in back. For a bras type tanner — tie three knots in two large kerchiefs. One behind your neck, one in front and one in back. But make sure they're large enough in both cases!

Some of the jokes in the *Shotgun* referred to the military culture that was visible both in the factories and on the streets. "Two girls were puzzled by a dead animal they saw on the side of the road as they were driving to work. One of the girls noted: 'It has two stripes.' 'Then,' said the other, 'it must be either a skunk or a corporal'." Other items in "Smile A-While" reveal a pervasive sexism. Women's work was taken seriously only as long as it was needed. "What is the outstanding contribution that chemistry has given to the world? Blonds!"

In addition to the *Shotgun* there were company-sponsored events such as beauty contests. A "Miss John Inglis Pageant" was held at the plant at the height of the war. The winner of the contest competed for the citywide war worker title. The final event was held at the Police Games.

Despite all of this attention, women leaving their employment at Inglis remained a

Inglis workers filled every inch of space outside the plant for the 100,000 Bren gun ceremony.

The 22 July issue of the *Shotgun* contained this advice:

What One May and May Not Call a Woman:

You may call a woman a kitten,
but you must not call her a cat.
You may call her a mouse, but
you must not call her a rat.
You may call her a chicken, but
you must not call her a hen.
You may call her a duck, but you
must not call her a goose.
You may call her a vision, but
you must not call her a sight.

In this photograph, June Pattison is No. 63. She recalls that all of the candidates were expected to wear the normal work attire of overalls and bandanna. Some women clearly found other clothing more attractive. Burford Trestrail, personnel manager, seen at the microphone far right, was the Master of Ceremonies. The names of the other contestants are not known.

problem. In September 1943, Irma Larson, head "forelady," surveyed her staff of supervisors throughout the plant for an explanation. Some of the reasons given included dissatisfaction with pay rates, the desire to find permanent work, the wish to join families, the need for a holiday, ill health, and shiftwork. Those who were "fed-up" had their own reasons: a disagreement with a set-up man, lateness of one kind or another, dislike of discipline, or the desire for a transfer to a new type of work. The unpleasant working conditions mentioned included dirty work environment, favouritism, no raises, a "lackadaisical attitude" in the department, and an unfair bonus system.

To set and maintain limits for the "girl" war workers, the company held training sessions for supervisors. While foremen were involved in the supervision of actual production, foreladies looked after the more personal side of factory life. They supervised washrooms and restrooms to maintain housekeeping standards. But they also looked out for any loitering. They were expected to advise female war workers about hygiene and "vermin" problems. This army of foreladies was expected to wear official dress: navy blue slacks and jacket with a long-sleeved white blouse.

For men, especially young men, working at Inglis during the war was a remarkable experience. Despite the complete transformation of the shopfloor at Inglis, men made up half of the number of workers in the Ordnance Division and accounted for roughly fifty-five percent of the total plant population in 1943. First and foremost, they enjoyed a sense of contributing to the war effort. For many of those young men who would have preferred serving in the armed forces, war work represented their first, full-time, regular job. It was their first chance to secure employment with a decent pay cheque, and their first opportunity to prove themselves as industrial workers.

War work also brought young men together with large numbers of women as coworkers for the first time. This created new opportunities for interaction between men and women. Dances were held at all hours to accommodate shift work, and there were always parties. To balance the grueling pace of work, the social life of both young men and women was an active one. Working shifts encouraged coworkers to socialize before and after the job. The Braggs were one of many couples whose

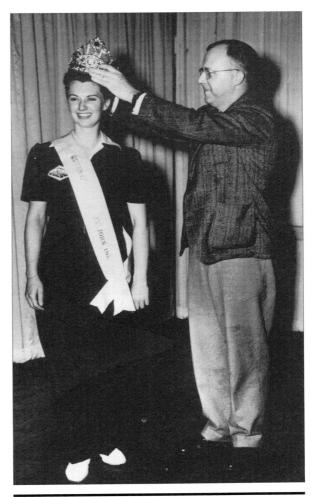

Lee Ainsworth, Inglis vice-president, crowns Miss John Inglis, June Pattison. The contest was held at the Inglis Girls' Club on Cowan Avenue.

June Pattison Lake began work at Inglis in 1940. In 1943 she was chosen "Miss John Inglis" in a contest held at the Inglis Girls' Club on Cowan Avenue.

I was excited when I won, yes. The only thing I didn't like was that I never wore make-up to work, and after I won they told me I had to wear make-up to work. I guess so I looked a bit better.

I was making $24 a week. I used to buy a bond every month. You used to go to shows. When you worked the midnight shift you'd go downtown and have breakfast, and you'd go to Loew's, see a movie. You did everything just turned right around. There were always lots of people to do things with. Their families were always west or up north. They had come from all over the country to work here.

You had to work — there was nothing else to do. We had a war. It was guns. We had a war going on. We had to make the guns.

Elizabeth and Roy Bragg recall: "We used to go to Centre Island, rent bikes, have a Coke, then come back and go to work. We went to the Tophat. There was a dancing place called the Acadian. And the old Palais Royale on the Lakeshore. We used to go down to the show at the old Imperial, and the Loew's, but then it was really an outing. We'd get all dressed up."

romance started at Inglis. Arrangements were easy to make, there was money to spend, and there was no lack of entertainment. The Braggs were young, not too long out of school, and grateful for good employment following the depression.

Roy Bragg remembers:

I started at 40 cents an hour. This was more than I'd been used to. I'd never been in the organized work force before. We were all on shift work. This was happening all over the city. They were having trouble providing social activities for the war workers, so the Y down at College Street jumped in and started having dances at midnight. You'd come out, and you could go to a dance at midnight.

Elizabeth Bragg adds:

I came in the fall of 1941. I went right into the tool room. I wasn't prepared for this work. We had to wear those bandannas on our heads, and none of us was used to those. You had to keep all your hair covered up. It was interesting work, I'll admit that. I broke lots of drills and different things. They had to depend on the women, because so many of the men in the forces were going overseas, because they were handicapped. They had to call on us.

Of women's role in the war effort, Roy said:

I often think that war work was the start of women's lib. Up to that time girls were office workers or house workers. They weren't normally factory workers. This was the start of it. And they did everything. I take my hat off to them. Welding, and cutting. They did a super job.

His wife mentioned the importance of her job to future employment:

I don't know whether it made me independent or anything. But it certainly didn't do me any harm in future years for jobs. I could stand up for myself. But I don't say I'm a real women's libber. If you wanted to get ahead you had to work. You couldn't slack off. Any of the other jobs I've had, I've worked pretty steady at.

Bert Bowler recalled activities away from the Inglis shopfloor. Much of the good wages he earned went to helping out at home, but he and his friends knew how to have a good time:

We used to do some weird things. If it was day shift sometimes we'd go to the track. You'd get in to the last three races free. In the afternoon shift, you wind up at about 12 or 12:30 [a.m.]. We used to go down to Chinatown and have dinner or sometimes we'd go to a house party. There was always things going on. They were conscientious, but they were also young and they wanted to have recreation from what they were getting every day. There was a limit to what you could buy, everything was rationed.

We had a camera — we didn't have any film — and we'd go down to the Lakeshore, over at Sunnyside. We'd start taking pictures and getting addresses. We'd get the address and phone number and then we'd phone them up and tell them the picture didn't turn out, but if they'd come out on a date, we could get more pictures.

Another thing we used to do, we'd get all dressed up on a Saturday and drive around till we found a wedding. Then we'd follow the last car and we'd go to the reception. Free drinks, dancing, and we never knew where we were going to wind up. We'd be at a Polish wedding one time, or Ukrainian or Hungarian, sometimes we'd be with the Irish or Scotch. We got into the habit of being able to pick out the mother-in-laws and the father-in-laws, and the first thing we'd do is go and congratulate them and give mum a big kiss and tell her how happy we were.

The transformation of both work and culture at Inglis through the creation of the Ordnance Division may have been disturbing for old-timers like Harry Goudy, who continued, as he always had, in the forge department of the original general engineering business. Marion Lindner, who worked from 1942 to 1967 in the Inglis payroll department, remembered Goudy's behaviour during the war vividly:

There was a blacksmith with a very unforgettable character in there called Henry Goudy. He was tall and thin. He always had this big leather apron on because they still manufactured some things on the anvil. He was a very difficult man to work for. A man of few words and I can remember well his temper … they hired a new man and he stomped into our office in a fury saying, 'He's no good and I can't use him at all. Get me somebody else.' He was a real character.

Old Goudy must have been quite a sight in his craftsman's garb. His temper may well have been fueled by the changes that he had fought to prevent so many years earlier. Over the course of the war, 16,000 new people had been hired, half of them women! The old John Inglis company was gone. Much of the equipment, patterns, and inner workings of the original plant had been sold for scrap. From the sound of it, Goudy had taken refuge in the last corner of the plant familiar to him. It was a part of the plant where there were virtually no women and the old union was still strong. The mass of semi-skilled and unskilled workers — industrial workers — may well have offended Goudy's old Inglis sensibilities. Goudy, one of the oldest workers from the original John Inglis plant, may not have thought these new workers deserved a union, which, as Goudy was about to retire, the workers in the Ordnance Division were seeking to gain.

Chapter Three

Hearts and Minds: Building USWA Local 2900

Inglis had always enjoyed a union presence. Yet as industrial unionism swept across wartime Canada and Inglis became a prime organizing target, it took several attempts by two unions to see the Ordnance Division of John Inglis become unionized.

The International Association of Machinists (IAM) and the Steel Workers Organizing Committee (SWOC) both mounted numerous attempts to organize between 1938 and 1943. It took over five years — despite the long union tradition, a number of committed activists, harsh working conditions, and two unions competing to add the growing legion of Inglis workers to their ranks. Complicated and interlocking events conspired to turn the organizing drive into a long, uphill struggle.

DANCE WITH THE C.I.O.

JACK EVANS
and His Famous Band

Featured By Jack Evans and His Orchestra

Royal York Hotel
Friday Evening, April 16th

Dancing and Floor Show, Get Tickets from Stewards

Tickets 75c   Dancing begins 9 p.m.

Just days before the union vote, the Steelworkers asked Inglis workers to dance in more ways than one. From the 16 April 1943 edition of The Inglis Steelworker.

When the Bren gun work started up, James Somerville, the IAM representative, was on the scene. The veteran official, whose relationship with Inglis predated World War I, was directly involved in the earliest contract negotiations for the Ordnance Division. His mission was to restore IAM Lodge 235 to its former greatness. Early discussions revolved around wage rates and job classifications. The starting point for these discussions was the long-time relationship that had existed with the original John Inglis company. But the machinists' forty-year history was no guarantee of a contract when Hahn began hiring. The Great Depression had severely weakened the old craft unions and the IAM representatives seemed confused by what was happening. The undertaking at Inglis stood outside the experience of a traditional machinist. Despite the hiring of many former employees, the enormous task of rebuilding Lodge 235 would prove a difficult one.

During these first contract negotiations for the Ordnance Division, the company and the Department of National Defense referred to the old craft-based wage schedule at Inglis. Wages there had ranged from a high of eighty cents per hour for moulders and a few other trades to forty cents an hour for labourers. The machinists' union seemed unprepared for the changes that would affect the labour process, skills, and male domination of the metal trades. The IAM invested considerable energy negotiating rates for jobs that would play a small role in wartime production. The company, for its part, seemed happy to discuss what it knew would soon be an obsolete wage schedule. In April 1938 a brief, six-clause contract between IAM Lodge 235 and Inglis was drawn up but remained unsigned, a relic of an earlier industrial era.

As the company sought to meet its production schedules, it encountered traditional union concerns that proved contentious: shop rules and methods of work that were decades old at Inglis. Hours of work and new shop practices related to Bren gun production soon became points of conflict. Within a year, Somerville complained that several union members had been dismissed without cause, apparently for involvement in union activity.

Organizing was further complicated by a split in the labour movement. By January 1939, industrial unions that were associated with the Congress of Industrial Organizations (CIO) had become the bitter enemies of the older craft-based unions affiliated to the Trades and Labour Congress (TLC), the Canadian equivalent of the American Federation of Labor (AFL).

This situation was exploited by both company management and the military bureaucracy. They were anxious to see that the CIO, which they considered the more radical organization, didn't get a foothold at Inglis. The IAM, which was affiliated with the TLC, was given the impression of cooperation and discussed wage rates for machinists, toolmakers, die casters, and assemblers openly and in great detail with both company and government officials. Somerville, with a history of opposition to the more militant wing of the union, was ill prepared for the extent and sophistication of these negotiations. It never occurred to the union that once production for the Bren gun was established, the vast majority of jobs would have little to do with traditional machining. The contract drawn up between Lodge 235 and the company had little relevance to mass production and was never signed by the company. Perhaps Inglis never really bargained in good faith.

While Somerville talked wages and job classifications with Lee Ainsworth, the company's vice president, Inglis management carefully screened new hires. Local union militants were especially unwelcome. At a meeting with Department of National Defense officials, the company was told to "make an arrangement with the Toronto Police Department for the purpose of investigating prospective employees before they are engaged, to ascertain any pertinent points concerning their record." Ten days later Major Hahn informed the military that the company was "laying special stress upon following up the record of any prospective applicant, through the references that are necessary on these application forms."

Once hired, production workers met managers who created unpleasant working conditions out of a sense of discipline. Jock Carroll, who was hired at Inglis in 1939, recalled that by 1940 there were growing numbers of women working in various operations of Bren production. They faced harassment in many forms.

One of the many flyers distributed by the USWA during the Inglis organizing drive. The experience of the depression was not forgotten, even at the peak of wartime production.

Management were very hastily recruited. There were some managers there that weren't very bright. One man in particular used to come around to our department and stand around the rifling machines. Working at a rifling machine involves standing and attending this machine for a half an hour or maybe an hour and watching it go back and forth. All the girl working at this machine had to do was take a little steel chip out of the end of it and of course, make sure the machine was running all right. So they got bored. They used to whistle or sing. This manager observed this and before you knew he had sent around a memo saying there would be no whistling or singing while working at the rifling machines. It was just the sort of thing that would make people want a union!

Erma Hughes, who came from Manitoba to work at Inglis, recalled the general atmosphere that motivated people to join the union:

I had no experience before that with unions, never. They never had any unions where I worked before. Sometimes there was a lot of favouritism. There were a lot of things that weren't quite right. If you were in with a cer-

tain clique, you got the better jobs. If you were not, you got all the dirty work. I wasn't in with the bosses and the clique. But I was a hard worker. That's why I never got fired, I think. I thought the union would see that everybody got their due, got the job according to how you worked and the way you performed.

The Secret War Against Organizing Takes Shape

The importance of the Bren gun to the pending war effort lent credence to the requirement that employees' backgrounds be thoroughly searched. Sabotage in such an important production plant could not be ruled out. But those labelled "undesirable" soon included a broad spectrum of trade union activists. Even prior to the signing of the Bren gun contract, intelligence reports were written about some individuals. By the start of the war in September 1939, a network of intelligence officers had been established throughout the plant. That this was carried out efficiently and quietly, may have been assisted by the fact that Inglis company President Hahn had himself served in military intelligence during the First World War. He may well have exploited his contacts in this regard, as he appears to have done in securing the contract in the first place. Some of these officers were there to ensure that the gun was made to strict specifications and that all conditions in the Bren gun contract, which had been signed with the Department of National Defense, were met. But other officers had additional responsibilities. They kept a close eye on all efforts to organize Inglis, just as the local police force did.

In 1938 and 1939, at least ten top secret reports about union activities at the Inglis plant were generated by the RCMP, Military Intelligence, and the local police department. Nearly the entire content of these reports remains secret to this day, protected through various clauses of the curiously titled Freedom of Information Act. Various levels of government regularly exchanged a range of secret information.

The Canadian military's ability to engage in anti-union activities and espionage was based on tradition. In 1932 a special branch of military intelligence was being trained by the RCMP to collaborate with local and provincial police departments. It later helped identify important industrial sites as possible targets of sabotage, as the country prepared for war. With the Bren gun

contract signed, the military had a direct and legitimate hand in the administration of the Inglis Ordnance Division. The RCMP had followed closely the actions of political organizations such as the Communist Party of Canada and unions that had close links to the party. Informants were used to keep these authorities appraised of "developments" and "subversive activities" such as strikes or meetings held by workers. Much of the secret infrastructure created to observe labour and working-class activism at Inglis was based on a closed community of men with little sympathy for the trade union movement.

The hostility that existed toward industrial unions in the military was only slightly less in other federal departments. A clear signal requiring employers to bargain with unions wasn't enacted until 1944 with the privy council's declaration of item 1003. Prior to that, the government had characteristically waffled on the question of industrial unions and their right to organize during the war. Prior to passage of PC 1003 there had been other privy council declarations that endorsed unions in theory, but had lacked the binding force of law. The accomplishments of the CIO in Canada were won with little public or legal encouragement from the federal government. And there was much that occurred behind the scenes, which suggests that various branches of government helped employers prevent organizing as long as production was not seriously threatened.

By the summer of 1939, Somerville was already complaining that a number of his men had been dismissed, apparently for being active members of the IAM. Continued disagreement about wage rates, hours, and classifications added to what was quickly becoming a serious industrial relations matter, with widening implications for the approaching war effort. Early working-class support of this effort was so important for war production that a number of senior government officials moved quickly to dispel any impression that trade union activists faced discrimination. But in reality they did. While Hahn gave assurances that "a number of members of trade unions were currently employed," this vague statement only calmed the situation publicly. It did little to change tense conditions on the shopfloor.

At the same time, the Steel Workers Organizing Committee, a CIO-affiliated group, had been working quietly without the benefit of direct meetings with the company. Industrial

I'M USED TO ROWING FELLERS BUT I'D LIKE TO HAVE SOME SAY ABOUT WHERE WE'RE GOING

WAR BOARDS

LABOUR

CORPORATION LAWYER

GOVT

A YEAR MAN

INDUSTRIAL MAGNATE

WAR PRODUCTION CHART

WAR EFFORT

This cartoon by an unnamed artist depicted the issue of labour having little say in the administration of the war effort. It appeared on 11 March 1943, in The Inglis Steelworker.

unionism was considered a subversive idea to many. The previous year, CIO organizers had successfully organized at General Motors in Oshawa, despite strong opposition from the provincial premier. The Inglis company's curiosity about its workers' political activities sparked a complaint from Silby Barrett, the newly appointed Canadian Director of the CIO. A question on Inglis job applications soon attracted the attention of the cabinet as well. Barrett wrote Labour Minister Rogers in July 1939, two months before the war began:

[Inglis] does not employ any man who belongs to a Trade Union. For sometime I have known this, but was unable to get

proof of this, until I received a copy of the application which a man applying for a job has to have filled out.

They ask him in this application, a copy of which you will find attached hereto, if he belongs to a Trade Union, either past or present, and the minute they find out they tell the applicant to come back in a day or two. If the applicant has been a member of a Trade Union, or is now a member, then there is no employment for him.

These men now come under the Steel Workers' Organization, and we intend organizing them. We have a number of them already signed up.

We would like your Department to have

This full-page appeal appeared in the 16 April 1943 edition of The Inglis Steelworker.

"Listen You War Workers . . .

"I am one of the 186,000 members of the United Steelworkers of America - C.I.O. now in the armed forces of the United Nations.

"I know what our union has meant. Because of the Union movement you enjoy your present working conditions. They can be improved by your adherence to the union cause.

"The industrial unions of the C.I.O. have led the way at all times in winning better conditions and wages. They can win the security that you as war workers and we as soldiers need in the after-war years.

"You girl workers, who have replaced the men in industrial jobs, the union means genuine equal pay for equal work—and security for your men when they return after the war.

"When you vote on April 19th, cast your ballot for the United Steelworkers of America - C.I.O."

The United Steelworkers of America - C.I.O. is a union of more than 750,000 members working in the war industries of Canada and the United States. As an affiliate of the C.I.O. it is associated with the more than 6,000,000 war workers, members of unions attached to that central labour body.

VOTE STEELWORKERS-CIO

this undemocratic practice stopped immediately, so that any workman in Canada may be able to join an Organization of his own choosing.

The IAM was active as well. In November 1939, after twelve Inglis workers attended a citywide IAM organizing meeting, one of SWOC's "best men in John Inglis" suggested that the group distribute union cards as quickly as possible. Charlie Millard, SWOC's central Canadian director, called a meeting within days, signing up forty-seven Inglis workers.

The company's practice of screening potential union activists was not the only barrier to union organizing. With informants in both the IAM and the SWOC, the company got wind of any union talk. One of the forty-seven who had signed up at SWOC's November meeting, Walter Camm, was a worker in the tool room. Camm reported being approached by both the machinists and the CIO and, after attending a meeting of the latter, he joined the CIO. Within ten days of his sign-up, Camm was fired for no apparent reason. Both Silby Barrett and Charlie Millard, with the assistance of lawyer J.L. Cohen, launched an investigation to find out why Camm had been dismissed. What followed revealed the extent to which employers like Inglis could intimidate trade unionists and ignore government inquiries to maximize production and ensure delivery of essential arms.

Several inquiries by CIO officials and local representatives of the Department of Labour proved useless. Soon after, the deputy minister of labour, W.M. Dickson, visited Inglis's vice president Ainsworth, who "met us in the most courteous and friendly manner, but explained to us that he did not care to discuss in any way the company's reason for Mr. Camm's dismissal."

Major Hahn provided a more detailed, but cryptic, explanation on 9 December 1939:

This organization has been built up on the general principle of employing the best men obtainable for the particular work to be undertaken. In doing so it is obvious, with the large number of personnel employed, that from time to time certain of that personnel may not, for one reason or another, fit into the organization.

The suggestion contained in your letter that any man is dismissed solely because he has joined a certain trade union is not in ac-

cordance with the facts, as a number of our employees belong to various trade unions.

In view of the important nature of the task we are undertaking, it is obvious that we must at all times assume full responsibility for the suitability of any employee to carry out the task. Views expressed by Mr. Camm came to our knowledge from sources which we are satisfied are reliable, but which we are not at liberty to disclose. These views were such that in our opinion his continued employment might jeopardize the successful completion of our work. The views expressed by Mr. Camm had nothing to do with trade unionism.

As suggested in your letter, we give this information in strictest confidence.

What Camm might have said that caused his dismissal remains a mystery. He may have made antiwar statements. However, it seems more likely that his recent activism in the CIO was behind the dismissal since the union took up his cause. There would be further firings of activists. Jock Carroll, a leader in the rifling department, had been working quietly to bring in the union. Carroll narrowly avoided the same fate as Camm. He recalled:

They eventually came to me and said to me they wanted to move me. I had been in charge of this one group, as I say, ninety people and they said they were going to move me down and run a lathe. I was going to be a machine operator again. I thought that was unfair or unjust or whatever you want to call it. I announced that I wasn't going to go down there and they announced that in that case I was fired.

At a meeting in the morning we had one night shift that was still on the job, the day shift was coming in, so most of my people were in the plant. So the security guard started to take me out of the building and about sixty or seventy people, most of the people who worked with me, followed me out. The company hadn't anticipated this. They took me and all those who had followed me and held us in a small hall downstairs before they put me out on the street. And lo and behold, John Inglis had been attacked in Maclean's *magazine by George Drew. He claimed there was a patronage thing going on, so they were sensitive about bad publici-*

ty. Major James E. Hahn himself came down to the place where this group of rifling employees was being held and addressed us all. He said this was all a misunderstanding, he didn't want any problems. Anyway he ended up giving a real speech. He said, 'Therefore we'll all just go back to work, Jock, you included.' And they had just fired me. All this happened before the union had really shown up.

Inglis's harassment of activists was not all that slowed the organizing drive. Events not directly linked to Inglis affected the SWOC's early drive at Inglis and elsewhere. The May 1939 appointment of Charlie Millard as Barrett's assistant paved the way for tension in the CIO's Toronto office. Operating some distance from Barrett, who was based in Nova Scotia, Millard feared SWOC had become a communist-dominated organization. Skilled organizers like Harry Hambergh, Dick Steele, and Harry Hunter, all left-wingers, were working away, trying to build Local 1039, when Millard arrived.

SWOC's early organizing strategy was to form a massive local, then called West End Lodge 1039, made up of members from numerous metal-fabricating plants in the area. As the organizers signed up majorities at individual plants, they would be split off to form distinct locals. But majorities sometimes failed to materialize, and lack of progress eventually became one of the reasons the communist activists encountered opposition.

Millard soon learned the extent to which the communists were active in the Toronto organization. A committed anticommunist, he slowly moved to isolate and limit front-line organizers like Steele and Hunter. By late 1939, SWOC's leadership in the U.S. was alarmed by the information Millard was able to provide. SWOC president Philip Murray threatened that unless the communists were cleared out, he would abolish the Canadian district and SWOC could start over again in Canada. SWOC's organizing efforts had progressed almost as slowly as the IAM's because disagreements between its activists were about tactics as well as ideology. The left-wingers were, in part, being blamed for SWOC's slow progress at plants like Inglis.

Ironically, it was Charlie Millard, working to reduce the influence of communists in the CIO, who was arrested on 6 December 1939 for making "statements prejudicial to security

in contravention of Section 39 of the Criminal Code." The police claimed that among other seditious statements, Millard had said, "The manufacturers would take advantage of this war as they did the last" and that "men were joining the army because that was the only way they could be sure of eating regularly." Millard was never brought to trial, but the RCMP's raid on the CIO's offices in Toronto provided it with valuable files and documents on SWOC's activities.

In June 1940, Dick Steele was fired and Millard was put in charge of SWOC's Toronto-based central Canadian organization. Steele's firing angered many of the CIO organizers at Inglis and elsewhere. But the communists didn't give up the organization without a fight. Soon after, four SWOC locals from southern Ontario, including Local 1039, which included Inglis, held a meeting in Toronto to discuss the firing of Steele. A statement drafted by the locals strongly protested the "political discrimination."

Later that fall, after the founding convention of the Canadian Congress of Labour (which included CIO unions), Harry Hunter and Harry Hambergh were also dismissed. An independent "Ontario Executive" opened an office at 966 Queen Street West, near the Inglis plant. It hoped to create a policy that was more in keeping with "the temper of Canadian workers." As late as February 1941, SWOC's head office in Pittsburgh was compelled to issue a bulletin to its SWOC membership in Canada, which began:

> Some months ago it was necessary for the Steel Workers Organizing Committee to dispense with the services of Messrs. Harry Hambergh, Harry Hunter and Richard Steele. These men were negligent and failed to carry out the policies of the Steel Workers Organizing Committee as enunciated by an International Convention. However, these men are at the present time representing themselves to you as being field workers or agents of the Steel Workers' Organizing Committee.

This situation turned some of the previously committed communist organizers at Inglis against the SWOC–CIO. Some drifted to the IAM. Efforts to build a union at Inglis also were disrupted by political infighting in the broader labour movement. With the signing of the

Steelworker organizers Eamon Park and Eileen Tallman. Park had been involved in organizing in Kirkland Lake, while Tallman came through the youth organization of the Co-operative Commonwealth Federation. This photo first appeared in the 11 March 1943 edition of The Inglis Steelworker.

Hitler–Stalin Pact in August 1939, communists remained opposed to the war, viewing it as a conflict between two capitalist countries. They remained committed to building a strong trade union movement, although their reasons differed from other CIO activists. For the duration of the Hitler–Stalin pact, a period of nearly two years, communist activists encountered considerable distrust from many workers and official oppression as enemies of the state. These internal differences diverted energy and time from the real struggle to organize Inglis.

Despite such disruptions, a small union or-ganization was built in this early period. Conditions both inside and outside the plant limited the success of the drive. The company continued to dismiss activists of both union organizations, especially those in the CIO. Under such threat, ordnance workers at Inglis publicized their difficulties in creative ways. Anonymous notices under the heading "DND Plant No.1" were placed in Toronto newspapers on 3 June 1940. These caused a furor in both the government and military hierarchy. Bureaucrats and military officers scrambled to decipher what "DND Plant No.1" was.

Ruth McCarthy, left, and Eileen Tallman were two of the organizers for the Steelworkers at Inglis during the war.

The notice read as follows:

The employees of DND, Plant No.1 feel that they are unfairly treated and below please find outlined the outstanding causes of the grievances which if not rectified may lead to serious complications at this critical time of very necessary co-operation:

1. Compelled to work seven full days of eight hours continually without any time off especially the night shifts who are working under artificial light.

2. Weekday lateness or time taken off deducted at rate of time and a half.

3. No preferences or alternation for married men on day or night shifts.

4. Suspensions for scrap caused by inefficient setters.

5. In case of quitting owing to existing conditions, other firms asked not to employ same men causing victimization.

Investigation is requested by those who must of course remain

"Unanimous [sic] Employees"

The newspapers notices described not only difficult working conditions, but the extent to which employees were forced to accept them. There was a war on, France had been attacked by Hitler, and production was paramount. Later that month, the workers in the Commercial Division, the "machinists and engine fitters," wrote to the minister of labour complaining of the rates paid for weekend work. The workers submitted a "round " of signatures that expressed their dissatisfaction in the tradition of the old craft shop. The reference to the former company management must have been a puzzling anachronism for ordnance workers.

The previous owners of the J. Inglis Company Limited paid double time for Sundays, time and one half for Saturday afternoons, also for all legal holidays. In closing, we wish to emphasize our loyalty to the prosecution of the war to a successful conclusion.

Union building was in fact complicated by the steady growth of both sections of the company, especially the Ordnance Division. There continued to be harassment of activists. By 1940–41 an increasingly complex bureaucracy had developed to oversee war production. As the war continued, the needs of Inglis workers for better wages and working conditions were hardly a priority. Everyone had a loved one or knew someone who was overseas. It was a time of sacrifice, and many felt production was paramount for the duration of the war.

Through 1940 and 1941, the IAM continued its organizing activities in the Ordnance Division. At the same time, they attempted to strengthen their presence in the Commercial Division. This division hired few women, who continued to be unwelcome by the more traditional machinists. The work in Commercial left job classifications largely intact when compared to the massive changes to metalwork taking place in the Ordnance Division. The IAM signed up seven men in 1940 and twenty more in 1941.

The wartime industrial relations bureaucracy also hindered shopfloor organizing. Virtually nothing could be decided between workers and employers without involving external panels or boards established by a government that was clearly comfortable with ignoring the needs of workers for most of the war. Even a brief sit-down strike in the autumn of 1940 failed to kick-start the IAM drive in the Commercial Division.

The SWOC approached organizing much differently, concentrating on the Ordnance Division where large numbers of semi- and unskilled men and women were working. In SWOC's massive West End Local 1039, there was still not a single member in good standing from John Inglis as of June 1941.

The network of military spies and general informants grew in sophistication and petty behaviour as well. A conversation involving an inspector from the Inglis plant travelling on the Bay streetcar was overheard by an informant. The worker had questioned the company's claim that 5,000 Brens were being produced each month, insisting that was "a lot of bunk. We're only producing eighty-three a day and haven't yet built one of the Colt-Brownings they've talked so much about." These statements were reported in the military intelligence branch's weekly report of subversive activity.

Communication had also been established with spy networks in the United States. Funds sent from CIO headquarters in Washington to the CIO in Toronto were intercepted by military intelligence. The names of those individuals cashing cheques to support organizing at Inglis were known to intelligence officers. But not all methods of intelligence-gathering were sophisticated. Jock Carroll, who helped organize Inglis for the USWA, recalled one of the company's fumbling attempts to gather information from him:

Mr. Ainsworth lived at the foot of Fallingbrook Road in a large house. As it happened, I lived on Fallingbrook Road in an old dilapidated house that my father had built many years ago. In the course of their approaching me to get rid of me as an active union person, they tried all sorts of things. Mr. Ainsworth had a very attractive blonde secretary whom I'd never met. At this point I had never met Ainsworth! One day she found me and you know it was quite a large place. She came to my place of work and said she was going to Mr. Ainsworth's place for dinner that evening and would I mind giving her a lift. I thought this was most bizarre, to say the least. That this secretary would be searching me out for a lift. I wonder what the hell she wants! I reported back to my colleagues. I didn't think it was for my body! I said sure and gave her a lift to his home.

The conversation on the way over became like an amateur spy session. The war was on by this time. Hitler was running Germany. Mussolini was running Italy. So she started prodding me about my feelings about the war. She started saying things like, 'Well after all, you have to admit that Hitler and Mussolini made the trains run on time.' I thought, is she trying to get me to say I'm an enemy of the country so they could get rid of me? I was so amused by this incident.

Now by coincidence, I was a bit of a literary person. I used to collect the writings of 'nuts'. There are lots of people around with very queer ideas, fanatics, whether religious ideas or whatnot. I had been getting a mimeographed paper from a man called John Justice Sunislow. He had weird religious ideas about bringing peace to the world and harmony to everything, typical of this sort of thing actually. Now I had several of these leaflets in the back of my car and so when

Mr. Ainsworth's secretary started prodding me for my ideas, I said, `Well I don't know anything about Hitler or Stalin or Mussolini but I have one man whose ideas are amazingly practical!' I handed her one or two of these leaflets from this man whom I regarded as a nut. Well she seized upon these leaflets thinking she had really stumbled on this nugget of knowledge. That was the end of that except I reported this idiotic attempt to make me look like an enemy of the people.

Hearts and Minds

By late 1942 both unions stepped up their organizing drives. In November the company finally signed agreements covering its machine and boilershops in the Commercial Division. The IAM and the Boilermakers' Union, craft unions with long experience at Inglis, represented a total of 1,200 workers, or less than ten percent of the Inglis work force. Wilbert Finch, who apprenticed as a toolmaker at Inglis during the war, recalled the long tradition of the craft unions:

I was working in the plant when the union was started up. The first union card to say I was a tool- and die maker says Toronto Lodge 235. This was the Machinists. It was the only union in the heavy machine shop.

The company may have finally signed with the machinists in the hope that this would improve their chances of representing workers in the Ordnance Division. In fact, in correspondence to Department of Labour officials, Lee Ainsworth was always sure to note that the machinists "already" represented some workers in the Commercial Division. The reality was that the company had dragged negotiations out for four years. The core of Inglis, the Ordnance Division, which now approached 13,000 and was still growing, would be the subject of a battle for the hearts and minds of the Inglis workers. The largest organizing drive ever undertaken at a single workplace was heating up.

Sensing the impending battle, the company positioned itself and continued to stall. On 27 November the IAM requested sole bargaining rights under its recently formed Bren Gun Local 1612. Three days later the USWA made a similar request. The company replied to both in the same manner, noting that there were two labour organizations seeking to represent the workers of the Ordnance Division and that they must first demonstrate "they had a substantial majority membership." It also requested that each union state what it believed its level of representation to be. Neither union replied, perhaps because they were unwilling to show strength or weakness to the other side, or were as yet unsure of a majority. A few days later a privy council order, passed on 1 December 1942, laid out procedures for collective bargaining in Crown-owned plants, which of course, technically speaking, the Ordnance Division was. The situation at Inglis had forced the government to provide a firm direction to labour relations at government-owned plants.

Not coincidentally, the company released a booklet entitled "Statement of Policy," in part to counter the widespread rumours that the company was stonewalling. It reminded readers that "the company cannot recognize any Union as a sole bargaining agency unless its membership represents a substantial majority among the total employees involved." The following month, the IAM claimed it had such a majority and urged that a plebiscite be held. Within days the USWA insisted that if a vote were to be held, it would be at the table helping to determine procedures and that the vote "must be under supervision of impartial authority such as the Dominion Department of Labour."

Vice President Ainsworth also polled other government officials and military men widely, trying to formulate the company's position when it looked as though the plant would soon be unionized:

Undoubtedly, I am going to be faced with negotiation with either the A F of L or the CIO, covering our Ordnance Division, in the near future, but considering the fact that the Ordnance Division is owned completely by the Government I should like to have some guidance from your Department as to how far we might be authorized to go in agreeing to some of their demands. Mr. Howe had told me that in any such negotiations as this we must consider ourselves a private company, but nevertheless we are custodians of Government property and funds and I would like to have your "off-the-record" feelings as to any concessions we might grant to the Union we negotiate with.

SWOC's drive gained dramatic momentum. The

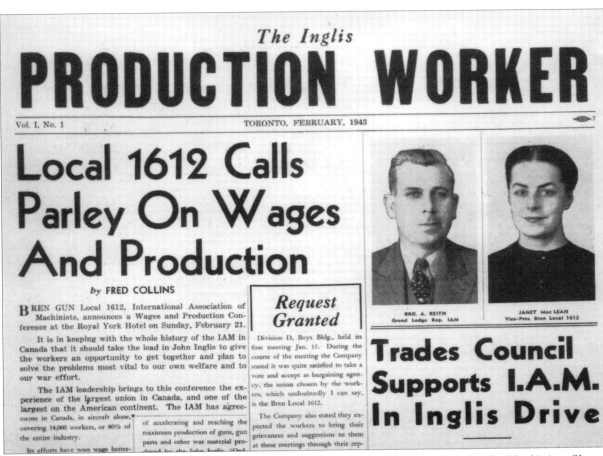

The Inglis
PRODUCTION WORKER

Vol. I, No. 1   TORONTO, FEBRUARY, 1943

Local 1612 Calls Parley On Wages And Production

by FRED COLLINS

BREN GUN Local 1612, International Association of Machinists, announces a Wages and Production Conference at the Royal York Hotel on Sunday, February 21.

It is in keeping with the whole history of the IAM in Canada that it should take the lead in John Inglis to give the workers an opportunity to get together and plan to solve the problems most vital to our own welfare and to our war effort.

The IAM leadership brings to this conference the experience of the largest union in Canada, and one of the largest on the American continent. The IAM has agreements in Canada, in aircraft alone, covering 34,000 workers, or 80% of the entire industry.

Its efforts have won wage better-

Request Granted

Division D, Boys Bldg., held its first meeting Jan. 15. During the course of the meeting the Company stated it was quite satisfied to take a vote and accept as bargaining agency, the union chosen by the workers, which undoubtedly I can say, is the Bren Local 1612.

The Company also stated they expected the workers to bring their grievances and suggestions to them at these meetings through their rep-

of accelerating and reaching the maximum production of guns, gun parts and other war material pro-

BRO. A. REITH
Grand Lodge Rep. IAM

JANET MacLEAN
Vice-Pres. Bren Local 1612

Trades Council Supports I.A.M. In Inglis Drive

Janet MacLean, pictured here on the right, was very involved in the organizing drive for the Machinists. She also was active in women's issues. She regularly met with other women war workers to discuss a range of topics and to share reading material. One publication she recalls discussing with other women was called Wenches with Wrenches. *Are there any copies of this still around?*

failed organizing drive at Kirkland Lake hardened the determination of organizers at Inglis and freed up resources and people. Several committed and gifted organizers came to Inglis from Kirkland Lake. Bill Sefton and Jock Brodie were hired at Inglis in February 1942. These Kirkland Lake veterans played a major role in building a more activist-oriented organization inside the plant. A third organizer, Eamon Park, had been involved in the Kirkland Lake drive as well. He became an important paid outside organizer for the Steelworkers. Park and Eileen Tallman began to hold meetings and to leaflet the workers at the gates. By 1942 the company had grown to 14,000 workers. Such large numbers demanded the attention of the CIO leadership. Membership dues were central in the economics of union organizing. Inglis simply *had* to be organized. With the arrival of the cold weather, union activity went into high gear. Tallman recalls the job of leafletting:

I remember meeting people off the midnight shift in a little shack that had a pot-bellied stove, on King Street. It belonged to the UAW, who were organizing Massey Harris at the time. Today I don't think there'd be very many women who would be meeting guys coming off the midnight shift!

One of my most vivid recollections of that whole organizing drive was how cold it was handing out the leaflets. With the size of the work force ... three shifts, going in at all kinds of different entrances, it was quite a task to organize, handing out the leaflets. We used to get some of the active union members to help until they had to go into work. One of the ones who always helped me was a woman named Beatrice Boardman, great gal. Her feet used to just about get numb. We'd sit in the car for ten minutes and then go out freezing.

Tallman and Park worked in conjunction with men like Sefton and Brodie on the inside. Meetings were held in a number of locations such as the Olympic Bowling Club on Yonge Street, the Polish Hall at Dovercourt and Queen, and the USWA headquarters at 1328 Bloor Street West. According to a company informant, the CIO's "first chief aim seems to be the women employees." Tallman recalls that there was growing dissatisfaction with the use of the bonus system and that this had a particular impact on the women who were concentrated in Bren production. Overseas, the war had reached global proportions and a number of important battles were being fought. Bren guns were needed badly and there was growing pressure on all workers to produce more of them, and faster.

The issue with the women was they did get considerably less at an hourly rate than the men, but they had a production quota system. Now undoubtedly some of the men had this too. But I recall particularly this: as soon as the women's group would reach their quota of production, then the quota would be raised. That was one of the major grievances amongst the women. That made it easier to organize them.

Mary Spratt, who worked in the Bren section, and became active in the local later on, recalled the slow process of organizing the women:

It was difficult to get women to join. You used to have to collect the dues from the person individually. You'd spend a lot of your time, your lunch hours, picking up dues, which sometimes you didn't get, and then there'd be a bigger argument the next time. It wasn't an easy task by any means.

Numerous meetings were held throughout the fi-

nal months of 1942 and the early part of 1943. Stickers were produced and distributed at the gates, and dues-paying members wore USWA buttons in the plant. Bill Sefton spoke of the "siege" at Kirkland Lake, describing how the "government had closed down on them and they were left holding the bag." On 17 November a shop stewards' meeting was held at which Sefton underlined the importance of the steward system at a plant "as large and poorly organized as the John Inglis Plant." As the drive gained momentum, the company fought back, dismissing those it believed were important activists. Overall, the CIO built a superior organization and was more effective at linking the issues of the Inglis drive to the broader politics of the entire war effort: the fight against fascism and for democracy.

While the CIO drive moved forward, so too did the IAM's. In fact, it was this union's request for a vote that seemed to accelerate the CIO's efforts. Despite being off the mark a little earlier and winning part of the Commercial Division in November 1942, the AFL's efforts seemed sporadic, poorly organized, and inconsistent. The IAM's drive at various moments appeared both bureaucratic, focused on wage schedules, and populist, calling for equal pay for equal work in the Ordnance Division, for example, in early November 1942.

In fact, the IAM's drive was really the effort of two distinct political tendencies. Much of the older, male IAM leadership took a bureaucratic approach, stressing wage schedules, avoiding "politics," and emphasizing its position of no strikes so that the war effort would not be harmed. This group issued a newspaper, published early in the drive. As the campaign continued, a small group of communist organizers joined forces with the IAM. Some communists working at Inglis viewed the USWA drive there as a raid, and the dismissal of communists from the SWOC office, still an issue in

Jock Carroll was a popular, very efficient worker/supervisor at Inglis. His struggle with a plant superintendent led to his deferment card not being signed. The National Selective Service required this information for all those called up for military service. The fact that Carroll was fired and reinstated more than once was a shining example to other Inglis workers of the need for union protection. From the 4 March 1943 edition of The Inglis Steelworker.

C.I.O. DANCE AT ROYAL YORK---FRIDAY, APRIL 16th

The Inglis Steel-worker

Published by United Steelworkers of America-C.I.O., 1328 Bloor St. West, Toronto

Printed by
HESS-TRADE TYPESETTING CO., 4 NELSON ST., TORONTO

Vol. 2, No. 12

TORONTO, APRIL 12, 1943

INGLIS WORKERS ON THE AIR

Tuesday, April 13th, 1.15 p.m.
CHML---900 ON YOUR DIAL

Machine Operators Get 80c Per Hour Under Steelworker-C.I.O. Agreement

see page 3

LABOUR SUPPORTS LOCAL 2900 STEELWORKERS-C.I.O.

Unions from Coast to Coast Urge Vote for Steelworkers-C.I.O.---see page 4

Stewards Quit A.F.L. to Join Steelworkers-CIO

see page 2

STEELWORKER - C.I.O.

Stewards Meeting

To Name Union Scrutineers for Voting Day

Day Shift and Midnight Shift

Wednesday, April 14, at 8 p.m.

Afternoon Shift

Thursday, April 15, at 1.30 p.m.

Both Meetings at

STEELWORKERS - C.I.O. HALL
1328 Bloor West (at Lansdowne)

Finished Colt-Browning Gun receives final o.k. as Inglis workers turn out thousands of small arms each month. Fifteen thousand Inglis workers all contribute to victory in war. They can contribute to victory in peace by voting Steelworkers - C.I.O. on April 19th.

WHEN YOU VOTE NEXT MONDAY---VOTE STEELWORKERS-C.I.O.

The real organizing of Inglis workers began after certification. This leaflet was distributed 31 August, 1943.

1941, had not been forgotten. Further, with the collapse of the Hitler–Stalin Pact in June 1941, many left-wingers may have felt uncomfortable with the CIO's use of strikes and sitdowns. Communists increasingly viewed the defeat of fascism and the defense and survival of Russia as all important. After the summer of 1941, nothing, in their view, could justify harming the home-front production.

Such views put at least some communist organizers in the IAM camp. Ruth Weir and Janet MacLean were already supporting the IAM when they met Paul Pulk, a USWA steward working in the butt department of the Bren Gun Division. Pulk was initially collecting membership dollars for the Steelworkers during the organizing drive. He viewed the IAM as a narrow craft organization and, worse, "a company union." After meeting Weir and MacLean, he accused them initially of "sabo-

taging the war effort for joining and helping the IAM." The two women began the "reeducation of Paul" by introducing him to Walt Young, who lived across the street from Pulk on Hook Avenue. Young discussed the Steelworker "raids" at Anaconda Brass and Massey-Harris and explained to Pulk why the USWA organizing drive at Inglis was also a raid.

Pulk was convinced towards the end of the drive, but didn't switch loyalties quietly. The women helped him pen a leaflet, "Why I am not a member of the Steelworkers," which the IAM subsequently republished in its newspaper towards the end of the organizing drive. Pulk fingered the USWA for a range of sins, but with varying degrees of accuracy:

> When we joined the Steelworkers, we were told the IAM Bren Local 1612 was a company union. It was the Bren Local, however that fought for a two-way ballot, in opposition to both the company and our former union leaders of Local 2900. It was the Bren Local that asked our co-operation to fight for a strong Ontario labour bill, only to be ignored by our union officials.
>
> Doubts arose in our minds and we investigated the agreements of the two unions. We found only one Steelworkers' Agreement — and that over 3,000 miles away, contains a wage schedule, despite all the strikes they have called.

The leaflet continued by describing the machinists as being the only "strong, democratic workers' union," adding:

> The Steelworkers of Toronto had led the workers down a blind alley. At Acme Screw and Gear, the workers were led into two fatal strikes, a number of workers were left walking the streets and there is no union there today. At Research Enterprises, the company union rates still prevail. At MacDonald Tin, subsidiary of General Steel Wares, girls start this very day at 28 cents per hour. This suicidal policy of adventurism must not happen at John Inglis's; we have more important work to do. In conclusion, we wish to emphasize that we are not leaving one union to join another; we have joined the only real democratic union in John Inglis — Bren Local 1612, IAM.

Harry Gutkin is the cartoonist who provided this thoughtful political statement for the 22 December 1943 edition of The Inglis Steelworker.

This photograph, and the following three, were taken the day of the union vote, 19 April 1943. Polling stations were set up throughout the plant. Only about half of the Inglis workers actually voted.

The leaflet was signed by the former USWA stewards in Department 3 of the Bren Gun Section. It caused quite a stir. Many supporters of the Steelworkers were angry at those who had so publicly denounced the USWA. Pulk recalled threats. "One of the guys in the plant who was a boxer said he was going to beat the shit out of me. If I worked night shift my two brothers would come to meet me with pipes up their sleeves."

Company management kept abreast of what happened both at IAM and CIO meet-ings through informants' reports to its head of security, H.V. Waterhouse. These were rich in detail. The words and actions of individual ac-tivists were singled out. William Marchand was named for handing out stickers and for canvassing women workers. An assistant fore-man from the barrels department who was attending union meetings was described as "particularly sympathetic to the CIO." Two women activists also attracted the informant's attention.

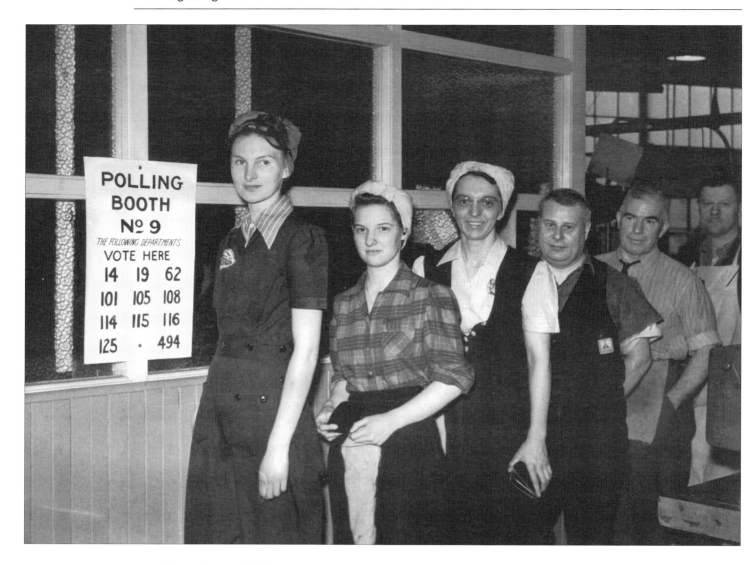

Mrs. Gwen Williams, secretary of Local 2900, reported at a union meeting that she was extremely busy in catching up with correspondence. She had told the company she needed to leave to take care of her children. The informant's report noted rather dryly, "Her explanation of leaving the firm to look after her children seems rather weak after above statement made about her being busy as secretary for Local 2900." Another woman, Mrs. Pearl Lewis, had transferred departments more than once within a short time period. "This looks like one person," the informant noted, "who has been sent into this plant for the sole purpose of organization of this CIO United Steelworkers of America."

Company records contain more reports on the CIO than on the IAM, which might be a reflection of several things relating to the latter: fewer meetings, politics, less competent informants assigned to the IAM, or simply the recognition, as Ainsworth seemed to note, that the CIO was winning the drive by a large margin. The regular informants' reports were hardly the company's only source of information on the union. Activists were watched closely in a number of ways. Any breach of rules could result in immediate dismissal. Sometimes a coworker unsympathetic to the CIO took the trouble to write to the company directly. One worker was reported as having approached a colleague on company time, making cynical statements about the war effort. Lee Ainsworth noted at the bottom of these allegations, "He should be fired at once with 7 days pay if this is true."

Companies also exchanged information about CIO organizers, though how they discovered so quickly where activists had been working previously remains a mystery. The speed with which records were exchanged and union organizers located suggests the sophisticated involvement of an outside authority. In December 1942 Inglis vice president Lee Ainsworth and Neil Petersen, the president of Acme Screw and Gear, exchanged details about Bill and Larry Sefton. The former had recently taken up his position as chief organizer in the Inglis drive. Ainsworth wrote to Petersen, providing him with some basic employment information. He closed:

> We are taking every step to see he does not devote any personal time to Union activities during working hours, but in talking to him it is obvious that is whole heart is in the CIO, and I know for a fact that he spends all his spare time in connection with these activities.

But soon no amount of harassment or intimidation could have stopped the union campaign. In fact, further harassment of Jock Carroll might have given the CIO a boost. Carroll, who had been fired briefly a few years earlier, was in charge of three shifts in Department 70 of the Bren Gun Division. The company had been trying to lure him into management for some time. Carroll was a knowledgeable group leader and an especially successful union recruiter. After he had signed up a large number of people, the company fired Carroll from his fairly responsible position. Carroll recalled:

A. L. Ainsworth, Vice-President and General Manager of the John Inglis Company, and Eamon Park, International Representative of the United Steelworkers of America, put their signatures to the agreement between the company and local 2900.

Eamon Park (left) and Lee Ainsworth sign the collective agreement. Park was an early SWOC organizer and then a staff representative for the Steelworkers. Ainsworth was vice-president and general manager of Inglis and carried much of the responsibility for the company during the war. From the 25 August 1943 edition of The Inglis Steelworker.

> *The drive was on, the union didn't want a strike. A majority of the people who worked for me had signed cards and eventually I was fired again. I was escorted out of the plant with my tool box and I was given a piece of paper to sign saying that I had resigned, which was crazy. I was marched out of the building but I refused to sign that. Then E.B. Joliffe, the solicitor for the union, got involved and the union decided that they would fight my case, they wouldn't try and organize a strike. They were going to fight my case on legal grounds. Some sort of a commission was formed.*
>
> *In the meantime I had no money. The Steelworkers put me to work in their office, assigning me minor tasks, paying me a salary equal to what I would have earned if I had been working at Inglis. There was a hearing, I testified. The result of this after a certain number of weeks was that Inglis was ordered to reinstate me at an equal position. So they*

> *reinstated me at what they perceived to be an equal position. I was assigned to be a set-up man for a small group of four people running some drill presses. At Inglis they could get military exemptions for certain positions essential to production. After I got put back at this new position I became aware that I was no longer on the exemption list. They wanted to get rid of me. I soon after joined the airforce and left Inglis, never to return.*

Carroll was a popular, articulate Inglis worker and his situation was soon fodder for headlines in the *Inglis Steelworker*. The union highlighted the unjust dismissal, reproducing the National Selective Service form that Carroll had refused to sign. Details of the case, revealed in *Inglis Steelworker*, emphasized "the need for a real union grievance procedure at Inglis." The case was closely documented in the issues that followed weekly. The company's moves to defend its actions were reported with little sympathy:

THE INGLIS STEELWORKER

Local 2900's President Bill Sefton and W. R. MacLachlan, Director of Manufacturing for the Inglis Company, signing the union agreement.

The first collective agreement between Inglis and Local 2900 was signed 19 August 1943. It covered basic areas such as wages, overtime, a grievance procedure, and seniority, but also a clause on post-war reconstruction. From the 25 August 1943 edition of The Inglis Steelworker

A flurry of activities by the company in an attempt to build its case has been evident in the last week. Major James Hahn, Canada's munition king, and President of the John Inglis Company, last week made a flying visit from his $1.00-a-year job at Ottawa, to lecture workers in Group 4 of Department 70 on the company's attitude. The penny lecture looked like a gratuitous insult to the workers and its effectiveness was not increased when Major Hahn hurried away after his remarks, refusing to hear the workers' side of the story. (Incidently, many workers were kept after hours to hear the lecture and it was subsequently announced they would be paid time and one-half for the overtime. The price of workers having to listen to financiers who live by the profits from munitions will be borne by the taxpayers of Canada — that means you and me.)

Both the USWA and the IAM had battled at the plant gates, handing out leaflets and publishing newspapers. In the final months, union leafletting was stepped up and both newspapers appeared more often. The *Inglis Steelworker* began regular publication in October 1942, reporting news from inside the plant as well as successes of the USWA and the CIO in general. The common themes in all of the issues were intense criticism of the way the company was run and the necessity for an industrial union.

Roy and Elizabeth Bragg were observers during the CIO drive. Many workers didn't come from union backgrounds, and industrial unionism was treated cautiously by many, including Roy Bragg:

> *The union started sending out pamphlets around, hand-printed pamphlets. A couple of guys handed them out at the gates. My father was an old-time bricklayer and couldn't stand unions, he had no time for unions. That was my initial response too.*

Specific issues were discussed, such as unfair promotions and transfers, the unfair bonus system, and the pay differential between "girls" and men. A mixture of broader political reporting from the industrial relations scene, cartoons, and photographs filled out the content.

Two editions of the IAM's *Inglis Production Worker* ran concurrently. The first was printed at the Morris Printing Company on Spadina Avenue and didn't appear until February 1943. Like the organizing drive, it was a staid publication. There were more calls to patriotism — the IAM endorsed a no-strike pledge — and fewer political issues discussed. Stories stressed the union's legitimacy, supported boosting production, and spoke of a lack of outside interference. The latter was a pointed criticism of the USWA's use of paid organizers on their drive. A second type of IAM newspaper was printed at Eveready, a known communist print shop. This was more openly critical of the USWA, issuing challenges and stating that the USWA was dividing workers by ignoring jurisdiction. The dual nature of the IAM's publications was a curious reflection of a campaign that swung back and forth between a lack of forcefulness and shrill overabundance of criticism directed at USWA. A last-minute story of imminent layoffs at the Inglis Plant, apparently emanating from the Bren Lodge 1612 leadership, was likely designed to discourage voters from going to the polls.

On 29 March 1943, after considerable manoeuvering on the part of both unions, a joint agreement was signed. The vote would take place 19 April 1943, five long years after both unions had made overtures to organize the Ordnance Division. The logistics alone of having 17,000 potential voters required considerable planning.

The vote was finally held using a simply worded ballot. At ten polls throughout the plant, the workers chose the USWA over the IAM by an overwhelming margin: 6,691 to 1,044. The victory for the USWA was decisive, but fewer than half the eligible workers had taken the trouble to vote.

Roy Bragg recalled the vote and how he felt about the union at the time:

They had a ballot box set up in the cafeteria when I voted; I think I was on shift. They had some representatives from the union and the company. At the initial time I voted no; I didn't want it. I couldn't see what the union could do for me. I knew it couldn't be a steady job; I knew this was war work, and maybe next year I wouldn't be there.

The low turnout could be explained by a number of factors. First, large numbers were totally committed to the war effort and felt a union would be disruptive. In their minds they were serving in an army as well, working on behalf of their loved ones dying overseas. Eileen Tallman observed that the war worker mentality was especially prevalent among women:

My guess would be that an awful lot of the women didn't vote because they figured they weren't going to be there after the war. Secondly in a plant that large it's virtually impossible to interest a majority of the workers ... in anything. You could just see by the hoards pouring out of that place when you were distributing leaflets that there was quite a large percentage that were interested in the bucks, and the beer, when you could get it, which wasn't very often.

There is further evidence that some were unhappy with either the Steelworkers' victory or that a vote had taken place at all. In May 1943, immediately following the vote, the turnover rate increased to more than twice what it had been in any other month that year. The second highest rate occurred in June 1943. Some, it seems, voted with their feet.

After the USWA was democratically chosen as the bargaining agent in 1943, Paul Pulk was encouraged by his chief steward to rejoin

Local 2900's Negotiating Committee caught in a rare (?) good mood outside the plant during a noon-hour recess. From left to right: Ed Collom (Bldg. 23); Barney McCarney (Boys Bldg.); Jock Brodie (Colt Bldg.); Harold Stevens (Bren Bldg.); Bill Sefton (Colt Bldg.); Eamon Park, International Representative; Bill Griffiths (Maintenance). Missing: Roy King (23B).   —Photograph by Bob Van Evera.

Women, whose votes were eagerly sought before the balloting, were not part of Local 2900's first negotiating committee. From the 8 July 1943 edition of The Inglis Steelworker. *Jock Brodie later was elected president of the local.*

In 1944, Fred Spratt, the former plant chairman for the AFL, was fired by the company. He was dismissed because he had refused to participate in a time study conducted at the plant. The Steelworkers defended Spratt, Mary Spratt's father, and won him a week's wages in lieu of notice. He was not rehired at Inglis.

the Steelworkers. Men and women in his department had continued to pay him their union dues because they trusted him as a trade unionist.

Industrial unionism had been established at Inglis. In the following year a three-way vote would decide that the Commerical Division would also be represented by the USWA. Tremendous effort had been put into organizing the largest manufacturing plant that ever existed in Canada. By the end of 1943 there

Members of Local 2900's negotiating committee sign the first collective agreement with the John Inglis Company. From left to right: Ed Collom, Barney McCarney, Roy King, Harold Stevens and Bill Griffiths. Seated is Jock Brodie, the local's first president.

were already 4,000 fewer Inglis workers. Production of the Boys and Browning guns was winding down. The decline would continue through 1944 to the end of the war. Workers at Inglis and elsewhere began to turn their attention to a world without war. In 1942, as the union drive was gaining momentum, the USWA looked ahead:

Those John Inglis employees who remember what happened after the last war must stop and think occasionally when they see the enormously expanded payroll of the company at the present moment. They realize that some day, the special war work will end and that the men overseas will be demobilized. What happens then?

Chapter Four
Transforming Inglis: The End of the War

At the height of wartime production, thousands of women worked in factories across Toronto. Many were involved in a type of work that they had never done before. Female labour became absolutely necessary to meet production goals, and although aspects of this experience may have seemed liberating to women, in many ways life for working women did not change radically.

At Inglis and elsewhere, for the most part women were still segregated into jobs reserved for female labour. Participating in nontraditional jobs did not free women from the responsibilities of domestic labour. Homework was still considered women's work. If real gains had been made for women during the war years, these changes would have carried over to peacetime. Instead many women returned to more traditional types of work — clerical, retail, hospitality — or were encouraged to put their energies into home and family. Although women were eligible for postwar training programs, their choices were directed towards so-called "womanly" occupations.

There was some belief that women were entitled to the same postwar treatment as men: retraining, adequate pay, and opportunity for advancement. Instead, the federal government began to cancel incentives put in place during the war. Women were expected to make way for men, and positions in domestic service were encouraged. Not only did this mean a drastic cut in pay, but women also lost their right to unemployment insurance if they entered domestic service. To make domestic responsibilities more attractive, women were encouraged in the media to no longer be the competent, independent "Bren girl," but instead to be "little women," happy at home, glad to consume. Inglis, which had employed unprecedented numbers of women in production, would soon strive to appeal to them in a decade of record consumption. Making the right purchases meant a fulfilled domestic existence, and marriage and motherhood were presented as primary goals.

This unnamed Inglis worker was one woman who was able to keep her job after World War II ended.

Women's participation in the work force reached a high of 33.5 percent in 1944 and then began to fall again. The 1944 level would not be topped again until 1967. But a closer look at who remained employed demonstrates that it was young, single women who left active work following the war. Not surprisingly, the rate of marriage for young women rose considerably at this time. But the participation of married women in the work force remained almost at 1944 levels, despite an overall decrease in female employment. The enormous growth of the service sector in the Canadian economy found good use for experienced women workers, but once again they were limited mostly to low-wage jobs.

Canadian women had entered the industrial wartime work force only in part out of patriotism. Well over half, in a 1943 survey, indicated economic reasons as the prime motivator. After the war, many continued to work outside the home, although not in well-paid industrial jobs. For many families, paid employment for women was the key to improving a family's financial position. This was understandable given the depression and war years, which added up to fifteen years of material deprivation. Cars, furniture, and, of course, appliances such as those Inglis produced were perceived as necessities. Better education and health care were desirable family goals with a price tag.

Both Elizabeth and Roy Bragg remained employed outside the home after leaving Inglis. Elizabeth recalls:

I left in 1944. I could see sooner or later it was going to stop, and shift work was beginning to get to me. I decided that was the time to leave. They were cutting back about that time. They had a big pile of stuff. The boys were coming home, and they got first crack at any job.

Roy adds:

It was kind of tough. You felt that you were booted out and you're a second-class citizen now. But I guess you understood it. The fellows were coming home and going back to their jobs. That was the law, that if you left a job to join up, they had to give you that job back when you came back.

I guess Major Hahn made a lot of money. And his executives, I would think. A lot of people made money during the war. I honestly think this is why we have wars, because this is the bottom line. A lot of people make money during war. Unfortunately it's the ordinary person who gets killed or maimed, but he doesn't make too much money.

The Economic Dream

The reorganization of the John Inglis Company was part of a conversion of Canada's entire industrial profile. The unprecedented growth experienced during the war could not be reversed. Yet two economic conditions were unchanged in the country: the market limitations of a vast country with a relatively small population, and foreign domination of corporate life. At the war's end, both factors would affect Inglis, a thoroughly Canadian company. In another respect, the industrial clock could not be turned back. Wartime production methods had effectively put an end to craft-based production. Entrepreneurs would have no motivation to permit a return to traditional power relationships on the shopfloor.

As munitions production for war began to wind down, conversion to peacetime became a dominant issue. Manufacturers needed to find new products for new markets. Trade unions had to define their role in relationships no longer dictated by wartime regulations. The year 1946 was a notable one for work stoppages. For the Canadian work force, conversion signified the return of thousands from the armed forces and other military jobs. It meant extraordinary changes in life style, as most workers adjusted to shorter work shifts and reduced wages. The public was also anxious to purchase those consumer goods that had been unavailable during the war.

Canadian workers had demonstrated that the homemade economy was capable of growth and development beyond all expectation. There were many who believed that this potential could continue in production areas previously unrepresented in Canada, creating a truly Canadian economy. In 1945, serious attention was given to postwar industry in a report for the Department of Reconstruction and Supply, a section of the Directorate of Economic Research in Ottawa. This optimistic report was called "Location and Effects of Wartime Industrial Expansion in Canada, 1939–1944."

It was clear that Canada would probably need fewer facilities for iron and steel and

Three unnamed Inglis workers in the postwar plant.

The two Inglis-built tanks are typical of the huge engineering projects which the company undertook in the years following World War II. The name of the worker giving the tank a friendly pat is not known.

that employment in secondary steel would decrease correspondingly. The same situation applied to other basic industry such as nickel and aluminium. Other sectors would grow in post-war production capacity. In textiles ... this backlog of civilian domestic demand in addition to the need for reclothing Europe is like to keep the mills operating at capacity for some time. Also as rubber for automobile tires becomes available, the demand for cotton cord for linings will grow. The production of rayon will undoubtedly increase. The potential peacetime demand for textiles should then substantially replace the wartime demand ...

Overall, there was the hope that the Canadian economy would develop in strong and independent directions:

Canadian manufacturing industries are planning to expand and produce many new lines, including at least one hundred major products never before manufactured in Canada. For example, end-products range from inter-city buses, prefabricated houses, glass fabrics and plastic products to a myriad of household articles. The development of the toy industry in Canada gives promise of an end to reliance on foreign countries. Primary materials and components of manufactured articles include ball and roller type bearings; polymer flake, an important material for nylon fabrics; special type yarns; synthetic resins; titanium dioxide for all types of paints. The list of new products includes medicines and chemicals as well as many types of plant machinery and equipment never before made in Canada ...

The report saw increased employment and expanded markets abroad. Instead of exporting raw materials, Canada would begin to sell manufactured goods. In a reversal of past industrial practice, imported products might be raw materials and semiprocessed goods.

Summarizing, Canadian industry, grown in stature and capacity, has demonstrated in recent years the potentialities that lie in making full use of the resources (human and natural) of the country. If adequately utilized, the experience gained, the techniques developed, the capacities created and the skills acquired in the field of manufacturing industry hold promise for increased returns for the Canadian people in terms of raising their standard of living.

It would go far beyond the content of this book to explore the reasons why the Canadian economy failed to live up to the hopes expressed. Certainly, an entrepreneur as savvy, influential, and committed as James Hahn would have been a driving force in such a development. Perhaps other business people lacked his vision. Perhaps the forces of foreign capital, from Great Britain and later from the U.S., were too powerful to resist.

In hindsight, Canadians missed a chance to control their own economic destiny. Immediately following the war, the Inglis company purchased controlling interest of the Canadian subsidiary of English Electric. Inglis, an attractive Canadian company with international aspirations, attracted the attention of the subsidiary's parent. In 1950, Inglis itself was purchased by English Electric of Great Britain and, for the first time in the company's history, corporate leadership was no longer Canadian.

Restructuring Inglis

The management at Inglis thoroughly explored the possibilities for converted production. In connection with new product development, the company was able to purchase the government-owned Strachan Avenue buildings from the War Assets Corporation. The total price that Inglis was to pay for both buildings and equipment was $750,000, only a small percentage of the $2,100,000 the government had invested originally.

The Ordnance Division became the Consumer Goods Division, a name change that symbolizes postwar manufacturing in Canada. In late 1946, the Inglis work force in the Ordnance Division had dropped from a peak of 17,000 to a total of 1,500, one-third of whom worked in the Consumer Products Division. The Engineering Division became an essential part of industrial expansion in the 1950s and 1960s. Through licensing agreements with British and U.S. companies, Inglis researched, designed, and built industrial facilities throughout Canada and in other countries as well. In the heart of factories, ships, breweries, steel mills, refineries,

CANADIAN WAR PLANTS SWITCH FROM PRODUCING PISTOLS TO PANS, BREN GUNS TO FISHING R

FROM PISTOLS to pans is part of the reconversion program at the John Inglis Co. Many sizes of saucepans are reaching production and will be available to the public soon. Post-war planning started on Jan. 2, 1943, when president wrote about it to the directors

THERE'S NO DIFFERENCE between making a Bren gun and a fishing reel from an engineering standpoint, according to Maj. James E. Hahn, president of the Inglis Co. The same machinery is used

Tribute to Jock Brodie

Shortly after Jock Brodie was appointed to a Steelworker staff position, his local paid tribute to him. From the Minutes of the Local 2900 Executive, 21 September 1948:

> Presentation on behalf of Local 2900 to our past president Bro. Jock Brodie, who I am sure will be missed by all those who had the pleasure to work with him, during his tenure of office with Local 2900.
>
> Being appointed to the staff of the United Steelworkers of Amer. is the good fortune of the staff in this area. In being able to call on men of Brother Brodie's caliber. And from the ranks of Local Unions, throughout the country, there must be many more in the Steelworkers Union. It is to be hoped that such will continue to be policy of those who have the power to appoint men, from the ranks of Steel.

sewage plants, skating rinks, and mines, Inglis products pumped away. As in the early years of industrial expansion at the turn of the century, Inglis products were found in nearly every Ontario industrial establishment.

Major Hahn had begun to explore new manufacturing possibilities as early as 1942. He realized that to utilize the plant's capacity, he should pursue a double strategy:

> We had one set of equipment and a group of people well-suited for heavy engineering; in this type of engineering the products tend to be custom made and large, and a high degree of skill lies with the individual worker. We had another group well versed in the art of gunmaking, which involved large quantities of like items, well-tooled and meticulously planned, where, in some cases, a large degree of skill was required of the individual worker, but an even greater degree of skill was required of the planners, tool designers, and toolmaking personnel. This division of skills indicated to us the need for two types of operations, after the war, one carrying on the heavy engineering part of the operation, the other utilizing our gunmaking skills and practice in new lines. This second group formed what later became our Consumer Products Division.

Another fact that became obvious as we laid our plans was the need for something to fill in the transitional period ... we felt that it was vital to find some means of keeping our personnel together during this period so that they would be available when the time came for the manufacture of the new lines. We therefore set up what we called "the Bits and Pieces Programme." This called for our taking immediately upon the cessation of hostilities, any sub-contract work or order for bits and pieces that could be put into production with a minimum of tooling delay ...

The new union local, for its part, also pursued a strategy for postwar production. Local president Jock Brodie asked the company to reduce the regular hours of work at Inglis to forty per week, which would help reduce the number of lay offs. But the company had other plans.

In a handsome book published by Inglis just after the war, all of the company's products are illustrated and described. The General Engineering Division was still the major force. In the book's introduction, Inglis employees are stated to be "its greatest asset. The creative ability of its engineers, the skill of its craftsmen and the experience and demonstrated stability of its production staff are the major force behind the Inglis organization."

Building and installing boilers, both of Inglis design and under license, remained a primary activity for the Engineering Division. Compressors and pumps of every nature and for a multitude of uses were made in cooperation with Worthington Pump and Machinery Corporation. Related to those products were complete refrigeration systems installed and serviced by Inglis for the food and beverage industry and for ice rinks. Forging hammers and hydraulic presses, again built under license, were crucial for the expanding metalworking industry.

Both the brewery and dairy industries purchased Inglis-made glass-lined tanks. Inglis brought to Canada, under an agreement with the A.O. Smith Corporation of Milwaukee, Wisconsin, the single-piece steel tank with a fused glass liner. These tanks would be fired in huge furnaces in the Inglis plant.

By combining these products with Inglis engineering know-how, the company was able to supply shipbuilders with engineroom necessities. These included engines, boilers, steam

War Plant Now Makes Fishing Tackle

New rods and reels are being shipped out to all parts of the world. Some of the rods are made of glass. Here are workers fitting the new tubular steel rods into the "offset" handles and preparing them for shipment.

—Globe and Mail.

POTENTIAL CUSTOMERS for the post-war products of Canadian industry examine the latest unit to be developed by the John Inglis Co., latterly producers of Bren guns and other war equipment

VERSATILITY is the keynote as war production facilities are converted to peacetime needs. Here Jean Bogart finds out the Inglis company also makes 45,000 h.p. turbines

This is the title page of The Story of Inglis *published by the company shortly after World War II. Beautifully illustrated and designed, the book highlights the incredible range of products the workers at Inglis made.*

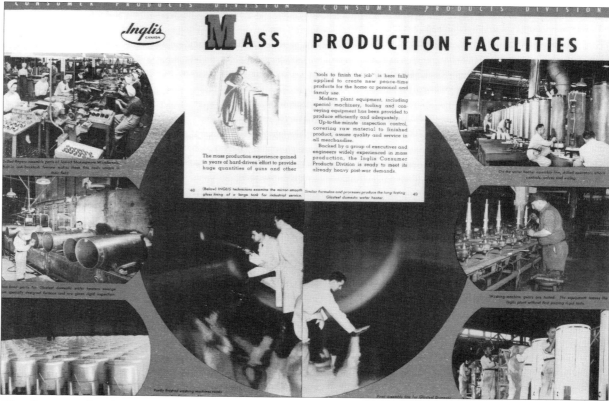

The Consumer Products Division of the post–World War II Strachan Avenue plant manufactured an impressive array of products. From fishing tackles to washing machines to glass-lined tanks, the company applied the lessons learned about mass production during the war. Many of the products were built under licensing agreements with American and British companies.

Mel Lastman, also known as the "Bad Boy" after his appliance business, became His Worship, the Mayor of North York. Here he is selling the merits of an Inglis washer to a customer. Appliance sales were an important part of the post-war economic boom.

New Business for Canada . . . New Worries for Fish!

How Strong Is Nylon Line? How Balanced Is A Casting Rod? How Precise Is A Reel? How Rigid Are Tests And Inspections? It's A Long Way From Fishing, But It's Important To The Fisherman — And The Fish.

DURING World War II, John Inglis Co. Limited operated one of the largest ordnance plants in the British Empire. Specialized skills, developed in the high-precision manufacturing of arms and war weapons, are now serving industrial peace-time requirements. One of the new departments at this plant is the Sporting Goods Dept. where fishing reels, rods and nylon lines are manufactured. Shortly after the cessation of hostilities, an agreement was signed between the Shakespeare Co., Kalamazoo, Michigan, and the John Inglis firm. As a preliminary step men were sent by Inglis to the Shakespeare Co. to learn just how these reels were manufactured. With the constant aid of the Shakespeare Co. they are now manufacturing six models of reels, nylon line in five weights from fifteen pound test to thirty-five pound test, and have three rods available.

A visit to this department at John Inglis will find a large section of one building set up with expensive machinery for the manufacture of the Shakespeare line, and possibly the most outstanding feature of the

operation of the department is the rigid inspection to which all of the products are subjected.

For instance, in the nylon line section, each individual skein of nylon line is tested for its tensile strength before it is wound on the spools, thereby insuring the fisherman that the test indicated on the spools is absolutely correct.

The Shakespeare slogan "Built Like a Watch' is a very true statement. The tolerances to which Shakespeare reels are manufactured are just as exacting as those to which watches are built, but Inglis have the best machinery available for this type of work in their plant, and are quite capable of doing the job with the utmost skill.

Probably the most difficult operation in the manufacture of fishing rods is the binding of the line guides to the rod so they are properly spaced, and set at exactly the correct angle on the rod. Each guide is wound to the rod with nylon thread, fastened by a special knot, and then varnished to insure securely bound guides.

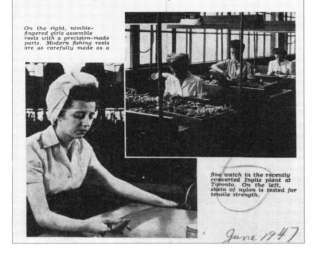

On the right, nimble-fingered girls assemble reels with a precision-made parts. Modern fishing reels are as carefully made as a fine watch in the recently converted Inglis plant at Toronto. On the left, skein of nylon is tested for tensile strength.

June 1947

turbines, condensers, evaporators, and pumps. Below ground, the company could supply the mining sector with everything from cages and mine cars to boilers and jaw crushers. The same combination of expertise, licensing agreements, and product was available to the growing petroleum, chemical, rubber, and pulp and paper industries in Canada, and to the gas and oil sectors.

Even more diversified was the Consumer Products Division. Home appliances were intended to help fulfill the dream of domestic harmony and tranquility following the unruly war years. The Inglis Company explained, "The mass production experience gained in years of hard-driven effort to provide huge quantities of

guns and other 'tools to finish the job' is here fully applied to create new peacetime products for the home or personal and family use."

Inglis built and marketed glass-lined domestic water heaters, too, originally designed by the A.O. Smith Corp. Such a high-capacity water heating system was clearly needed to accompany the new home laundry equipment. Inglis also signed a licensing agreement shortly after the war with Nineteen Hundred Corporation of St. Joseph, Michigan, the forerunner of the Whirlpool Corporation. The Inglis assembly line turned out wringer-type washers, portable models, automatic washers and dryers, and electric irons. It also turned out convection heaters and oil burners with an Inglis fuel pump. The Consumer Products Division also manufactured mobile homes, fishing reels and rods, lighters, pots and pans, powder compacts for women, and lipstick holders.

Any opportunity to modify work organization on the production floor was clearly overlooked. Lynn Williams, former international president of the Steelworkers, was a dues-paying member of Local 2900. He worked at Inglis in 1947 before becoming a union staff representative. "Working smart" had unexpected consequences for him and his coworkers.

We were working on hot water heaters, the assembly-line work. The core of the heaters was downstairs. They shipped the heaters themselves upstairs and there they put insulation around and a case around and painted the case. Assembly-line work is interesting in its dullness. In a sense, it's interesting what people will do on an assembly line to sort of entertain themselves and communicate and keep from going crazy. This was a young crew; we were all kids. One day, we got humming — we got really into sort of making this thing work and doing it well and took some sort of satisfaction — and, as a result, we got way ahead of the folks downstairs with their heaters. They sent us home at noon, and we all lost a half a day's pay for our efforts.

I've often chastised management about that because we made sure then the rest of the time I was there that that never happened again. We made sure that we knew how many heaters were coming from downstairs and if we were getting ahead, we didn't stay ahead. It was just such an inter-

No question about gender identity in this 1958 ad for Inglis appliances. This illustration depicts the "ideal" family: two children, one of each sex, a home in the suburbs with a family room, and all kinds of home appliances to make life easier. While the females in the family pursue book learning, dad passes on more practical skills to his son.

A Working Wage

Inglis was always a male-dominated workplace, despite the presence of 9,000 women workers during the war. In the 1950s the shopfloor at the Strachan Avenue Factory returned to what many men would call "normal". By 1961 only 50 women worked in manufacturing at Inglis. The shop floor culture of Inglis drew on traditional concepts of male behaviour and pride. Married workers usually supported their families without the need of a "working wife". Good industrial wages fed the paternalism of the times, reflecting in turn the skilled tradesmen's attitudes of the pre-war factory. The marketing of consumer products in the post-war era reinforced these stereotypes. The corporate transformation of Inglis, while affecting the long-term future of the factory's working-class community, left intact traditional values of wage-earning men.

David Hahn's association with Inglis began when his father, Major James Hahn, bought the company. Along with his twin brother Jim, David Hahn worked during his summer holidays in some of the dirtiest departments at the company. During those work periods, he was a member of USWA Local 2900. His father didn't mind, he said, as long as the sons didn't throw bricks through his windows. After completing his university education in business, David Hahn was hired in the 1950s at the plant which his father no longer owned. He became Works Manager under English Electric, whose very British management style, according to Hahn, affected the long-term health of the company.

esting lesson. If the company had been smart, they would have paid us for the afternoon off as a reward. Who knows what might have happened to productivity. But they just figured they would save some money and send all these folks home.

There were more damaging errors made when English Electric took control in 1950. Hahn remained as president for the first year or so, but the changes on the shopfloor were noticed quickly. Being run from Great Britain as part of a multiplant chain put the Strachan Avenue plant in a new position and changed both the style and substance of its operations. English Electric's method of management soon led to

difficulties. Hired in 1952, Paul Ryan's shopfloor perspective was common among many of his coworkers:

We had Major Hahn for a while. He was quite good. He understood you had to spend a buck to make a buck. Then top management was the old English system of doing things. While we were owned by English Electric they milked us. They didn't put any money back into the scheme. We used to have the best tradesmen in North America. We had everything going for us. We were building turbines for the Royal Canadian Navy, and Seaway stuff and Chile, and for papermills all over the world — we had a good business going. When English Electric came in, they brought the efficiency expert in from the States. It cost them a million and a half dollars to go around and study tradespeople. These are office people trying to study tradespeople to decipher that the welder should be able to weld so many feet in so many minutes. You can't do that. These are Class A welders. That's where the business went. Taking short cuts.

New shopfloor methods were just the beginning of deepening frictions between the foreign owners and the workers at Inglis. The haughty attitude of much of the upper management also made the Canadians bristle. By the 1950s James Hahn's son, David, was working for the management of English Electric. He recalls the hierarchy that the British ownership brought with them:

English Electric was a huge company. In one facility, I think it was the Preston works, they had seven different levels of cafeteria for lunch. There was blue collar and shopfloor, then staff, then office workers, then senior staff, then foremen and supervisors; finally you got to the executive holy of holies. I mean terribly class conscious. In a British plant if [senior executive] Hurton was going to come or Sir George Nelson, the line-painting machines would be out three weeks before the visit and you would know he was coming tomorrow, he is coming in an hour, he is in the next building and everybody would be twitching. Tactics that our Canadians wouldn't put up with.

Aside from these attitudes, there were also incidents of incompetence and mismanagement that cost the plant important business. One example from the mid-1950s is noteworthy. Large glass-lined brewing tanks were an important part of the plant's business in that decade. A young British engineer decided to make the product a different way one day. Frank McCuaig, who worked in the plant from 1953 to 1966, recalled:

That was another thing they lost a lot of orders on. They wouldn't listen to the superintendent and some British engineer got in there and said "It has to be done this way." They put this tank on there, which they'd done hundreds of times before. This

engineer persuaded them to take off four ribs. They had a hell of a lot of steel work around these tanks, because they were so hot that if any air got near them much and they weren't held, they would collapse. So the engineer wanted to take off four ribs; the superintendent said, "You can't do that!" The foreman flatly refused to do it. They told the superintendent that if he wanted his job, he'd do it. So he did it, but under protest.

The tank was sixty feet long. It was glass-lined. Beautiful tank. They put the tank in, and drew it out red-hot. I was working in the main shop at that time. Suddenly I hear this bang. I was over to the boiler shop like a shot. Here's this bloody tank; it just collapsed in the middle. Right flat, both ends were still round. I said, "What happened?" One of the guys said, "Oh, they got smart, as usual. Some engineer ordered the ribs out. You remember the extra ribs, the double ribs we used to have on top? He ordered them out. He was going to do it cheaper; less time to do set up. There it is!"

Molson heard about it. That's it — no more tanks. They finished the two tanks they had, but they were going to renew the Montreal plant, they had finished their quota for that. So they got them built in the States.

There were similar stories involving other products, notably papermaking machinery and tank welding. The outcome was the same for all of them. Bit by bit, the plant lost large contracts by failing to provide the quality products on which its reputation was based.

The structure of the company was also altered with lasting implications. In 1951 some steam turbine contracts and some large defense-related work was transferred to the recently constructed Scarborough plant on Eglinton Avenue, which operated under the English Electric name. When the government-related work dried up, the plant was downsized and became a factory with an unclear purpose. John Fitzpatrick, then president of the USWA local at American Standard, was told by a relative working there that the plant "lost money, they had no control over it, they'd get parts in and let them lie out in the field and rust away." The plant was eventually sold to General Electric for $5 million in 1965. The diversity of the Strachan Avenue plant was also slowly eroded. In 1958, the refrigeration

This pamphlet was distributed to the Inglis sales force in a 1952 promotion. It depicts the then popular notion that technology, in this case in the form of an automatic washer, would make women's lives better, happier, and more free. This image is in stark contrast to that of the woman war worker who fulfilled her job competently.

and air-conditioning divisions were shut down. The elimination of other products would follow in the years to come.

The shrinking range of products affected the quality of working life at Inglis. One of the things that made the plant an attractive place to be was the diversity of work that was available. Bob Higgins, who began at the plant in 1951, recalled, "You could apply to work in different areas in the plant, especially if there was going to be even a seasonal cut back. I would say that at that time the range of goods they made was a

strength and an attraction."

The Heavy Engineering Division experienced growing losses. Soon the Consumer Products Division, which manufactured home appliances under license for Whirpool Corporation, was the only moneymaker at Inglis, not because the other divisions were not viable, but because they were so poorly managed. Yet the British managers of Inglis understood the Consumer Products Division the least of any part of Inglis. Profits were earned by selling the higher-end models and offering a range of features. The then head of the division, David Hahn, struggled, with little success, to explain this to his English managers:

> *They had their loss leader that they advertised and that was the one that was supposedly the one they nailed to the floor; so the salesman was to do everything not to sell it, but it would be advertised and it would be a cheapy. Then they did step up selling. You know, 'For an extra five bucks we'll put this bell on and boy is that going to make a difference to your laundry,' and so on, up to the top line of models. Their equipment was technically the best on the market, their washing machines were the best, and the features they put in were innovative. The one at the bottom, nobody made money on. Whirpool sold it to their retailers at a loss. They made a modest profit on the next one up and, you know, up it went.*
>
> *English Electric couldn't understand this. It was anathema to them to sell anything at a loss. They just didn't understand. Why did they need all these "bloody models"? And our job, at Inglis, as far as Whirpool was concerned, was to keep Simpson Sears happy. We were the only one at that point in 1955, '56, '57 that was profitable. The other divisions, English Electric was losing money, general engineering was losing money. So we were the only one that was profitable and our profitability depended on Whirpool.*

The realities of where the company's profit was being earned eventually led to a growing emphasis on white (or household) goods, generally, and a growing dependence on Whirpool, in particular. Decisions taken in the 1950s, a period of apparent prosperity for Inglis, were in fact, extremely damaging to the long-term health of the Strachan Avenue plant.

The Legacy of Women in the Union

At the end of the war, thousands of women lost their jobs at Inglis. Some, like Mary Spratt, were able to stay on, and they changed the nature of factory work forever. Women began to play a role in local union activities, as stewards, negotiators, and members of the executive board. Many broke new ground as the view was challenged that women couldn't do certain jobs.

Women continued to work at Inglis, primarily in the Consumer Products Division. Karen Mills started at a time when there were still separate wage scales and seniority lists for men and women:

> Some of the women were older women that were here from the war years. It was strange because they hadn't changed the way they dressed. They wore coveralls and they wore bandannas. Some of the women still dressed the same way until the day that they were retired.

It was still difficult for women to break into certain types of factory work, especially higher-paid jobs. Mills continued:

> After about eight years, I decided I wanted to do something different. I reported to the department where the assembly line was — automatic washers. The foreman told me, 'No way, no women are working on this line.' He gave me quite an argument 'til my break, and I told him he had no choice, that I had the right to work on that line. I wasn't on the line for very long when they asked me to work as group leader. I was all set to say no, but one of the men started getting mouthy and I thought that if he was going to get too mouthy, that I should go and be group leader.
>
> You always had to be better than any man back then. There were men that ended up helping you, but there was some men that didn't help you especially if you had more seniority than they did.

For women like Bonnie Smith, working at Inglis was a continual challenge as well. In particular, she struggled with the eternal belief that smaller size made women unsuited for hard factory work. The job of "floater" was considered especially inappropriate for women, because it required a range of skills.

By the late 1950s, the Inglis Consumer Products Division concentrated on producing white goods. The end-users of these products were, of course, the many women who no longer had jobs in factories and other industrial establishments. The role of women, as expressed in the company newsletter, Scope, must have puzzled the "Bren girls" still employed in production at Inglis. A column in the May 1958 edition gives "Credit Where Credit Is Due":

> Wives of employees make a big contribution to industrial progress. They represent the indispensable link between the home and the shop and office.
>
> ... Good, home-cooked meals are no less important to the army of industrial workers who, by their efforts, help to build Canada's economic future. Without the vital assistance of wives who plan and cook nutritious meals, this modern army would soon lose its vitality — and its ability.
>
> Much of the assistance provided by wives are so-called "little services." This probably accounts for the fact that the total extent of our wives' contribution to progress is so often overlooked. The darning of a sock may seem relatively unimportant. Yet many a bachelor has put in an unsuccessful day at work because of the discomfort caused by a protruding toe.
>
> The losses sustained by employees and industry because of illness run into millions of dollars annually. The figures would at least be doubled if it weren't for the ministrations of wives.
>
> A man with a sore throat or cold might underestimate the seriousness of his condition. By continuing to go to work he would infect others and perhaps run the risk of developing pneumonia.
>
> A wife insists that her husband go to bed. With proven remedies and tender care she has him back on his feet in half the time he would have needed to recover if left to his own devices.

Bonnie Smith

They didn't think I could handle the work because I was small. They didn't think I could do it. But I told them they had to let me prove myself. If I couldn't, then they could send me back. But I proved myself. That's why I became a floater. Because I had to prove myself. And I had to prove it for all the other women, too. I've done just about every job in fuel pumps that the women did. I could have probably done some of the men's jobs too, I just didn't apply for them. I could probably build a washing machine in [my] garage. I've done repairs, I could probably do most of it.

Bonnie Smith, a single mother who started work at Inglis during the sixties, could not rely on any "little services" to lighten her role. Smith's son, Brad, was boarded out during the workweek.

If I went to get him through the week, to take him for a day, I had one hell of a time getting him back. You know, I've seen him get sick, where he wasn't sick but he made himself sick. If you've ever had your child where they actually get sick, and then once they know everything's okay, they're okay. All of a sudden he's burning up with fever and so I'd phone work and say I wasn't coming in. It was hard, so I got to the point where I couldn't even go and get him through the week. I sometimes would go over and visit and just stay at the baby sitter's for an hour or two. Because if I took him out of there, I couldn't get him back.

Chapter Five
The Workers' Factory Defended

Labour Day in Toronto, 1961

For producers and consumers, for companies and unions, the sky was the only limit to unprecedented growth in the three decades following World War II. It seemed as though the boom would never end. There would be minor peaks and valleys, but these short downturns of a year or two were eclipsed by steady economic expansion.

The Second World War had changed industrial relations dramatically. Management emerged from the war with a new range of technologies and products that the public was happy to purchase after the fifteen years of depression and war. Unions, for their part, organized thousands of new members in the booming economy and sometimes were able to temper the growing power of corporations.

Toronto experienced an extended boom in nearly every area of its economy. The strong demand for goods created plentiful opportunities for workers in thousands of factories across the city. The city's labour movement, like the city itself, also grew dramatically in the postwar era. Industrial unions, such as the USWA, sought to consolidate their wartime organizing successes and those from the period that immediately followed.

In many factories, there was a certain tentativeness on the part of activists right after the war. Even at Inglis, it was unclear if the new found strength of industrial unions would be lasting. Older trade unionists recalled that after World War I, the power of unions was rolled back significantly. This had happened to the ma-

Two unnamed Inglis workers pause from their job on a turbine blade. Inglis produced turbines for dozens of projects across Canada and abroad.

chinists' union at Inglis. Unions seemed without political direction for most of the 1920s, but events were different after World War II.

Workers' struggles focused more narrowly on economic and job-related issues, and less on general, working-class conditions. USWA Local 2900 had to tackle the job of establishing and entrenching the union at the Inglis workplace. This process was typical of postwar collective bargaining and included the compromise of accepting recognition in exchange for control of the shopfloor environment and the "rule of law." This transformation was only reluctantly accepted at Inglis and would break down consistently during the three decades that followed.

A Culture of Defiance

While the era was characterized by the growing power of business, rampant consumption, and a vastly expanded state, fragments and pockets of an earlier time persisted. The old plant on Strachan Avenue capitalized on the heightened demand for both industrial and consumer prod-

ucts. Home to a relatively young industrial union, it was also part of a neighbourhood that was marked by highly developed independent working-class attitudes. Worker discipline, demanded by postwar compromise, rankled many old-timers at the plant. The increasingly controlled production environment challenged some of the most fundamental values that the workers' culture at Inglis had defended. Many workers, especially those in the boiler and machine shops, viewed the demands of "modern" management with distaste and suspicion.

Through the 1950s and 1960s, members of Local 2900 continued to challenge the authority of management. The number of members in the local increased during this period as the company broadened the range of standardized products through numerous licensing agreements for fuel pumps, water heaters, domestic dryers, and other consumer products. The two divisions of the plant made for a confident and potent local of considerable depth and experience in both its leadership and membership. The workers in

Consumer Products grew in terms of militancy alongside the skilled trades in Heavy Engineering, with their politicized views and positions.

The size of the local also became a source of strength and made it independent of the expertise and resources available from the greater USWA organization. As independent attitudes developed, the local attracted militants who might have avoided a local so close to the offices of both the area council and the district.

Local 2900 militancy was also made possible in part through the inheritance of the old workers' factory itself, where the physical layout defied many of the new management controls that became dominant in the 1950s. What was also inherited was a traditionalism that deepened the contradictory attitudes of the workers. While the plant had changed dramatically during the Second World War, there was also some continuity of a craft perspective. This was reflected in perceptions of masculinity, paternalism, and gender-controlled skill.

Despite the tension between militancy and traditionalism, members of both camps reacted with similar anger to management's breaching negotiated rules. This shared anger arose for different reasons. A more traditional worker would not tolerate an insult to his sense of dignity and skill. A militant one might react to management's mistreatment as an unacceptable increase in employer power.

The factory's location, too, contributed to its powerful legacy. Convenient to a solidly working-class environment, its place in the city's western downtown area offered a number of comforts and attractions. The mixture of geography, personalities, politics, and the nature of production at Inglis allowed a strong union-based culture to once again flourish at the Strachan Avenue plant.

While the formation of Local 2900 during wartime represented a distinct break with a half-century of craft union control, the industrial union maintained the plant's militant tradition of shopfloor action, which was just as old. The steady growth of the work force allowed the

The huge components of this industrial project dwarf two unnamed Inglis workers.

The Negotiating Committee for Local 2900 holds a meeting in 1976 or 1977. From left to right: Mary Spratt, Syl MacNeil, Paul Ryan, Carl Bailey, Charley Kelly, Mickey MacNeil, and Jack Pingle. Ryan is wearing a Steelworker jacket.

Members of Local 2900 hanging out together. From left to right: "Butch" McKinnon, Charley Kelly, Syl MacNeil, Albert DiPinto, Paul Ryan.

union to reorganize so that camaraderie could develop among the members. Jack Hill began work at Inglis in the 1950s. He became a union activist and eventually president of Local 2900. He helped develop a programme that went beyond just the signing of a union card.

We also did another thing there — we devised a new membership program when a new member came in. The steward would go and spend lunch hour with the new guys. It may take two weeks at lunchtime with the new members, telling them that when we got the dental programme, when we got all these things, the company just didn't give them to us. We were very aware that the company would take the people in and say, `Here's a dental card, fill this in. Here's an Ontario Hospital card, fill this in. Here's this card, fill this in. And here's a union card. We've got a union here, fill this in.' And we're very aware of that and we wanted to tell the people they didn't give us those things. They didn't give you all these cards — we had to fight for them and we told them how we fought for them and how the people achieved them so that the people had an understanding.

The unionized Inglis tradition and the famous wartime organizing drive also attracted members from politicized working-class families in the area. Many people who came to work at the plant had been raised in a trade union environment. The memories of Bill Townley, who started in the plant in 1949 and became a steward the following year, were typical and supported the membership's sense of historical struggle.

My father was in the union on the railroad, when they were just starting out. When I was very small, there was a big strike in a fur factory on Davenport, near where we lived. The police would not allow the people on strike to go within four blocks of the factory. The people were in the field on the south side of Davenport. It was in the winter, and my mother would send me around with a wagon with one of these big kettles of tea we used to take on picnics, so they could have a hot drink. I was on my first picket line when I was seven or eight years old. There was a feeling in my family that you should be involved in things.

Throughout the Inglis factory, workers personalized their work stations. This was one example of the culture they created on the shop floor, a culture which disappears with the plant.

Quite a few of those workers from outside the neighbourhood had grown up and been trained overseas. They were comfortable with a more politicized style of trade unionism. Bert Bowler, an Inglis worker who stayed on after World War II, recalled the perspective this overseas experience brought to the local:

We had a lot of welders and ex-shipyard workers, people from Britain and Scotland. They seemed to have a stronger feeling for their rights in the union. They were more liable to pursue a problem and a grievance. If they didn't get the right answer, then they just shut her down. They were taught this from the time they entered the shipyards and boilershops in Britain.

These were gentlemen who had been through rough times, through the depression. These men had been through all of this. I can remember one fellow getting up and saying that when they timed him on the

The men who built this turbine pose with management personnel. The photo was taken in 1955.

job, they wanted to know whether he wore a belt or braces to hold his pants up. 'Why?' he said. 'You can get out of a pair of braces faster than you can undo a belt.' This was to time the time spent in the washroom.

The experiences gained from wartime production were also maintained in the plant. Former war workers were toughened by their experience of arms production and the lengthy organizing drive. World War II for Inglis workers meant a crash course in shopfloor politics. The product made may have changed to pots and pans and aluminum lighters, but, as Mary Spratt recalled, quotas and a bonus system still were maintained, along with some old-fashioned supervision that inspired defiance.

We were enclosed in a fenced-in area, with one small door. One fellow — I won't name him, but he was a son-of-a-bitch — he was forever watching you, forever on top of you. If you went to the washroom and you were a little long, he would tell you off. If you got up off your stool half a minute before the whistle blew he'd make you sit back down. He was lead hand. He was just hard to get along with. I couldn't see eye to eye with him. I didn't want to be in prison. It was bad enough to be fenced-in; I didn't want to feel that I had a whip over me.

Little incidents happened. The girl working beside me, Sally, had been on that Western Tech Course with me, so she and I decided we would fix him. There was a quota to meet every day, maybe 1,000. One day she'd do 999 or 997 or 998 or whatever and maybe I'd do 1,001, but between the two of us we worked this. We could pace ourselves. Some days we both got 1,000, so he couldn't say anything. But we'd always end up being done by three or four pieces. He watched this for a while; it made him very angry, but he couldn't do anything about it.

Such subtle manipulation of production or the creation of bottle necks, along with a detailed familiarity of the plant, all formed an important part of workers' control on the shopfloor. In many parts of the plant, managers hired from within the bargaining unit exercised their authority with divided sympathies. Bill Townley recalled an incident during a work stoppage in the late 1950s that made a deep impression.

In '57 or '58, it was required that the foremen do some work in the shop. Two foremen, who were Scots, and who had been promoted because they were really good in their job — they were excellent fitters and one was a lay-out man — were asked to do some work. It involved finishing off some big fabrication, getting it ready for shipment and operating the cranes to load it on the flatcars. They said, 'We've been working with these guys, and we'd prefer to get a leave of absence, rather than be in a position of doing the work that these people on the picket line would normally do.' The company said, 'You do it, or get out.' They actually put on their coats and walked out. This was quite a thing for two people to do. They had good jobs. They were management foremen. They made that sacrifice. That was an amazing thing to see happening.

Mary Spratt (front row, far right), who joined Local 2900 during World War II, is seen with other local members at a Labour Day parade in the 1970s. The two men enjoying a smoke (on the left) are brothers Tom and John Powers.

Bill Townley, Doreen Palmer, and Bev Brown use airguns to assemble washing machine doors.

Work in the Strachan Avenue plant took many forms. The welder in the corner is Clifford Lindsey. The name of the other worker is not known.

The dominance of union values extended beyond the plant into the neighbourhood. The continuity of production in the same place had allowed several generations of working-class families to establish roots at Inglis. Many postwar workers had known the plant through family connections or because it was part of "their" neighbourhood, or both. For example, Paul Ryan, who worked at Inglis for thirty-seven years, had been living in the area and came to Inglis because of a sister who had been a union activist during the war.

I was a union man before I ever worked. My mother taught me that. She came here as an immigrant just after the First World War. She worked for CPR as a boxcar checker. She found she was getting lesser wages than the men were, so she took herself into the president's office and demanded to know why. She got her raise. That's where we got our union fighting, and the sense to stand up for ourselves: from my mother.

I believe in socialism; that is, that the

The most favoured drinking spot for Inglis workers was the Palace Tavern on the northeast corner of King and Strachan. Countless pints were enjoyed, engineering projects developed and union strategy planned in this tavern. The owners rotated the brand of beer served, but always ensured the brew was union-made. Service staff at the Palace belonged to the Bartenders and Waiters Union. At the top of the photograph, above the "On Draught To-day" sign, is the union certificate identifying the Palace as a "Union House." The sign to the right says, "Keep Your Temper to Yourself, No One Else Wants It." The photograph is probably from the early 1960s.

wealth of the land should be shared equally. It shouldn't be inherited from their forefathers, who most likely got it by stealing and abusing the working class. That's the way I was always brought up.

The culture of Inglis workers did not start with World War II, but was based on a much longer and more complex series of historical relationships. This cultural continuity was symbolized by many things, none of which was more colourful than the Palace, the working-class tavern mentioned earlier in this book that served several generations of Inglis workers. The Palace served many purposes, but above all, it was a place where workers could discuss things on their own terms. For some it was a place to exchange ideas about what was being made in the plant, or a place to find out which company was hiring. Bill Townley recalled:

Facing Substance Abuse

Lifeline is a joint labour and management employee assistance programme. It is intended to help Steelworkers fight any addiction, or mental or personal problems which could interfere with work. While neither union nor company leaders know the nature of a worker's difficulty, the Lifeline agreement usually helps a troubled worker keep a job during treatment. Lifeline has successfully found appropriate treatment for Steelworkers since 1974.

Retired Local 2900 member Mary Spratt remained active in the labour movement. Here she is seen serving as a marshall at an anti-poverty rally in 1989 at Queen's Park in Toronto. Spratt was also active in the local Labour Council to which she was a delegate for many years.

There was the old Palace Hotel. It was the local pub. There was many a turbine and boiler built there by these guys. They'd get in there, and inevitably start talking about work. You'd meet a lot of people from the old Massey Harris that became Massey Ferguson, there. They knew people here, and we'd worked in and out of the two shops. I worked there three times. They always needed welders. Sometimes you'd be on lay-off from Inglis, so you had a lot of people moving back and forth between the two plants. Inglis was really the better place to work. Massey was more of a plant where people were just passing through. Inglis seemed to be a place where you could feel a little more comfortable.

The familiarity of the Palace gave Inglis workers a sense of ownership of the neighbourhood as well as of the plant. The workers at Inglis knew the area well. There were secret haunts, private clubs, and shadier forms of activity. Bert Bowler recalled a close encounter with the law:

There was a bootlegger on Strachan Avenue too. I nearly got killed there. I was sitting in the bootlegger's on a nice summer evening having a nice cold beer up in the rec room, and the window was wide open. We hear bang, bang, bang on the front door. Then we hear police hollering and saying, 'We're going to arrest everybody.' I had just bought a new suit, that I'd worn to work and changed. I was going to go downtown and instead I went to the bloody bootlegger's. I got out of there and I went to get off the roof. I jumped and landed on a darned clothesline. It caught me by the knee and spun me around and I landed flat on my back, knocking every ounce of wind out of me. I crawled over the fence and got on the other side. I hear the police coming around and saying, 'Well, we got everybody.' I'm laying there saying to myself, 'Oh God, I got away with it.' Well. I had torn my pants to my new suit. I had a bruise you wouldn't believe and my back was sore. They would only have charged me $10 for being found inside. I never forgave myself, I damn near got killed.

Drinking wasn't limited to local haunts; Inglis employees figured out how to bring alcohol into the plant, as well. While those at Inglis worked hard and turned out a product of which they were proud, they were also hard drinkers and partiers. In this respect, they did not differ from workers in hundreds of other industrial plants. One particular method for sneaking bottles into the factory was especially creative. Syl MacNeil revealed the long-held secret:

Here people had taken out a brick. It was a double brick because it was a double wall, and you just went to the phone. If you wanted a bottle in the daytime, you would just phone the cab number and just say, 'The hole in the wall,' and you stood there with your money and you passed your money out to the cab driver. He used to drive up to it, roll down the window, and pass the bottle through. And we had a lot of bottles. That was a pretty hot little corner, at times. We had a lot of wine come through that hole.

The union eventually took on the work of fighting alcohol-related problems. The local became involved in Lifeline, an agency associated with the steelworkers' union that helps provide rehabilitation programs for substance abuse.

Naturally, there was also time for healthier pursuits. Stanley Park, at the north end of Strachan Avenue, served as a convenient playing field for the workers at Inglis and the surrounding factories. Union-sponsored sports leagues took advantage of the park throughout the 1950s and early 1960s. Production workers and office workers competed against each other, and there were larger interplant industrial leagues in the area as well. With a large number of workers tied to the area, events could easily be scheduled for the off-hours. There were also club and social functions that took place in the neighbourhood. All of these social activities were as important as the economic functions of formalized collective bargaining. The union served as an institution through which diverse activities could be enjoyed.

Dances and Christmas parties, organized and paid for by the union, were held. The union insisted on keeping its celebrations separate from company-sponsored events. A Christmas party for members' children was held for many years in competition with one thrown by the corporation. Mary Spratt helped to organize a few of them. "We used to have Christmas parties for the kids, but then they got so expensive we couldn't carry them on. But we had much better presents! One year the company wanted to put it on with us, but we said no." Paul Ryan also remembered the Christmas parties of the 1950s. "We were spending five dollars a toy, back in the '50s. It was a lot. We'd have oranges. Some guy would dress up as a clown. In those days I was too skinny to be Santa Claus."

Less public gatherings also interested some members of the local. The Masonic Lodge, with its long history in the nineteenth century as both a benefit society and a secret fraternal network, had a long, exclusive history with Protestant men in the plant. Machinists' Lodge 235, the earlier dominant union at the plant, began as a railway lodge in which the Masons played an especially active role. The organization had both workers and managers in its membership; both John and William Inglis had been members. Lodge 235, which emphasized ritual in conducting its meetings, created a paradoxical, common bond between labour and management, alongside the equally long history of troubled industrial relations in the Strachan Avenue plant. Into the mid-twentieth century, the Masons maintained a powerful presence, especially in the skilled trades. This Masonic network often was present in trade union politics, as well. Several former workers reported that they had found jobs at Inglis through their Masonic connections. "Sportman's clubs" served as fronts for gatherings of Masons, and the lodge was involved in many elections for local officers who were also lodge members. Jack Hill recognized the power of the lodge when he became president of the local in the mid-1960s.

When I took over, there was a good group in the United Steelworkers' that were Masons. My father was a Mason and he even asked me to join and I said, 'No, I don't believe that I would like to join any type of situation that disagrees with another type of religion or anything else.' I guess he was using it politically too. I put the first Catholics on my executive and they were not Masons. I think I broke that barrier when I was president of the local and stopped that type of situation. I wasn't going to have that Mason type of thing.

In addition to the strong presence of working-class values and institutions in the postwar period, there was always a highly politicized and experienced group of activists inside the plant. The flavour of discussion within Local 2900 was linked to a tradition of class politics that the machinists' union at Inglis represented during World War I. During the organizing of Local 2900, many communists and their supporters contributed to the building of the USWA at the plant. Jack Hill's father, Edgar, was a socialist who had worked at Inglis and had helped Jack find a job at the plant. The Hill family was steeped in a style of class politics that didn't end at the plant gate. Hill had strong memories of the 1930s and his father's activism:

My father, who was working at John Inglis, asked me if I would like to try and work at John Inglis and he got me a job there. My father was the vice president of the union at John Inglis and had been very active in the union over a long period of time. I can remember at our house on Weston Road, there was two people on the front door and one on the back door. My father would have been taken and put in a labour camp if they could have got him 'cause of his organizing in the trade union movement. So there was lots of discussion around the kitchen table with union people and different people in our house. I was brought up in the union movement, I understand it. It was basically our religion in our house, which I thank my father very much for.

But Edgar Hill didn't practise his brand of trade unionism at Inglis without difficulty. The isolation of activists, communists, and sympathizers that affected the organizing drive during World War II continued unabated in the decade that followed.

Some local union activists, because of their political associations and beliefs, worked in a growing atmosphere of fear and mistrust — especially in relation to the USWA hierarchy outside of the local. The pressure that left-wingers experienced in Local 2900 occurred throughout the trade union movement, but the factionalizing effects of "red-baiting" were particularly strong in the Steelworkers. Local 2900 had been formed by a broad coalition of political forces, including communists and other left-wingers who worked at the plant. The long history of union activism, well known among the neighbourhood's working class, may have been especially attractive to politicized union mem-

bers. There was always a healthy range of trade union politics, from the relatively conservative to the fringe groups of the left.

The familiarity that made the workers comfortable in the neighbourhood and in the plant was put to use by the local. Its tactics went beyond the abilities of a specific leader to borrow management's tools. For example, the plant's paging system was hijacked at opportune moments for several years and permitted the union to shut down the workplace in a matter of minutes. Syl MacNeil describes its effectiveness:

We used to have a paging number, I think the paging number was 69, and whenever you heard that page, everybody just sat

Union Work

The local spent time and resources on issues outside of union business. Jack Hill relates an example:

We were very active. At one particular time that I can remember, we adopted an African student and were paying for him, his education at school in Canada. He came to our membership meeting to thank us and he was sitting at the back of the hall. I had finished the meeting and I went down to meet him and talk to him.

Many workers spent time at Inglis events even before they were hired. Dave Parker's mother took her young son to an Inglis Christmas party. Parker, here on Santa's lap, may have filed a grievance.

This photograph from the union publication Steel Labor *shows the negotiating committee for Local 2900 for the 1950 contract, of which Edgar Hill was a part. Hill is in the back row at the far left.*

down. We knew that somewhere — the plant was vast, the number of employees in here when I started was 1,700, and there were more before, so you couldn't get to everybody to tell them, so 'Sixty-nine!' Everybody sat down. You knew that there was an incident happening in Consumer Products or General Engineering and we looked after each other pretty good. This went on for years until the company realized that and so then they removed the paging system.

The local also had a convenient, neutral meeting place for impromptu work stoppages and walkouts. Marching to the old soldiers' graveyard across the street near the Stanley Barracks became a defiant ritual during disagreements with management. Nearly every activist from the postwar period recalled the importance of the graveyard as a workers' meeting place. One incident, though, was sparked by a misunderstanding. MacNeil recalled:

There was one particular time, when the company got wise to the paging system and took the paging system out, we ended up down in our graveyard. Some guy went

home early, had a pass and went home. So some guy from Consumer Products said, 'There's some guy been canned in Engineering. So Consumer Products said, 'Well piss on that!' and they walked out. General Engineering, seeing Consumer Products walking out, they all left. Everybody got down to the graveyard and you had the steward body from both sides, and they were both saying, 'So what happened? What the hell did you guys walk out for?' 'Well we walked out because you walked out.' 'Well, we walked out because you walked out.' 'Well, WE walked out because YOU walked out.' And nobody knew what we were down in the graveyard for. So in order to save face we had to stay out.

Walkouts were usually sparked by the suspension of a fellow worker, an unreasonable change in the pace of work, or some other production-related reason that challenged what the workers believed to be just. Anything exceeding the local's sense of fairness could bring the entire membership out in a matter of minutes. Shared values and the certainty of shopfloor control were never in doubt. The graveyard became an important forum for the exchange of information and rallying the troops on the sins committed by management.

The politicized nature of the shopfloor was seriously tested during the English Electric years. Inglis had sold a majority of shares to the British company. Jack Hill, who began working at Inglis during that period, described how the "classist" actions of some English managers elevated militancy in the factory.

They had the idea of putting people in white coats and they were trying at one particular time to get us to wear certain types of coveralls so that they could find out if we were out of our departments and if we were going to the washroom too much. At that particular time, they had a works manager who ran around with a bowler hat on his head and an umbrella. He was real English. They were very, very classist and egged us on. They didn't give too much thought about us.

Members of Local 2900 refused many of the controls that management attempted to impose on them. They were a capable, highly skilled work force. These workers were responsible for creating the astounding array of products that flowed out of the plant in the two decades following World War II. Many workers maintained paradoxical feelings about the plant. They could express their dislike for much of what management did, but that coexisted with their pride of being part of the Inglis tradition. Bert Bowler described his love of the work and the control he exercised over how it was organized:

I used to love lathes. I got along with the machinery so well. I could get my day's work done in about four hours on a lathe; I could make that thing sing. I had all the rest of the day to loaf around in. I'd do four hours in the morning real hard, and in the afternoon I'd take my time.

The kind of workers' control that Bowler describes existed throughout the cavernous factory and should not be confused with laziness or job indifference. This control over the pace of work meant that the abilities of all workers on any given day were accommodated. It was one of the conditions that made Inglis a good place to work; it attracted people who would work at the plant for decades and who would invest en-

Edgar Hill played an active role in Local 2900 following World War II. In 1949, as the cold war frenzy gained steam, Edgar Hill was removed for alleged improprieties involving the distribution of some literature from the communist-influenced United Electrical Workers Union. Hill was subsequently victimized by an internal trial, engineered by more conservative elements in the local and in the Toronto Steelworker hierarchy. An experienced local union activist, Hill sensed he was being set up. After it became clear that the charges would be brought by the broader union, he telephoned Charlie Millard, Canadian director of the union, desperately seeking an explanation. While Millard assured Hill he would "be protected," Hill noted that protection would be useless if it waited until "he was swinging from a rope."

Hill escaped the rope but was stripped of his union office. He took a job outside of the bargaining unit a few years later. Shortly after, he was laid off and the union did not defend his interests. Hill left the company in 1953 and it appeared that the company had used Hill's non-union position to get rid of him altogether.

Hill's removal sent a message to left wing activists at the local level that was largely ignored. The divisive character of this red-baiting didn't alter the style of the local very much. Hill was just one of several militants. New, equally militant leaders would come to Inglis after Hill's departure, and two decades later Edgar's son would be elected to the office of local president. The militant character of the local was based on more than just radical leadership. Many politically more conservative members at the local level believed in direct workplace action and continued to practice it. Coalitions were formed which included members from across the political spectrum.

Former Inglis worker and Local 2900 president Syl McNeil may have used the hammer in his left hand to produce the effect in the right lens of his safety glasses. Maybe MacNeil learned this in the coal mines of Cape Breton before he moved to Toronto. His first day at Inglis was marked by a sit-down strike.

Versions of History

Like all past events, aspects of Local 2900's history were recalled differently by those interviewed. What people remember, and how they remember it, is, of course, one of the central challenges of writing history. Many personal reminiscences contained in these pages were confirmed through printed sources or through multiple testimony. Among the most painful episodes of the local's history was the intense friction between communists and their supporters and trade unionists with a more social democratic perspective. Today, both sides agree the movement was weakened by this conflict. In Local 2900, Edgar Hill was persecuted for his politics and attacked for his vision of trade unionism. Some of his detractors claimed his troubles were self-inflicted and his aspirations based not on idealism but self-promotion. Today, through the filter of human memory and years gone by, the truth, if there is such certainty, cannot be known. All we have today are fragments from this chapter in this union's history. Events often appear veiled in both oral and written sources. The minutes of Local 2900 of just one meeting reveal the emotional quality of these political debates. The charges brought in just one of the political trials of Edgar Hill are discussed in this entry from January 1950:

> Brother Slaven gave a brief review of questions asked at trial. It was then asked that charges be again read out by the Rec. Sec. [recording secretary].
> Bro. Slaven stated that Bro. Hill was found un guilty [sic] by a vote of 3 to 1 and moved that the recommendation of the trial committee be accepted.
> The meeting at this point became rather unruly with speakers supporting Bro. Hill, denouncing Bro. Hill. There being so many speakers, the noise being so great it was impossible to record all the pros and cons on the subject. Bros Goodine, McMullen and Burke repeatedly stated this trial was out of order. Bro. Hill gave a complete and extensive defence of himself.
> After much discussion by several other members it was moved by Bro. White, Sec. by Sis. Sprat [sic] That all discussion be tabled till next monthly or special meeting be held.

ergy in defending those conditions, which, in turn, strengthened the union. The union's shared control of the shopfloor with management allowed for an increasingly rare phenomenon: a workers' factory. But in the process of defending what made Inglis a good place to work, many battles would be fought.

The Friction of Production

The culture of USWA Local 2900 translated into significant power at the point of production. Management wanted to have the plant running all the time, but the union insisted that some aspects of production would take place on its terms. Workers here would stand up to the petty requests of foremen or the harsh treatment that front-line management often used to intimidate and push people to work harder. Coworkers and the union stood behind those people who refused to be intimidated. The confidence that Paul Ryan felt in his first two days at Inglis in the early 1950s was indicative of the union's strength on the line.

I've never experienced any abuse, because I wouldn't take it. The first day I worked here I had a fight with my foreman. The second day I had another fight with another foreman. The first day we were working on end plates, putting them on a little skid, I had them all counted up to go to the fuel pumps and the second shift foreman came along and said, 'You can't use that skid, it's a day shift skid.' He dumped them on the floor. I thought that was ridiculous. So I picked half the skid up and started chasing him down the aisle. I threw it at him. But I missed.

The second day, I was unloading zinc agitators for the wringer washer. They gave us big trucks to unload them with. I noticed the wheels were loose, and I informed the foreman that the wheels were going to fall off. He said, 'Never mind that, just do it.' So I got the first load on, and when I was taking it off the elevator the wheel came off. It fell all over. He came over and started

Some sense of the size of engineering projects can be gained in these photographs. The men are welders.

yelling at me. I took the handle off the truck and I chased him down the aisle, because it was his fault.

Not all conflicts between workers and management were physical, but if workers felt justified, they challenged management. The context of relations between union and management gave workers like Ryan the *right* to stand up for himself in the way that he did. Any disruption of production was a demonstration of rank-and-file control and militancy that extended beyond the formalized, increasingly bureaucratized, "legal" strike.

Frank McCuaig, a long-time trade unionist and former United Electrical activist, came to Strachan Avenue in 1953, the year that Edgar Hill left the plant. His arrival underlined the continued participation of activists in the local. McCuaig eventually served as its president for almost a decade. His open and democratic style kept the shopfloor informed and involved, and he continued the tradition of work stoppages. He described the importance of work stoppages to maintain the balance of power with management, and its relationship to the broader union hierarchy:

When I first came to the plant, they used to have at least one stoppage a month, in the skilled trades. Generally in the boiler shop or the machine shop. You'd be out for one or two hours. They were about small things. I used to try to settle them. Brodie was the international rep. He used to tell them to go back to work. I would say, 'Why should we go back to work? Let's talk to the company now and settle it before we go back to work.'

Other changes also influenced how the Strachan Avenue work force related to management. After being purchased by English Electric in the 1950s, the Strachan Avenue plant was joined by two other plants, one in St. Catharines, the other in Scarborough. Production was reorganized and, for a time after 1952, some of the General Engineering Division was moved to the Scarborough plant. The broad mixture of heavy engineering and standardized products that had existed in the factory was affected with lasting implications. As management mismanaged the future viability of the plant, Local 2900 consistently took the most militant position of the three locals in the system. Bargaining became more complicated. As Frank McCuaig, who first became president in the mid-1950s, recalled, "You were bargaining with two companies."

The Strachan Avenue local distinguished itself in 1954 by holding out for a better contract, after one had been accepted by the two other Steelworker locals. While the Local 2900 executive admitted most aspects of the package were adequate, they wanted wage increases and the adoption of the cooperative wage study, a job evaluation system developed by the Steelworkers. A surprise sit-down hit the plant in late May as local members expressed frustration that a contract had yet to be signed. "The employees were disgusted with the long drawn-out negotiations, " international representative Jock Brodie was quoted as saying. The sit-down ended after four days and the local finally signed the agreement, which was different from the other two in its rejection of the company's new wage classifications. The new package included a broadened health insurance plan and the provision for a paid Christmas day, even though it would fall on a Saturday that year. It was the first time that Local 2900 had accepted a wage freeze, but the membership was always willing to trade money for better working conditions. It was a sign that the members were committed to the Strachan Avenue plant for the long term.

The continued militancy of McCuaig's local also led to problems with some of the staff in the USWA office. Local 2900 became known as a rogue local that treated the staff representatives with little respect. The constant walkouts, marches, and sit-downs made the local too militant from the perspective of some in the USWA organization at the district and the International level. The seriousness of the problem of local discipline became clear during several incidents that occurred in late 1950s. The local and the company had disagreed since the end of the war over the amount of time local union leadership could spend on union business. A letter to Local 2900's president from J.A. Farr, the manager of industrial relations for Inglis, discussed the issue of control and union rights in detail:

Union activity, particularly that for which the Company have [sic] agreed to pay, has been the concern of management for some time. We have been reminded often by the

Paul Ryan worked at Inglis for more than 30 years. He was always active in the union and was one of Local 2900's past presidents. Ryan grew up in the neighbourhood around the Inglis plant and remembers when the whole area was home to vibrant industrial activity. He is pictured here in 1978.

Frank McCuaig, his son Jim, and another Local 2900 member whose first name only is known — Sid — prepare the local union's banner for the Labour Day Parade in 1959. Such displays of labour's strength in Toronto were important rituals for trade unionists.

union when we sought to curtail it that it is within management's control. In recognizing this fact, we have more recently endeavoured to establish some reasonable control.

Despite the company's attempts to water down the entrenched practices, the local defended them passionately. McCuaig recalled that even the number of representatives at the bargaining table became contentious.

They didn't like the size of our negotiating committee. We had six members and they tried every way to get me to reduce it. They got to the point where they wanted us to come down to one man each, the president of each local. 'No way! I'm not going to go for that. No representation from our plant at all? No. Our local wants six.' We try and get them from each section of the plant, so each department is represented.

A strong tradition of participatory trade unionism developed in the local. Members expected to be informed of bargaining strategies, union administration, and grievance procedure. Nothing took place in the dark. By entering the factory and joining the union, members became part of a proud tradition. Jack Hill recalled that one of the earliest presidents, Jock Brodie, who went on to service the local, used a ceremony to add meaning to joining the local. It was quite a deal.

I remember being sworn in. The stewards' offices were up in the old church on Shaw Street. The union used the auditorium as a meeting hall and I remember it being a very smoke-filled room and I remember Jock having all the new hires come up to the front to be sworn in accepting the union and making quite a ceremony of it. Meetings I was at at John Inglis were always quite well-attended.

In the summer of 1957, Local 2900 president McCuaig called a local union meeting during work time and expected the company to grant leave to the workers to attend. Permission by the company was denied, but that didn't prevent approximately 600 people, nearly every worker in the plant, from attending at noon. They gathered in the old graveyard across the street, the place where Inglis workers traditionally met. At the meeting, President McCuaig provided an overview of a number of outstanding grievances. He recommended that the grievance procedure be ignored and that his members walk out immediately unless the company settled these differences on the spot. The workers voted narrowly to respect the grievance procedure and return to work.

The uneasy calm was broken when some of those who attended the lunchtime gathering were suspended for leaving without permission. The suspensions escalated the anger of the work force and a second meeting took place at about 1:30 that same afternoon. This time, the workers voted 450 to 250 to shut the plant in sympathy for those who had been suspended and to further protest the outstanding grievances between the company and the union. The company was shut down for several days until the workers voted to return. The entire walkout had been a local action and was viewed unsympathetically by both District 6 and international leadership.

A staff representative, concerned about the legality of the walkout, had broader misgivings regarding the militant style of the local leadership and of McCuaig in particular. He provided district director Larry Sefton with some interesting observations. In red-baiting style, the unnamed writer described contact with the left-leaning United Electrical Workers, but this may have been alleged to justify increased surveillance on militants within the local. The report read:

It is my opinion that there is a well organized left-wing group within this local, and from scraps of conversation, the general attitude, I am convinced that there is a definite move toward the U.E. I have contacted some of the employees department in order to watch for any development along this line. This I believe should be carefully followed up and must in my opinion be watched very carefully ... This is a serious situation in the local and I believe it is necessary for someone to spend a great deal of time close to the situation, since in my opinion Frank McQuaig [sic] is a clever and scrupulous individual who has all the ear-marks of a trained Communist but whose approach is disarming and extremely "democratic."

Welding was always a big part of engineering projects at Inglis. Many skilled welders left the company in the 1950s to help build Toronto's subway.

During the next major strike, in 1959, the lack of agreement between the union locals within the Inglis–English Electric corporation deeply affected collective bargaining. This dispute lasted four months and involved issues other than money, as had previous disputes with the company. At stake was the right to a paid, full-time union president and the in-plant union office, both of which had been established years earlier.

The 1959 negotiations were difficult from the very beginning. They proceeded slowly and it soon became clear that the company planned to isolate the local from the Scarborough and St. Catharines operations over issues that were dear to the membership of Local 2900 only.

McCuaig recalled what he said in his address to the members before the strike-vote meeting:

'I'll tell you frankly what's going to happen. It's up to you people to decide. Here's the score. Scarborough and St. Catharines are holding votes tonight. St. Catharines' vote is a certainty. The president of the negotiating committee said they have no reason to go out. They're not interested in our office business, so they're not going to strike; that's for sure. They're going to settle. That's the first time that this has happened. It's going to make it very difficult for us. Scarborough is meeting now. They've indicated they can't be bothered with this side issue.'

Boy, our workers really got mad. One guy stood up in the hall. 'Let's kill them now!' The welders and the fitters — these really tough guys. I had just finished talking when a guy from Scarborough came in and

*Three picketers
outside the
Strachan Avenue
plant during the
1959 strike.
Their faces are
remembered but
not their names.*

Three picketers outside the Strachan Avenue plant during the 1959 strike. Their faces are remembered but not their names.

a guy from the back yelled, 'Scarborough's voted 90% to accept.' I said, 'There you are. We are on our own. It's up to you people.' Well, they all voted. Ninety-four percent to go out! I couldn't believe it myself. But they were a strong local as they say. Always had been.

The 1959 strike was a good example of the kind of grassroots organizing that Local 2900 could accomplish. Within twenty-four hours of the strike's beginning, the local's union office was shut down and, in the words of a terse 14 July 1959 letter, the company requested "that any furnishings belonging to Local 2900 be removed from the premises not later than 5:00 p.m., July 15th, 1959."

As McCuaig had indicated, this was not a strike over monetary issues. The core issues were union rights and worker power. Differences over job evaluations, reducing the number of stewards, the size of the negotiating committee and lay-off provisions were the reasons for the strike. The local union sensed that these

were important issues which went directly to the heart of the union's militant character.

The militancy exhibited by the local was based on a disciplined, yet politicized, trade unionism that used the increasingly bureaucratic tools to their limits. Paul Ryan, who later served as local president for five years, recalled the extent to which the local was committed to the education of its membership and benefited from solid leadership:

First of all we always had integrity, which is the most important. We had honest executives all the way along, and people who were concerned about the working class. We trained our own people. As soon as we got a new contract, we trained our stewards — in safety, in CWS [Cooperative Wage Study], in time study. We didn't wait for other Steelworker schools to do it. And we were not reluctant to send people to learn more about it. If you have an educated local, they can dispel any problems on the floor right away. If you're ignorant of the situation, you can't argue. So our people were well trained. They came and appointed me a steward. The first thing we had to do was learn the contract. You'd look in the book, and quote it to the foreman. You're abusing this and abusing that. Right away he'd back off, and try to rectify the situation. Just knowing the contract was the most important tool.

While a militant culture dominated the shopfloor, the incompetence of management slowly threatened the integrity of the plant and narrowed its range of products. During the English Electric years, the Engineering Division experienced a series of losses that undermined its long-term viability. The company slowly shifted to becoming a producer of consumer products only. In the boardroom, removed from the shopfloor, David Hahn, now a senior executive with the Consumer Division, was getting frustrated. He proposed that the company sell a small stake in Inglis to Whirlpool to solidify what in the past had been a short-term licensing agreement.

Every five years we could be led to the scaffold. It was a crazy way to do business. So I was concerned about two things. One, the fact that English Electric didn't understand how we had to work with Whirlpool. That attitude coupled with the license renewal every five years. I kept trying to tell these guys that sooner or later they were going to lose the ship.

In the 1960s, as concerns over the growing foreign control of Canada's economy became the subject of public discussion, Inglis workers experienced its implications first hand and fought back with the tools available to them. Of course, the union wasn't privy to boardroom decisions. The broad powers of management left all the business decisions that determined the viability of the plant, and therefore the survival of the local, to themselves. The workers sensed that their plant was being mismanaged, but in the narrow terms of collective bargaining, there was little that could be done. They continued to defend the quality of factory life at the plant, but long-term decision-making was, of course, removed from the shopfloor. The diversity of production was slowly eroded, but the atmosphere of workers' control was maintained. The institutions that had enhanced life at Inglis in

For many years Local 2900 sponsored an elaborate Christmas party for the members' children. The union competed with the company until the expense led to the end of the parties. The 1961 celebration was held in Masaryk Hall, once the location of the Inglis Girls' Club

the early '50s were still around fifteen years later. Syl MacNeil, whose history at Inglis began in the early '60s vividly remembered starting there as a chipper-grinder in the boiler shop:

First day I walked in at 7:30, there was no noise in the plant — there was a sit-down. I was grabbed by the shoulders by the shop steward, and he said 'Siddown.' So I sat down. The foreman said I wasn't in the union, I'd better get my ass up and get going, but coming from a mining town in Cape Breton, I gladly took the advice of the steward and sat down. They tried to let me go, but the union said if he goes we sit down again. That strike was about safety. A worker was hurt and we sat down until the steel ladder was properly fastened to the tank. Oh God! All my days in the coal mines, and we had plenty of work stoppages there, I never seen the likes of this place.

Stephen Lewis, former leader of the Ontario New Democratic Party, visited the picket line during the 1974 strike.

Local 2900 and the New Democratic Party

As the New Democratic Party was forming in 1961, Inglis workers started up their own New Party Club. It was named after Fred Goodine, a former 2900 president.

Clubs were formed to encourage grassroots participation in formulating party policy. Underlying club activities was a firm belief in the parliamentary system. This assumption was intended to eliminate extreme left or right positions within the party. Any club with at least 50 members, all of whom paid one dollar to join, was entitled to a delegate at the national founding convention.

In November 1961, the Fred Goodine Club sponsored a dance. An eight-piece union orchestra provided the music. Tommy Douglas, then premier of Saskatchewan, was the speaker.

The union had earlier ties to the Co-operative Commonwealth Federation which preceded the NDP. During the 1943 union drive, organizers were recruited from the CCF Youth Movement (CCYM). Enthusiasts like Eileen Tallman and Eamon Park had been trained as organizers in the 1930s by the CCYM. Several of the Goodine New Party Club founders had also been active in the CCF.

From these beginnings, Local 2900 maintained strong ties to the NDP throughout its history. During the 1974 strike, Stephen Lewis, then leader of the Ontario NDP, walked the picket line with Local 2900 and 4487 (office) members.

Through the 1960s the local continued its tradition of "spontaneous" stoppages. Grievances and arbitrations were pursued in an equally militant manner. Workers from other parts of the country, like MacNeil, deepened the trade union culture of the plant. Syl MacNeil held many local executive positions, including that of president.

A dispute in 1963 underlined the continued defense of shop-based work rules as well as the creeping influence of the Whirlpool product licensing arrangements. After some of the company's American efficiency experts called for changes in workloads to certain jobs at the Strachan Avenue plant, the membership of Local 2900 revolted. On 29 March all 1,200 production workers walked out, and they were joined by the entire office staff the following week. The work force didn't return until it was agreed that its complaints would be investigated.

Friction continued within the broader Steelworkers' organization. At the Steelworkers' convention in 1961, Frank McCuaig, now head of Toronto Area Council as well as of the local, ran afoul of the leadership many times over Local 2900's tradition of walkouts and its constant desire for independence in all of its affairs. Many in the politicized membership were active in party politics. There were communists, CCF members, and non-aligned socialists who saw the struggles in the factory in a broader social context. In the early 1960s, Local 2900 was very active in the New Democratic Party, sending delegates to the founding convention and every one after that. Jack Hill was instrumental in bringing the local and the party together.

I motivated the group into being the first members of the New Party. We were talking at that time. We became the first club in the city of Toronto. We joined the New Party and what we did is we put out leaflets and told the workers and, over a period of years, we convinced the workers that the New Democratic Party was the party. I think at that particular time we, if I recall, signed up pretty close to seventy percent in the New Democratic Party from the John Inglis work force and we worked at it in that way.

Class politics continued to be combined with a tradition of playing hard. Drinking, partying, and joking were very much part of life on Strachan Avenue. There was a constant banter and healthy competition to outdo each other in practical jokes. Occasionally there were excesses. Syl MacNeil recalled one specific incident. When one worker went on a binge, MacNeil sent a union steward to bring the drinker back to work and save the man's job. Then he sent a second steward to find the first two. The second steward disappeared as well.

I got a call from the foreman, and he said, 'Look, either you go up and get them three or they're all canned.' So I left. The three of them were sitting in the kitchen, stoned, there was no way of getting them back to work that day. I phoned the foreman and told him, but said I'd have them all back in on Monday. He agreed. But I couldn't believe the

place. It was infested with cockroaches. They'd switch off the light and get the can of Raid, and there was an albino cockroach. They sprayed and sprayed that cockroach and the damn thing kept going and going. Finally, one of them said, 'Sonofabitch, must be a union cockroach, can't kill it.'

There was also fighting. Union meetings sometimes broke up over fistfights and the police were called to the Palace on more than one occasion. John Fitzpatrick, who observed the local for many years and eventually serviced it as a staff representative, recalled:

I wouldn't say that 2900 was difficult. They were very reactive. You might say difficult in one way only. They enjoyed themselves when they went out. They had a good time. They were good drinkers! But that's ever since I've known them. They used to have meetings in the basement next door, Christmas dances, that would end up like a Donnybrook, just a goddamn barroom brawl. And the next minute they'd all be laughing. One day I was kicked in the groin trying to stop it. I could hardly walk. And I could see everyone sitting on boxes laughing to kill themselves! They would all be friends the next day.

Under the relatively stable employment conditions of the 1960s, Local 2900 thrived. The union local remained healthy and democratic, but the same could not be said of the company itself. While workers were exercising their power on the shopfloor, the strength of Inglis executives in Canada was beginning to wane. A 1966 company announcement about the complete shift to consumer products put these developments in the best possible light. "For almost twenty years Inglis has manufactured and sold laundry equipment in Canada under a license agreement with the Whirlpool Corporation ... We wish now to extend our line of consumer products to include domestic refrigerators and freezers which are manufactured by Whirlpool in the United States. This will require the expansion of our manufacturing and warehousing facilities and substantial capital expenditure."

On the surface, the shift to white goods, or appliances, seemed positive, but the company's announcement failed to mention that the Inglis corporation, for the first time in its history, would be entirely dependent on the sale of a product, the production and design of which were ultimately controlled by another company. The Inglis tradition of Canadian-designed, -manufactured, and -marketed industrial products was over.

The strength of the market for these consumer products hid the innate weaknesses of the strategy at first. Indeed, former workers recalled that other lines, such as fuel pumps and water heaters, were pushed to the margins of the operation to make more room for the household laundry appliances. Short-term profitability was preferred over a long-term, varied production strategy. No one thought to ask what would happen when the demand for these appliances waned. At the time, sales were high and employment at the Strachan Avenue factory increased slightly through the 1960s, making the consequences of the decision less noticeable.

Since employment seemed secure for the workers, the union pursued new issues for the local, adjusting to a faster, entirely standardized form of production. The growing age of the plant and its productive equipment placed new demands on the workers and required a high degree of ingenuity among them. The same militant style continued despite the growing dominance of Whirlpool Corporation in the factory's product line and the company's management. It was no secret, however, that Whirlpool did not tolerate unions in its U.S. operations.

The narrowing product base was met with equally significant changes in the way Local 2900 faced management on the shopfloor. The bureaucratization of union activism soon began to mirror the bureaucratized management hierarchy. According to Syl MacNeil, the shopfloor wildcat strikes ended through changes in legislation in the late 1960s, when they were ruled illegal:

I think it was the worst thing that ever happened to the labour movement. I think we had the power then. There's no delaying in the justice. Now all you can do is grieve, and end up in arbitration. If you go through arbitration it takes months and months and this brings hardship on the person that's been wronged, hardship on him and his family, there's no money coming in. I think there's no better way than, 'We ain't gonna

work until ...' A one-hour sitdown, one hour lost production, hurt the company, but it did justice to that person that was being wronged, being suspended or being fired. And usually when you got down and got into the thing, it was a mistake on the company's part, or something that they'd done to cause the incident. So who should pay, the worker or the company? I think the company should. When they screw up they deserve to be hurt, and hurt in the pocketbook. It's the only way to hurt them.

With the gradual erosion of Canadian control, there was a parallel erosion of the Inglis neighbourhood culture. But the vibrant social life in the plant continued. Bobby Sim, whose father also worked at Inglis, began in the early 1970s and remembered the Palace with enthusiasm. The tavern still remained the gathering place for Inglis workers.

You knew everybody. You'd walk in there and you didn't even order and they'd have your beer in front of you. We used to go up on a Friday after work. I tell you, you would just make a pig of yourself because you go up there at 12 o'clock [midnight] and you've only got 'til 1 o'clock. So you wash as much down your throat as you could possibly get. They made great hamburgers and the food was fantastic, brilliant in the Palace. The service was good most of the time. There was probably ten to twelve thousand guys walked up the road all over that area. I knew a lot of guys. I knew welders from Massey used to go up to the Palace. That was the only time you'd see them sometimes was at the Palace. It was mobbed. You couldn't get in some days. I would say it was probably the best joint in Toronto. The atmosphere was great.

Such continuity in the institutions that members enjoyed initially hid subtle changes in the neighbourhood of the plant and structure of the working-class life, though. The return of some heavy engineering production from the Scarborough plant in 1965 left a group of workers living in Scarborough, commuting downtown. Other, younger, workers wanting to own homes moved to the suburbs. This integrity of the neighbourhood, where people had both lived and worked, was slowly eroding. The working class of Toronto

Jack Hill

Muriel Monteal spent her entire nursing career at Inglis, beginning in 1940. She saw firsthand a number of serious accidents, some fatal, before retiring in 1978.

During the war, Monteal attended to a woman whose hair was caught in a machine. The worker lost part of her scalp. "There was lots of amputated fingers through carelessness. Not using their guards. They weren't as rigid then about safety." Soon after starting at Inglis, Monteal saw her first accident victim, a man crushed on a beam between two overhead cranes. Welders were called from the Boiler Shop to remove the body.

Later in the Boiler Shop, Monteal had to deal with more than one fall from a ladder when proper supports were not used. In the 1950s, there was an explosion involving an outside contractor. "They had been using propane to do something or other inside the tank, and then somebody went in to do some welding. The tank exploded. You could hear it all over the place. There were two badly injured, one guy died. The doctor went in and pulled him out of this tank. The other man was going to be married that week."

Her recollection of a later accident reveals the dangers associated with factory work. Monteal was on her way out of the building when she heard yelling.

This guy was at the hopper — it was a great big thing — and it was heated by coal at that time. He went down in the hopper and was trapped there with the hot coals. They had to get him down the rest of the way and bring him out. He was black from head to toe and burnt. He was a mess, but he did survive.

had became more diverse and more dispersed. Slowly, this reality affected the social life of Local 2900. Still the parties continued. If work in the maintenance department was done on a Friday evening of an afternoon shift, indoor barbecues in that department became a regular affair. The grill itself was installed beneath a powerful fan that was part of the plant ventilation system. Bobby Sim recalls the huge steaks with corn bread, popular menu items. When the men became bored with steak, Yugoslavian coworkers brought in homemade sausage full of onions, black pepper, and garlic.

It was absolutely fantastic. We always had a few beer too. It was a feast. It was like going to a big, fancy restaurant and spending 100 bucks. I remember we used to have Indian grub. An Indian electrician brought in Indian food one time. It was fantastic. I brought in Scottish bacon and Scottish sausages. I once brought in about five pounds of shrimps and we got rice and we got celery and green onions. We just chopped the

Former Local 2900 president Syl MacNeil speaks to a crowd of trade unionists. Staff representative John Fitzpatrick, left, listens carefully. At the time, MacNeil was also president of the Steelworkers Area Council. Former USWA Education Director George Butsika is seen at the right.

> whole lot of it in the frying pan. And what
> came out of that frying pan was utterly
> beautiful. It was a good time.

The sharing of meals like these demonstrates how the ethnic make-up of the plant changed over the years. The multicultural workforce was a far cry from the anglo-saxon, protestant, and male Inglis worker in the skilled trades tradition. More women were hired on in the 1970s, and they became part of the celebrations as they learned the ropes. Bonnie Smith remembered this and the friendship that existed between coworkers:

> We used to work all week to get ahead so
> that Friday nights we partied, you know. It
> wasn't that we didn't do our work, we had a
> rate to make so we just stockpiled. It was
> even better for me when I was down on mid-

> nights, 'cause you'd be surprised how much
> work you can do when there's nobody else
> around, you know, no distractions. I used to
> get ahead on midnights and save it. We actu-
> ally used to hide parts in our lockers. That
> was our bank. One of my friends that
> worked opposite me on the same job on a
> different shift, she'd get talking on the day
> shift so she wouldn't get her work done. So
> she'd go to my locker and take my bank that
> was saved for Friday nights.

The Inglis tradition of working hard and partying hard continued.

In 1971 English Electric sold its shares of the Inglis Corporation. At the same time Whirlpool increased its control of the company by purchasing what amounted to forty-three percent of the company's stock. Simpson Sears, the largest appliance customer of both Whirlpool

= LOCAL 2900 =

MEMBERSHIP MEETING

8:00 P.M.

TUESDAY, APRIL 21, 1964

33 CECIL ST.

Agenda

GENERAL
BUSINESS

S P E C I A L

Film showing of the Last

LISTON - CLAY fight from Miami.

* * * * *

REFRESHMENTS   DOOR PRIZE

Issued by:
United Steelworkers of America

WHAT YOU DON'T KNOW
YOU CAN LEARN
AT YOUR MEETINGS

April 15/64

This meeting notice highlights the male-dominated reality of union membership. To encourage attendance the union showed a film of a boxing match. Refreshments were always available at the meetings, but we don't know what the door prize might have been.

Members of the Maintenance Department enjoy one of their regular food fests. On the left, from front to back: John Horoszko, Bela Franc, Ray Flaubel, Joe Lange. On the right, from front to back: Eric Holt, Mehfooz Shaikh, Bob Sim, Pat Thornton.

Cooking up spicy sausages with a Balkan flavour is Jack Lalic.

and Inglis, purchased a twenty-percent interest in the Inglis of Canada Company. By the end of 1971, two-thirds of the company's stock was indirectly controlled by outside interests — not coincidentally, U.S. interests.

This shift in control set the stage for a new era of bitterness in labour-management relations. As usual, Local 2900 was up for the fight. The particularly bitter strike of 1974 was typical of relations at the plant until the very end. In discipline and style, this strike had much in common with the massive stoppages in which Inglis workers had participated in the past. Not only had the dynamics of ownership in the company changed, but the structure and health of the general economy had changed as well. The postwar boom that owners and workers had ridden for nearly three decades was coming to a close. Members of Local 2900 took to the pavement in an atmosphere of high inflation, flat sales, shrinking rates of profit, and pay cheques that were squeezed by inflation. The outlook was the bleakest it had been since the depression of the 1930s.

Companies in Canada, recalled John Fitzpatrick, USWA staff representative, were concession-driven in the early 1970s:

> The 1974 strike happened because the company wanted to take things away. We were one of the few locals in Toronto that had a full-time president, a union office, a telephone. The company used to pay for arbitrations — there were about twelve things that the company was determined to take away. It wasn't a money strike at all.

The 1974 strike lasted over five months and was characterized by "old-fashioned bitterness," according to the *Globe and Mail.* Local 2900 faced a tough opponent in Inglis president Maiden. He rekindled the tradition of William Inglis, who had opposed the union in his plant sixty years earlier. The Australian-born Conde Maiden explained his philosophy of industrial relations: "I grew up with militant unions in Australia and there is one way of handling them if they step out of line … If there is any nonsense, you just wallop them."

Maiden's philosophy and the company's demands antagonized the union. This period saw the beginning of "concession bargaining," a phrase that soon became familiar to trade unionists throughout North America. This

Sometimes the connections to the Strachan Avenue Inglis plant stretched further than expected. Bobby Sim first knew about Inglis while still in his native Scotland.

I worked in the shipyard before I came to Canada, and they were famous for building certain boilers. They were experimenting with what was called torpedo boards. They were classified as destroyers and driven by steam turbines. Now between the main office and what we called the shed, where they actually built parts of the ship, there was an exhibit there of this place. And the reason I noticed it was because my family was in Canada at this time. It was the very first steam turbine ever built for a ship. Guess where it was built. Here. Strachan Avenue. I mean, this is what I think that bugs me. This Inglis was famous for turbines, boilers. And yet these Yanks come up here and say, `You people, you're of no value' and `you're costing us too much money, you're gone.'

This barbecue was officially sanctioned by the company and held between Inglis buildings. Those wanting to eat big steaks paid for the meal themselves. Peter Tsakiridis was the chef who supplied rare, medium and well-done. Sharing meals, both formally and informally, was an important part of any work day.

Sim father and son — Jack and Bobby — worked at the Strachan Avenue Inglis plant. Bobby was there the day this photograph was taken when his father retired. From left to right: Paul Beaumont, Andy McIsaac, Eric Holt, Ian McCreadie (making presentation), Stuart Sinclair, Jack Lalic, Bobby Sim, Jack Sim, Wesley Campbell, and Milan Djordjevic.

would mean that the union was expected to give up gains in the areas of wages, benefits, and working conditions. The company, according to a negotiation bulletin that was distributed to local members, wanted to take away paying for the full-time president of the local, reduce the number of stewards, and give the company the right to impose compulsory overtime on any day of the week.

In this struggle, the local embarked on a highly innovative consumer boycott, which appealed to the consumer's sense of Canadian loyalty. During the strike, the company had been importing machines from other Whirlpool plants to meet the sales demand. The local used this fact effectively to influence public opinion. By calling into question the quality and standards of the American-made models, the local coordinated a "corporate campaign" against the company.

The plant was situated not far from a large gathering of potential purchasers of the company's product, and so Local 2900 began leafletting families attending the Canadian National Exhibition (CNE) just around the corner. Access to the nearby exhibition made the leaflet campaign especially effective. William Inglis, who had served as the CNE's president in the 1920s and had used it to showcase his company, would have raged at the union's strategy. In the end, the company was forced to back down from most of its concession demands.

The late 1970s continued to be financially troubled times for workers. Wage and price controls were imposed by the Trudeau government, and unemployment rose steadily to what were then the highest levels of the postwar period. A significant first wave of deindustrialization had also hit Toronto by the late 1970s. This urban transformation put additional pressure on the old downtown manufacturing plants. Despite the beginning of rumours that the plant would soon close, Local 2900 continued to fight for good wages and working conditions. Even a recession that hit Ontario's manufacturing sector with a vengeance failed to weaken the local.

The traditions of the local served the members well as they entered the 1980s. The plant was still a workers' plant, but the more intensive demands of production in this period strained the membership. The new partner, Whirlpool, had different expectations of its staff, and the rules of manufacturing had changed since the '50s and '60s. Global production systems, such as those which Whirlpool

controlled, could beat a militant local like Local 2900, not by battling it in the factory, but by threatening to move the factory elsewhere. Workers' factories, tied to the neighbourhood institutions and communities that had given them strength, were far less mobile.

In 1981 and again in 1983, Local 2900 struck against the company. The strike in 1983 was especially illustrative of the union's determination to maintain the living standard of its membership, despite the steady decline many other workers were experiencing. Mike Hersh, who had started at the plant in 1970 and was Local 2900 president by 1983, recalled that it was the federal government's suspension of sales tax on home appliances that really bolstered the union:

In the 1983 strike they really wanted to beat our faces into the pavement, and we really lucked out. It was a depression at the time, 1982–83, and it wasn't a so-called "smart" time to go on strike. Then they [the federal government] removed the federal sales tax, so you could get appliances without a sales tax, for a limited time only. So Inglis all of a sudden came back to the table. I think they had really wanted to ruin us. They had wanted to get rid of our cost-of-living and our SUB [supplementary employment benefits]. A lot of employers did and they were getting it. We were the last short-week benefit in the whole appliance industry in North America.

The way the union operated its strikes was to create a maximum presence around the plant. A message was being sent to management. During the 1983 confrontation, it took all of the organizational experience of the local to run the strike. Mike Hersh described some of the difficulties:

We encouraged people to find part-time jobs and we gave them strike pay even though we're not legally supposed to do that. Because we want people to survive. It makes for a stronger picket line. But there was NOTHING available in 1983. There were actually petitions to go back to work. It was kind of rough. We had a lot of special meetings to encourage people and to encourage people who signed petitions not to do that. It was never voted on. It was very difficult. I don't know how much longer we could have kept them out.

The company failed to beat the union, but it gradually picked the plant dry. The following year the dryer line was shut down at Strachan Avenue and moved to another location, costing the plant 250 jobs. The plant had only one product, washing machines, left, a huge reduction from the half-dozen the workers had produced just a decade earlier. The shutdown of the dryer line foreshadowed what was to come. Bev Brown, vice president of Local 2900, recalled the effect on the membership:

I saw how devastating that was. Anybody with ten years or less was gone at that time. Now two years before that they kept saying the dryer line is going and everybody knew it was going to happen for two years. But right up until the day the last dryer went down the line, we all thought something was going to happen to change it.

But nothing happened to change it, and the appealing diversity of work that the Strachan Avenue factory had once offered workers was eroded. Nevertheless, the way washing machines continued to be made at the plant provided a wide variety of jobs. The machine had been designed and manufactured for the Canadian market. Sourcing decisions were

Inglis workers on strike in 1974 distributed this flyer to visitors at the Canadian National Exhibition. The company displayed and sold its products in the Better Living Building. The appeal to nationalism and safety concerns demonstrates Local 2900 members' understanding of the issues.

These Inglis workers were on strike in 1974. Local 2900 members were out for six months.

Inglis workers and their families gather to listen to one of many visitors to their picket line. These 1983 photos document the union's continuing commitment to include families in its activities. The two offspring pictured are Billy Joseph's children.

made in Canada, and most of the raw materials were purchased from Canadian suppliers. In addition to these national benefits, nearly all components, from the name plates to the agitator, were made inside the plant. Very few parts were purchased from outside suppliers, so the members of Local 2900 had the pleasure of watching the product come together from parts they had manufactured. But that, too, would soon be threatened.

In Clyde, Ohio, Whirlpool had designed the LEAP washing machine for the U.S. market a few years earlier. It was twenty percent cheaper to produce and had twenty percent fewer parts. As Hersh noted, "I think they'd definitely made up their minds they were going to produce something different from what we were doing." After the 1983 strike, the old belt-drive washer was slated to become obsolete in the Whirlpool product line.

Union leadership saw that ownership of the company was slowly giving way to U.S. in-

terests. They included this knowledge as part of the union's strategy in dealing with local management. Mike Hersh knew by heart the exact date when ownership of the company defaulted to the U.S. "Whirlpool, as of July 12, 1985, became the majority shareholder of Inglis, and so far as I was concerned, they were the enemy. So I started to work with local management to see if I couldn't win them on-side against Whirlpool."

The historical relationship between office and production workers at Inglis, once part of the same local, helped 2900 keep in touch with managerial decisions. The office workers kept the local well informed. The traditional practice of hiring local management from within the bargaining unit continued to be a distinct characteristic of the plant. The last two plant managers had been active in the union during their early years at Inglis. This created a dynamic at the plant that teamed local Canadian management and the union against Whirlpool, the American owners. The appeal to local management using a nationalist argument was effective, for the future of local management was also tied to the survival of the plant. Many of the managers maintained sympathy for the union years after they had left the bargaining unit.

How union leadership and local management related to its foreign owners, first English Electric and later Whirlpool, had become an important part of the plant's identity. The blurry line between local management and production staff was significant when the plant was U.S.-owned in its final years. Mike Hersh described the intricacies of this relationship:

I managed to win local management on-side to us as much as possible. That's why I was

Bev Brown, pictured here in 1982, made a place for herself both on the production line and in the union. Women at Inglis both tolerated the rough factory atmosphere as well as challenged it..

able to get as much information as I had. I had a very good relationship with them, with a lot of local management. They had a lot of confidence in me. They confided in me things they wouldn't confide in their own circles. It's difficult to maintain that without having the members see that. That kind of relationship has to really exist behind closed doors. The members would immediately think I'm suck-holing.

Had they known about it, the members of Local 2900 would have disapproved of such a close relationship with management, and so it was kept a secret for the last years of production on Strachan Avenue. The partnership affected the last and longest strike that took place at Inglis. The six-month shut-down in 1986 spoke volumes about the determination of, and the growing dislike that Whirlpool had for, this militant Canadian local.

Senior management in Canada, Hersh learned through his information pipeline, had taken the defeat in 1983 personally.

Collins-Wright took the 1983 strike as a terrible personal loss for him. I think he realized that they had us, in a way. They were in a better position and they didn't beat us. The tax thing came in and we ended up getting a wage increase and holding on to our cost of living, the only one to hold onto a full cost of living, and the only SUB. He got beat. I'm not saying it becomes a personal thing but it does in some ways. He took it as a personal thing.

By 1986, concessions were once again being demanded by employers across the continent. The job classifications that had helped protect the integrity of life in the plant were on the negotiating table. Management claimed that the classification system and traditional time measurements were preventing efficiencies necessary for the implementation of a redesigned washing machine. But the union was determined to maintain what had taken decades to build. In addition to the issue of cost-of-living increases, supplementary unemployment benefits, and several other monetary issues were also on the table. As members of USWA, Local 2900 prepared for what would be its longest strike; it countered concessionary bargaining with a sophisticated analysis. Members knew their labour was only a

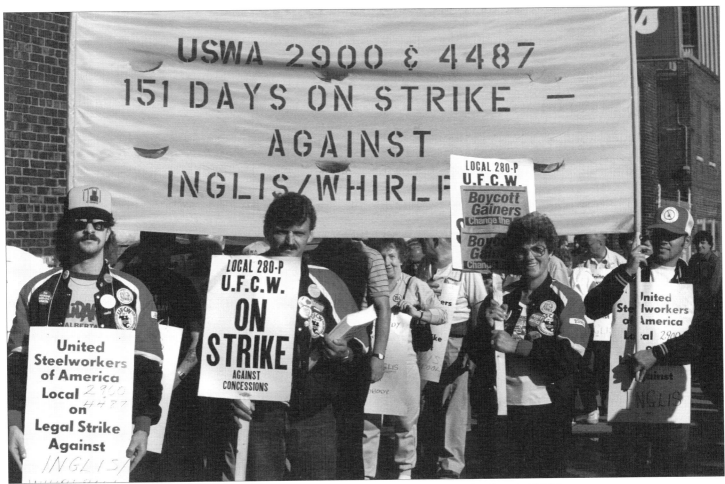

Members of both Inglis locals, 2900 and 4487, are joined on the Strachan Avenue picket line in 1986 by representatives from other unions such as the United Food and Commercial Workers (UFCW). Former Inglis worker Joe Evans is seen at the far left.

small percentage of the product cost to the company. The president of Inglis Canada had come to the local a year before and discussed what effect free trade would have on the industry in Canada. The members knew that giving back their hard-earned wages and benefits was not the answer. Hersh explained:

> *I knew the cost of making a washing machine at Whirlpool and I told management and our members that even if we cut our production costs in half, under free trade, even with the exchange rate (which at that time was 74 or 75 cents), they could still land a machine cheaper than we could make it for them. So I said wages are not the problem. Cutting wages in half was going to cut the cost of a unit by $10. And that just wasn't enough. Concessions were useless. It wasn't going to save a job in that place.*

Management checked every number that Mike Hersh gave them and they all proved to be correct. He had contacts at Inglis's competitor, the Camco plant in Montreal, so he could compare what its unit costs were. The union's analysis was flawless, yet the strike continued. The local, with privileged data, had determined that the company had enough inventory to keep the plant closed for eight weeks. During the strike, sources in the Camco plant provided Local 2900 with production data, and these figures were compared to those from the monthly Statistics Canada reports. The local was soon able to calculate how many units the company was importing from the U.S. The local's years of experience during bargaining allowed it to assess what effect the strike was having on the company. The union's networks, as Hersh described them, extended in a number of directions, including to Whirlpool's plant in Michigan:

Two Local 2900 members, Betty Carew (left) and Lynn Bayley (right), make their thoughts known during the 1986 strike. This would be the last time that the union would organize picket lines and strike pay.

I was in contact with St. Joe's, Michigan. So I knew when they started production, because they made consoles for Clyde, Ohio, and St. Joe's made some of the parts, so they kept me informed of when the production had changed over to Canadian. So we knew how many and when. I had contacts at the Canadian border, at customs. I knew when all the machines were coming and what trucks they were in. We also knew when they were faking it. When they brought trucks in to try to demoralize the picket line and I knew the trucks were empty, because they hadn't crossed the border. We knew everything they were doing. I mean everything.

The strength of the local seriously weakened the business of the Toronto operation. In July 1986, the company and the union met and, to the local's surprise, there was no settlement. In retrospect Hersh realized that the "defeat" the company experienced in 1983 continued to bother the Canadian president. "He wanted to get back something terrible." Equally important, the company's bargaining strategy was increasingly affected by the U.S. ownership. In Hersh's view, the lengthy strike fit Whirlpool's expectations.

It fit right into Whirlpool's policy. So they thought that maybe this union is like American unions. They also thought that local management had a grip on the situation and that they would bring us to our knees. It's actually amazing how much of a loss an anti-union management will accept. There's actually no limit.

Canadian management was an observer to much of this and was asking why there was no settlement. It became clear that the future of the Strachan Avenue plant was expendable. Whirlpool soon began to search for other Canadian locations. The plant was old and would have required upgrading before the redesigned washer could be manufactured there. However, Whirlpool hadn't significantly invested in the plant for over a decade. Hersh also noted that the company refused to budge on improving the severance pay component of the contract. He considered this sign to be ominous.

The decision to end the strike came from Whirlpool's head office. From this point, the U.S. parent was really biding its time. The independence of the Strachan operations decreased after the 1986 strike. The Canadian president resigned and there were new appointments to nearly all of the Canadian vice-president positions. Whirlpool's people took their places. From the perspective of the U.S. operations, Strachan Avenue had two strikes against it: a growing obsolescence, and a militant union.

The demise of Strachan Avenue had happened slowly. In the 1950s, short-term profitability had been traded for long-term viability. What happened to this plant happened elsewhere in the country, with subtle variations. By the mid-1980s, even local management was now beholden to Whirlpool. In October 1988, confidential information was passed to the local: Whirlpool had decided that there was not going to be a new Canadian-designed washing machine. It was unnecessary. A free trade agreement with the United States was a virtual certainty after the Tory election victory.

For almost fifty years, USWA 2900 had been active on behalf of its membership, and for all but the last decade, workers at Inglis had enjoyed a long period of plentiful work and relatively good wages. There was hope it would always be this way. Whirlpool was handed the chance to write the 650 remaining workers on Strachan Avenue out of the corporation's future, and it took it. The Free Trade Agreement of 1988 simply provided the plant's owners with an excuse to shut the place down.

Family Day during the 1986 strike found Inglis workers and their children and spouses joining the picket line.

"The longer the line, the shorter the strike" is a philosophy to which Inglis workers subscribed. Workers were encouraged to find temporary, alternative employment to supplement strike pay.

Leo Gerard, then Director of USWA District 6, addresses families attending a rally in support of the 1986 strike. The local was able to win broad support from the membership because families were involved in the activities.

Three of Local 2900's officers posed for this picture during the 1986 strike's family day. From left to right: Bev Brown, Mike Hersh and Dave Parker as clown.

The union had established a workers' community, rare in an increasingly harsh, conservative climate. The neighbourhood around the plant had changed — a sad reflection of a lack of industrial policy, weak government, and the globalization of the corporate landscape. Important decisions about a workers' plant that was over a century old were made, not from the office next door, but by strangers in another country.

Chapter Six
Waiting for a Miracle: The Final Closure

There is no single reason why the Inglis plant closed. It closed as a result of a long and complex series of historical forces. Nothing is simple when it comes to the end of a factory over a century old. According to the collective agreement, the factory closed in April 1991. For some, however, Inglis closed the day of the official announcement. At least, that day was seen by many as the beginning of the end. After weeks of rumours and speculation, the company, at the union's urging, called together all employees and confirmed what for most was their worst possible nightmare.

For those who placed hope in a possible worker buy-out, the closure came with the release of the feasibility study. Many months and dollars later, Inglis employees had to accept the fact that there would be no worker-owned parts factory, no white goods company, no appliance repair service.

For the union members concerned with assisting the displaced workers, the closure was an ongoing event. Instead of building washing machines on Strachan Avenue, they put in their hours helping rebuild their friends' and coworkers' lives.

Inglis workers clear out their belongings and head home for the last time.

Paul Ryan, Cecile McAlister, Paul Goguen and Pauline Rogers, driving the tow motor, share a joke in the final days of production.

For the few who negotiated the closure package with the company, the end came on a Friday morning, just before Labour Day, in one of those indistinguishable meeting rooms of a west-end hotel. Nine union and four company signatures finalized a hard-fought document that sealed the fate of 650 workers.

Economic Context

If "misery loves company" and "there's safety in numbers," former Inglis workers were happy in a crowd. According to 1989 figures collected and released by the Ontario Ministry of Labour, 17,526 Ontario workers lost jobs that year due to plant closures or reduced operations. Since the ministry does not count lay offs involving companies with fewer than fifty employees, the true figure is likely higher still.

The list of companies in the ministry's tabulation reads like an industrial *Who's Who*: Alcan, Arrowhead Metals, Ault, Bendix, Black & Decker, Budd, Carlton Cards, Control Data, Domtar, Echlin, Eddy Match, Fiberglass, Fruehauf, John Deere, Kendall, Mack, MacMillan Bloedel, Maple Leaf Mills, Midas, Monarch, Ontario Bank Note, Pemberton, Samsonite, Union Carbide, Westinghouse. Workers were not recalled to any of these operations.

Corporate streamlining could not prevent the process of massive deindustrialization still occurring in the manufacturing sector of the Canadian economy. Since Ontario is home to such a large proportion of industry overall, it was inevitable that this province would be affected profoundly by such a basic transformation in Canadian society. It became inefficient to produce small amounts of any product for the Canadian market. Goods can be manufactured instead in one afternoon-shift in a larger U.S. facility. Or goods can be made more cheaply in offshore economies, where workers are paid a fraction of Canadian wages.

While some politicians tried to make the public believe that this change in the economy was for the better, that it would herald the beginning of a great Canadian service economy specializing in "high tech" industries, the fact remains that in numbers of jobs, in value of jobs as measured by wages, in the creative spin-off effect of manufacturing, service-sector work is no substitute. While holding companies played real games of Monopoly, one factory after another was boarded up. Wheelers and dealers, merger specialists, and corporate lawyers were the main beneficiaries of deindustrialization.

Paul Ryan worked at Inglis for thirty-seven years and saw many changes.

When I first started, I lived just up the street, on Stanley Terrace near Stanley Park. In the '50s, this whole area was working people. You couldn't get into the Palace at noon hour, you had to stand up to drink your beer. After work people would line up outside to get in. They worked here, Massey, Dr. Ballard's, the paper company that's behind us, Loblaw's over here, Irwin Toy Company. Today I wonder, Is this going to become another New York City? It should be a mix of different industries, but Toronto has become a service centre, especially in this area. Where Massey is, it's all high-tech banking. They don't produce anything. They just manipulate working-class money.

Most of the displaced Inglis workers identified the 1988 U.S.–Canada Free Trade Agreement as the final nail in a coffin that had been years in the making. It was stated that Inglis workers were the first of its victims. The terms of the agreement include the removal of a 12.5 percent tariff on imported household appliances over ten years. Consequently, Whirlpool can now manufacture washing machines in its plant in Ohio, ship them to Canada, and still make an admirable profit. While there may have been political mileage to be gained from the claim that the FTA was responsible for the closure, it is far too simplistic an answer to the question of why Inglis chose to shut down this plant. At the heart of the issue, was the fact that the foreign management felt no loyalty to the Inglis name in Canada.

Inglis executives insist that free trade had nothing to do with the decision to close the Strachan Avenue plant. John Utter, director of corporate industrial relations for Inglis, was one of the main company negotiators during the closure.

We had a joke about when the free trade thing started to come up. The free trade thing came up long after '86. It wasn't even dreamt of. When it came up, I said, you know what's going to happen if we close this plant, it'll be called a free trade issue. Everybody on the union side just laughed, what a

Bobby Sim expresses his anger in front of the plant on the day of the closure announcement. Gord Palmer looks on grimly.

joke that would be. But that was the theme when it closed, that's the one that Mike [Hersh, local union president,] pushed. And that's the one I never forgave him for. The union went out to the press and said, free trade closed this plant. Well, that's pure nonsense. They said it, and said it, and they hurt us very badly, and it had nothing to do with free trade. I can't convince anybody of that. Strachan Avenue was a made-in-Canada decision.

The deindustrialization of Toronto had devastating effects on companies across a broad spectrum of sectors and in almost every part of the city. While the effects of this trend appeared most serious during the final years of the 1980s, in fact deindustrialization was part of a thirty-year process. Perhaps it was the inability to recognize deindustrialization in its early stages that made it impossible to stem when it reached its worst form. The mobility of capital has always been flexible enough to create and destroy industrial facilities at will.

Particularly in times of political conservatism, restrictions on the flow of capital are almost nonexistent. There is little incentive for investors to keep money in or to bring funds into an economy with high interest rates and a high-valued currency. It is far better to invest in undertakings in developing countries where labour and environmental restrictions are much less stringent or in the changing economies of Eastern Europe. The climate in Canada wasn't right for entrepreneurial risk-taking.

Toronto's associated real estate frenzy was part of the closure parcel. The Inglis factory was located in the heart of the city, steps from Exhibition Place, a short walk from Lake Ontario, and just blocks to luxury condominiums. Development was creeping further and further west along King and Wellington streets. In the hoopla and hysteria of Toronto's Olympic bid for 1996, the proximity of the Inglis lands to the Exhibition Grounds, the Skydome, the lake, and other potential event facilities probably drove the paper value of the lands sky high. Strachan Avenue would be, it was rumoured,

Mike Hersh speaks to the media on the day of the closure announcement. Dave Parker and and Bev Brown look on.

the site of the competitors' Olympic village. Clearly, selling the land and making goods elsewhere was seen as an attractive alternative by Whirlpool executives.

Announcement

The bitter cold weather of 15 February 1989 was no match for the icy chill that overcame Inglis workers when the closure was finally announced. For months workers had anticipated news of the location of a new Ontario plant. But after weeks of rumours, company officials finally gave in to union pressure and held a meeting with all employees. Production of washing machines would end early in 1990, leaving just a skeleton staff to see to the final shut-down.

The company found no consoling words to offer in its sober, official announcement of the closure:

On August 16th, 1988, Inglis announced that it was initiating a study to determine the best possible future use of its Toronto facilities. As a result of this study, a deci-

In a letter to Gerard Docquier, then national director of USWA, Local 2900 member Paul Ryan expressed opinions shared by many union members:

Dear Brother Docquier:

...The negotiating committee of Local 2900 attended a seminar on Plant Closures, at the C.A.W. Centre in Port Elgin ...We spent four days at this seminar and to our amusement, we learned that there is no expertise on plant closures.

During the week we were at Port Elgin, it was the conclusion of the students, who were from a variety of unions, that there is no concerted effort to mobilize the forces of all unions to combat the continuous plant closures... We are all standing by watching, while one plant after another closes and attempts to negotiate a plant closure contract, that will only assist the workers in a short term basis, are made.

The retraining program of all governments is all propaganda and is not properly funded or initiated at the proper times ...

It is about time that National Unions stop sitting on their hands, get up off their asses and start mobilizing the workers for a concerted effort in protesting the actions and attitudes of our present day government. This could be done by a Canada-wide strike or demonstrations across Canada, sizing [sic] property by occupation and getting our problems and messages across in the media. Let's start kicking asses.

I hope your office will start action immediately, before you are laid off, because there are no workers left to pay union dues.

Fraternally yours,

Paul Ryan
Local 2900, USWA

sion has been made to close the Toronto Plant during the second quarter of 1991.

In view of the previous decision to delay plans for producing a new automatic washer for the Canadian market, Inglis has decided to source washers from Whirlpool Corporation's Clyde, Ohio, facility. Based on current projections, plans are being developed to cease production of the current full size and compact washers in early 1990. Service parts operations will be gradually phased out until closing.

In addition, approximately 85 employees at our Cambridge Plant and 25 employees at our Montmagny Plant, which supply parts for our current washer production at Toronto, will be affected.

The Toronto Plant, with many dedicated, long-service employees, has been the cornerstone of Inglis operations since 1881 and it is with deep regret that this decision has been reached. The Corporation will be immediately establishing a Manpower Adjustment Committee to develop programs to assist its employees through this difficult period.

Many of the Inglis workers affected were very angry and felt betrayed after years of service to the company. Others were moved to tears at the prospect of a job search following decades spent at one company.

Paul Ryan not only spent most of his working life at Inglis but he was also past president of the local. He continued to serve the union actively as a member of the executive committee.

Everybody's feeling bad. After thirty-seven years. If you're turning 58 or 59, and you've spent most of your life inside of a plant here ... I've never been out of a job. Now, who wants me for six or seven years of my life? I want to die working, I guess. I didn't think I'd have to go and fill out an application and say I'm 58 years old, I'm looking for a job. Who in the heck wants a guy at 58?

Others had short, to-the-point comments:

Inglis is changing its name to Whirlpool Canada.

That used to be a source of pride to say I worked at Inglis.

The old central prison was a distinctive landmark on the company grounds. Inglis workers in the early days saw prison labour making brooms there. At the end, the building housed hundreds of blueprints and records.

We make the best machine in Canada. The company made lots of money.

High atop the Inglis plant is a large electric sign which each day carries a short motto-type message. The words can be seen from a busy downtown Toronto expressway. On the day following the closure announcement, commuters to the city could hardly be expected to appreciate the irony of the chosen message for that day: "When anger rises, think of the consequences."

Negotiating the Closure Agreement

For months, company and union representatives danced around the negotiating table, as those workers affected second-guessed and anticipated the severance package. Thousands of dollars were spent in theory and in dreams. The low-key signing ceremony, the handshakes all around on 1 September 1989, did not begin to reflect the fancy footwork of the union's strategy.

To outsiders, it appeared that the three levels of the union involved in negotiations — the local, the district and the international — were operating at cross purposes. Company representatives dealt with the local president in the plant on a daily basis. The international union was at the bargaining table through the presence of rep, John Fitzpatrick. At the District 6 level, the director, Leo Gerard, watched carefully, ready to intervene with corporate staff. Each player in the negotiations had a different role to play, but the goal was a common one.

It was clear that Inglis management most

Peter Arsenault managed the last Inglis
baseball team.

Lorne Drody, David DiPinto and Carl Bailey (left to right) march in the 1989 Labour Day parade. Members of Local 2900 were
out in large numbers.

feared a consumer boycott of company products that might be organized throughout the Canadian labour movement. This threat became the negotiating committee's primary weapon. In fact, the 1 September deadline for the signed document is no coincidence, as company representatives believed that an Inglis boycott would be the theme for the 1989 Labour Day parade in Toronto.

Leo Gerard had once served as the Steelworkers' business agent for Local 2900. He had marched with the members on more than one picket line. In his position as director of USWA District 6, he was part of the overall union strategy.

A role that I often play in my function as director is to bring the full weight of the institution down on the employer, to make sure the employer knows that the corporation is not just dealing with a group of workers at a single plant. The role that I played was to prepare a national strategy to boycott Inglis products if we didn't get the kind of closure agreement that our members would accept. We prepared the campaign and sent a letter out and copied it for the president of the company. Then I met him and told him that we intended to launch a national campaign against their products. At the very least, the corporation had an obligation to our membership to give them a decent closure package, so we could move on to a different life with some dignity. I made it very clear that we understood that the biggest part of their profits were not made at the front end of their sales, but at the back end. They make eighty-five percent of their profits on the last three percent of the products they sell. Our goal was not to put them out of business but to simply lower their sales by four or five percent. And I was sure we could do that.

No strategy or plan, Gerard knew, could work without the cooperation of the plant bargaining committee and the members it represented. Feelings were divided about the best way to apply pressure on the company.

There were some of them that just wanted to end it. They were tired and there were people biting at their ass and they wanted to tell people that the plant was going to close.

We knew we needed to do something just before Labour Day. That was the plan that we cooked up. We put it to a vote, and just before the vote, the guys said to give it two more weeks. That's when we did the thing about Labour Day and made Inglis the centre of the Labour Day parade. We took out ads in the newspaper.

I called the company president and had this package of the things we were going to do and the analysis of the company. I had never met this guy that we called up — I forget his name, but he's an American — you could have cut the air with a knife. He was cold, just like talking to the devil. I introduced myself and told him that I was calling as a result of the closure and I was hoping that he and I could talk. He said the decision was done and he didn't see the benefit in talking. And I said that I was sorry he had that attitude and that I intended to do something to his company and that I owed it to him to let him know. It would be in his best interests to hear me out. The next morning we met at the Delta Hotel. I went in and sat down, ordered a coffee and said I didn't have a lot of time and neither did he to dick around. What was on the table was inadequate and our members deserved better than that. I told him that we were going to have a dealer list,

Leo Gerard: "I don't think it's sufficient to operate in a country or city, to use the capital of that country or that city, use the land and use the people, then, all of a sudden, one day decide on your own you're going to reshuffle the deck, only the deck doesn't happen to have any workers in it this time."

Nearly all of the components for the Inglis washer were made in the plant. Dozens of sub-assembly lines like this one fed the main final assembly.

WHERE WOULD YOU LIKE IT

OHIO

Inglis

500 JOBS

THE LITTLE TRUCK DRIVER MAKES ANOTHER DELIVERY

which at that point was a lie, but he didn't know that. I told him we were gonna go after the dealers. And ours was going to be 'buy Canadian'. I told him we wanted a decent severance and closure package.

In a time when many workers in other plants were left with no severance pay, this was considered a very good closure package. The first two paragraphs of the signed close-out agreement deal with union assurances that there would be no participation in or promotion of any type of product boycott. Union reps hastened to assure company negotiators that the Labour Council of Metropolitan Toronto could revise plans for the parade in a matter of days.

Although the local union members wanted an end to the uncertainty, USWA District 6 leadership was eager to get as much political mileage out of the Inglis closure as possible.

Once terms of a "benevolent" settlement became public knowledge, there would be less advantage to highlighting the Inglis situation as an example of free trade devastation. District 6 representatives saw no reason to hasten the signing of a closure agreement.

When the signed document was at last available for general distribution, Inglis workers knew how hard their representatives had bargained. There would be one and three-quarters weeks' pay for each year of employment for all those with five or more years of seniority. Employees received paid worktime to attend job interviews. Monthly benefits under the group insurance plan would still be paid by the company until a total of $250,000 had been reached. The continuing benefit payment was a particularly unique and useful agreement, as most companies pay only for a fixed period of time, regardless of employment status. Former Inglis workers would receive this assistance for as long as they required it until the total amount set aside was exhausted.

Payment of severance could take one of four forms: full payment two weeks after termination; later payment with maintenance of recall rights (those who chose to remain on the recall list would avoid the penalty imposed by the Unemployment Insurance Commission and could receive benefits after a short waiting period); payment could be in the form of Registered Retirement Savings Plans (RRSP), an option offering substantial tax savings; finally, severance payment could be made after 1 January 1990, avoiding a huge personal income tax burden for many. The leadership of Local 2900 recognized that union concern for the membership went beyond the last day worked.

This payment-option palette was rare in closure agreements. In a climate when businesses were stealing away or declaring bankruptcy, intense negotiation was necessary to achieve more than minimum standards as required by law. The Inglis agreement demonstrated the broad knowledge its leadership possessed so that the full usefulness of the severance pay was protected.

This agreement ended decades of confrontation between the union and the company. In the '80s, Inglis had wanted to reorganize the shopfloor. To sell its new ideas of rationalization, centralization, deindustrialization, specialization, and a so-called more competitive economy, management embraced new techniques. In the globalized marketplace, old techniques were no

As half-finished washing machines drift by on a conveyor, George Spurrel hunts for the right part.

longer viable, so the hard-sell began, and labour and management were frozen in an adversarial relationship. The company suggested that a team approach to managing a business would have to replace old-style unionism. In reality, the company simply wanted to eliminate unionism.

A team approach erodes the shopfloor power of a union by cutting through traditional loyalties. Seniority and job classifications are just two areas that are supposedly incompatible with team management. Despite management's contention that the team approach is a win–win situation, Local 2900 steadfastly refused to give up hard-fought gains. Without such concessions, Inglis managers believed they could not recommend that the Strachan Avenue plant be renovated as the home of the new Whirlpool washer. However, another Inglis plant outside the Toronto area that had agreed to such changes did not escape closure, either.

The militancy of Local 2900 was also a factor behind the closure. Through the 1950s and 1960s, direct action was a common way to "negotiate" with management. Sit-down strikes, walkouts, and other job action were practised. Results could often be immediate and dramatic. The site of the old military cemetery near the plant had become the workers' town hall. Union records reveal that the local sometimes defied decisions made by the international union as well as agreements with the company to return to work.

But in more recent years, labour disagreements were settled through a formalized structure: the grievance and arbitration procedure. Workers were advised to "do the work and grieve later." Work refusals, walkouts, and other kinds of direct action became relics of labour history. With this development, a militant local like 2900 lost power at precisely the point that it had traditionally controlled — the point of production. In the name of labour peace, grievance committees, staff reps, business agents, and lawyers came between the workers and the boss.

It is easy to see why a multinational company, when making a decision to rationalize production, would look to a plant with a militant local as a good choice for closure. Local 2900 had hardly ever signed a contract without a strike. Over the years, the union had made many significant gains for the work force. By contrast, the Clyde, Ohio, facility where Whirlpool makes the same washing machine is not unionized. Strachan Avenue must have been a thorn in the side of the openly anti-union head office in St. Joseph, Michigan.

Certainly one of the most unusual clauses in this close-out agreement was the Inglis wind-up party. The company agreed to contribute $20,000 towards a final bash and to provide five Inglis appliances to be raffled off to those attending.

The Party

Plans for the party, which was held 10 November 1989 at an Etobicoke Lions Club, were avidly discussed from the moment the close-out agreement became public. Some union members were against attending a party with management. There were many opinions about what food should be served and how much alcohol should be available.

In the company newsletter, *Strachan Talk*, published 16 October 1989, the party was called "The Absolutely Best Bargain in Toronto."

For a $10.00 per person ticket you get a live band, food, door prizes and a heck of a good time with all your Inglis buddies. If you do attend this party — here is where the bargain comes in — YOU GET YOUR MONEY BACK!!

At the door, corsages were presented to all the women attending. Strips of tickets for drinks were distributed and invitation stubs were collected for the door prize draw. The food was sumptuous, the dance music live, spirits stoked to high intensity.

For the few outsiders present, there was sad irony in Inglis workers receiving appliances they had built themselves as door prizes. Leo Gerard felt rage at the possibility that any Inglis manager could win a USWA jacket in the door prize raffle. For Linda McKinnon, spouse of Inglis worker Stuart McKinnon, the evening had an unexpected bitter edge: that morning, Linda had lost her job with CKO radio, as the all-news station had closed abruptly.

Perhaps the wind-up party should have been held after the closure. Perhaps the union should have instead organized its own event. Perhaps there is no real way at all to celebrate a plant closure.

The Local's Reaction

The Local Executive Committee decided soon after the closure announcement that efforts on behalf of the membership would take three main directions: training and adjustment assistance, negotiating a close-out deal, and exploring a worker buy-out option.

The adjustment committee was made up of representatives from the union, management, and the federal government. Its main objective was to help Inglis workers find new jobs. Meeting this objective meant for many of these workers an upgrading of their skills. Others believed that retraining for a new vocation would best help them secure reemployment.

As part of the closure agreement, Inglis gave the Adjustment Committee $250,000 for employee training, with a matching amount from the provincial government. Responsibility for organizing training courses fell primarily to union executive board members Dave Parker and Bev Brown.

There was dancing and laughing at the company-funded party but under the festive surface lay anger and sadness.

Five former presidents of Local 2900 representing the years 1955 to 1989 were reunited at the closure party. From the left: Frank McCuaig, Jack Hill, Syl MacNeil, Paul Ryan and Mike Hersh managed to arrange themselves in chronological order.

Armand Girard checks washing machine components riding the conveyor belt.

Once more in her long association with the Steelworkers, Brown was called on to help union sisters and brothers pick up the pieces. One of the most active women in the local — she was vice president — Brown carried on the work begun by Mary Spratt.

In the last twenty years only one woman that I know of was on the Negotiating Committee. That was Mary Spratt. She ran several times for vice president and was never elected. I supported Mary because I like Mary and I knew she was a good trade unionist and basically, because she was a woman. I knew that there was a struggle to get support for women at the local level. Then I ran for vice president and was elected. That wasn't an easy feat in our local.

Women unionists struggled on at least two fronts: in the plant, and in the union hall. Brown believed that she had to work much harder to establish herself in both.

I had quite a bit of support from the Steelworkers when it came to anything that the Steelworkers were involved in. When it came to getting support for women being progressed through the union, there's no support there. There's no infrastructure. There's nothing. Women have to be progressed through the union. They got to be brought up from the grassroots and be brought all the way up. They have to be groomed the same way that staff men are. That isn't being done.

Like so many union activists, Brown's union work became all-consuming. In some ways, she played a very "mothering" role at the closure, leaving negotiations to others and looking after retraining and counselling. Life without union involvement was something Brown could not imagine.

My family is the union, the workers at Inglis. It's so much a part of my life, it's going to be something that I miss. I can't envision myself not being in some kind of trade union. I think I will have a harder time coming to grips with the fact that I don't have a union than I will with the fact that I don't have a company. It's going to be really, really hard. I just feel like my union's been shot out from underneath me. Of all the problems that I've had to see in Steel and the Steel establishment, I still like the Steelworkers and I'm still proud to be a Steelworker.

Although set-up time for the training programmes took longer than anticipated and the plant closed sooner than first announced, the breadth and depth of training possibilities open to Inglis workers were impressive. Courses included English as a Second Language, Literacy Training, Computer Awareness, Appliance Repair, Lift Truck Operation, Truck Driving, Welding, Air Conditioning and Heating, Heavy Equipment Operation, Math Upgrading, Blueprint Reading. Some of the instruction was provided by the Metro Labour Education Centre, a project of the Labour Council of Metropolitan Toronto. George Brown College also participated in the training and retraining efforts.

It was not easy, working a shift at the plant and attending courses afterwards. Some courses met four days a week, and although some of the class time was paid, participants had to be dedicated. Peter Chahanian, a twenty-year man, understood why the effort was worth making. He attended English instruction.

When I came here to this country, exactly twenty-five years ago, I didn't know one word. I came here with a wife, two kids, nobody knew nothing. Only $200 in my pocket. I worked very hard in this country.

I was very happy our union had English as a second language. I was very happy about that. Now, even when they close this company down, I know where to go, where to get some idea, what to do. I think I learn lots of things. These for me [are] big things.

I have difficulty with this language. For twenty years' time, I never had too much chance to learn because people like my age, it's very hard to learn language. You have too much pressure, you have your own problems no matter what. See, now lucky for me it's good relaxed time to learn the language. Good chance now to make English upgrading to learn more, because even my own kids, I cannot go, please read this letter and explain. Even if they don't refuse, sometimes you don't have that courage to go [to] them.

No matter what, I never work again factory. This is my point. No matter what. I have to try hard to do something, to do something on my own. Sure, not easy, but I'm going to try very hard. Something, if you have no choice, you try very hard. Because life is hope.

The Adjustment Committee identified 346 Inglis workers over the age of forty-five. Money from the provincial Transitions Program was made available for all those interested in training. This meant that a $5,000 retraining grant would be provided, to be spent over the following two years. If the workers about to lose their jobs started training while still employed, the union reasoned, there was a better chance that they would continue in the courses following shut-down. But there was a certain desperation in this race against the clock, and taking retraining meant admitting that in the future there would be no jobs at Inglis.

Dave Parker played an active role in organizing training. He recognized that for himself and for many of his coworkers, the Inglis work experience was not enough to find new employment. The skills developed on Strachan Avenue had not kept up with progress, something for which both employer and employee are responsible.

The management in this company didn't realize that they should train everybody. The company spends some money for retraining, there's no doubt about it. But not the type of retraining they should have been doing. They could have had computer classes in here a long time ago and gone computer, if it had some kind of efficiency for the plant. They chose not to do that. They took the money out and they didn't put it back in. The retraining that the people are getting now is mostly what the union-half of the committee pushed for. Some of the people just don't understand what the retraining is for, because some people believe that a miracle is going to happen at the last second and Inglis is going to say, 'No, no, we were only kidding,' which is a farce.

The earlier lack of commitment to training on the part of the company was also reflected in a lack of investment in the physical plant itself. An unsatisfactory business climate meant also that hardly any investment had been made at Inglis in technological improvements. It was no coincidence that structurally, Inglis looked the same as it had fifty years earlier. Much of the equipment on Strachan Avenue on the day of the closure had been brought in from other plants in the corporate extended family where modernization had taken place. It's easy then, but incorrect, to blame workers for poor productivity compared to other plants. It's hard to be productive without the right tools.

Yet from a marketing point of view, Inglis/Whirlpool had certainly bought into the concept of new technology. The new model washer planned for the Canadian market had many high-tech characteristics. Strachan Avenue workers may have believed that the old model washer was more steady and reliable, but the company was already making its plans around a newer, more marketable model.

Worker Buy-out

The idea that workers can own the means of production and run a factory for themselves is a dream probably as old as capitalism itself. In a market-driven economic system, workers' needs and abilities are not a factor in the corporate equation. A group of workers whose labour is no longer sought finally has no worth in that economy. When labour is in short supply, the lack of power is hidden under good contract settlements. Little time and effort are spent on strategies that would change this power structure.

Far too often, the possibility of a worker buy-out comes in poor economic times, in times of crisis. In the case of Inglis, a worker buy-out, whatever form that would have taken, was a long shot. The Steelworkers in the U.S. had carried out worker ownership several times with good success. Lynn Williams, international president of the Steelworkers, a Canadian and dues-paying member of Local 2900, took a keen, personal interest in the possibility.

I became very intrigued when the possibility of an employee buy-out started to be talked about. We talk a lot about workers' rights and traditional rights, having a right to have something to say about the management of the places where they work. The way we talk about that most frequently is that managers have screwed up enormously. And when the managers screw up, the owners screw up. It's the workers who suffer more than any-

body else. They're the least mobile, most tied to communities. They have the greatest amount of personal destruction in their own lives. And, therefore, we have a right to have a lot more to say about how these businesses are conducted and what their strategies are and what their futures are. In the end, the only plant shut-down strategy that works long-term is a strategy to have a growing, successful, job-producing economy where people can work and people can earn a living and they can function in some creative and decent and safe ways.

Dave Parker

Local 2900 leadership desperately wanted to keep as much of the work force together as possible, although no one had the illusion that all 650 people would be a part of a worker-owned Inglis. Many clung to the hope of this outside chance; some offered their entire severance package as investment capital. At the very least, the possibility of a worker buy-out could be used as a bargaining chip.

No one wanted a worker buy-out more than Mike Hersh. President of Local 2900, a lo-

Peter Chahinian (left), here with Dobre Curcic, was one of many Inglis workers who participated in English lessons at the plant.

cal with a history of militant leadership, Hersh brought both political experience and analysis to his elected position. Although he claimed never to have sought out positions within the local, he clearly enjoyed being able to both serve and lead the membership. Putting jobs first, keeping part of the membership together as a work force, was Hersh's top priority. But striking deals with capital must have created a contradiction that Hersh would have had to unravel for himself.

We're very flexible on how this thing should look. If we make washing machines, fine, or parts for appliances. But if not, whatever we make is good. Whatever we make is better than what we've got now, because now we've got no jobs at all as of 1991. We'd like to have worker control. That seems very remote at this point, to say the least. We've said we primarily want as many jobs for as long as possible, and that has to leave it open for all kinds of other things to happen. We've said publicly, and also privately, that we just want to maintain jobs. In my heart of hearts I would like it to be a real live worker buy-out where we would have the majority of shares and we would run the plant, with some assistance from local management.

To explore the buy-out possibility, District 6 director Leo Gerard pulled together a strategy team for a 17 March 1989 meeting: USWA Research Director Hugh McKenzie, Chuck Jacobs, a buy-out specialist from the U.S., Wally Brant and Ethan Phillips, from the Worker Ownership Development Foundation in Toronto, Mike Hersh, and USWA staff rep John Fitzpatrick. From the start, Gerard made it clear that developments surrounding a possible buy-out should not offer Inglis workers unjustified hope. "The only thing worse than the closure is having to announce it twice," he told the buy-out team.

Gerard's challenge to those meeting was to come up with a plan that would allow the Steelworkers to reassemble the Inglis work force using any number of options: a new product, an old product, a new location, the old Strachan Avenue site, in cooperation with Inglis, or in competition. But he did believe that whatever product was made, it should appeal to Canadian nationalism. "Stick the Steelworkers' flag on the back and the Canadian flag on the front, and we'll sell more fucking washing machines than Sears."

Jacobs warned that building a true workers' co-op took time, more time than was available in the case of Inglis. Some sort of interim agreement with Inglis itself might have gained additional months. He outlined some of the possibilities. The union could reach an agreement with Whirlpool, either to build or subassemble a product. A second possibility would be to manufacture something for Whirlpool that would not compete with other company operations. This could be appliance parts, or a selected product for niche marketing. A third route would entail signing an agreement with Whirlpool for repair and service work on machines the Inglis workers had themselves built. If Whirlpool failed to cooperate, a new partner could be sought. Such an arrangement would have to cover a multitude of areas: financing, manufacturing, distribution, marketing, necessary technology, and the politics of a new contract. Who would be this new partner with whom labour could work? Finally, the union could work towards a complete worker buy-out. This would require an enormous organization fed by economic information on product demand, price, cost structures, and so on.

The next step would clearly involve some kind of feasibility study. Neither the union local nor the USWA district office alone could afford to fund an investigation of such size and scope. McKenzie believed that the money could be found, but that a proposal was needed quickly to take to various levels of government. As Gerard left to begin setting up appointments with appropriate officials, Hersh could only warn, "I don't want to feasibility study this thing to death."

By April, the union was already approaching the city of Toronto for a grant. City Council had passed a recommendation at a March meeting to use community economic development funds to assist just such a feasibility study. Of the Local 2900 union executive, Mike Hersh and Hugh Walters attended the 17 April meeting of Toronto's Economic Development Committee. In his presentation, Hersh admitted that the union had no illusions about a worker buy-out, but the union's goal was "to maintain as many jobs for as long as possible." Such an objective was entirely compatible with the city's hope to stem the deindustrialization tide.

The rest of the meeting consisted of political posturing and grandstanding on the part of participants. Most of it was predictable. Council-

The only products made at Inglis in 1989 were washing machines. But at the Strachan Avenue plant, boilers, guns, fishing rods and turbines had once been produced by Inglis workers.

Syl MacNeil and Bobby Sim find it hard to say good-bye on the last day at Inglis.

lor Chris Korwin-Kuczynski said it was "too early" for a study. His colleague, Tom Jakobek, wanted to know where the Inglis employees lived. Robert Gordon, the president of Humber College, wanted to know about the employees' retraining needs. When it came to the money question, the union asked the city for half of the study costs or $37,500. Councillor Michael Walker asked, "If we are paying fifty percent of the cost, shouldn't we be running the show?" Walker continued to pursue the control issue, suggesting the city broaden the study and pay the whole shot. That way, he explained, it would achieve "our objectives."

Jakobek rode the anti-union horse, claiming that the Steelworkers did not contribute enough to the study. He went on to make four suggestions: that no rezoning of the plant site be approved; that City Hall staff report back on where Inglis workers lived; that municipal staff

ensure the study be conducted correctly; and finally, that other consultants be considered to undertake the feasibility study.

In the end, a consensus was reached that the Inglis workers should be helped. Mayor Art Eggleton had the last word before the vote. The company, he pointed out, paid taxes to the city, and now it was time for the city to do something in return. After the dust had settled, it was clear that any opposition had been token. The requested $37,500 was a lot less than what the city would pay to undertake a similar study itself.

Within weeks it became evident that government money-givers required a more acceptable, "more qualified," research partner to lend business credibility to the undertaking. Peat Marwick Stevenson and Kellogg agreed to participate, and by mid-May, a study plan was worked out. The feasibility study would take three months at a cost of $70,000. Peat Marwick

Finished washing machines were packed in cardboard boxes, made in Canada.

The base of the washing machine is assembled.

Stevenson and Cooperative Work would share the research tasks and the fees in a 65:35 ratio.

The final report to the union on the possibility of a worker buy-out made it very clear: keeping the work force together was never more than a dream. Inglis management refused any involvement from the start. The investigation started too late and much time was lost in efforts to obtain funding for the feasibility study. There were several other factors related to the closure that made worker ownership impossible. Inglis's decreasing autonomy meant

that Whirlpool paid the piper. The U.S. parent company had increased its share of the ownership to 71.6 percent. With relatively new management in place, Inglis could not successfully oppose Whirlpool's rationalization and consolidation plans.

In the corporate world of the '80s and '90s, rationalization and specialization were buzz words of the leaner and meaner managers. The only way to make "real money" was to make lots of one kind of product. Short-term corporate thinking and a bottom-line mentality made any economic policy based on social justice, loyalty, or community responsibility an impossibility, the dream of hopeless idealists. The corporate world could carve up manufacturing until the cost of production per unit reached bargain-basement levels. With the end of the Engineering Division in the 1960s, all the eggs were now in the consumer products basket, the most competitive basket of all.

To increase its share of the white goods market, Whirlpool had begun to enter the European market by purchasing the appliance division of Philips in 1988. Inglis Canada now accounted for only five percent of Whirlpool revenues worldwide. The European purchase cost Whirlpool US$350 million. A further option to buy the remaining forty-seven percent of Philips in 1991 meant that large amounts of cash would be needed, and the proceeds from the sale of the Strachan Avenue lands must have looked appealing to Whirlpool executives.

A further barrier to a worker buy-out could be found in the product itself. Whirlpool had introduced the LEAP washer, a lighter-weight model with direct drive rather than the belt drive of the older models. John Utter made the company's position clear on this point and on the worker buy-out in general:

> They wanted to continue making this washer for the Canadian market. They were convinced this was a damn good washer. One of the things they wanted to do was buy it and then continue producing the washer. That's not an option. We don't want the washer. We're making a decision to bring in a new washer. We're going to market that washer. We're not going to market this one in competition to it. We didn't think it was feasible. We didn't think it would turn out. It never went anywhere. They couldn't run the washer for us, we didn't want it. We didn't look at it seriously at all. We didn't think it would work, and we just stayed completely clear of it. We had no interest in it.

A further hindrance to the buy-out plan was, of course, the Canada–U.S. free trade deal, as mentioned above. At the same time, the value of the Canadian dollar was rising in respect to U.S. currency. Producing washing machines in Canada became less and less attractive to Whirlpool management. Instead, the company could produce the goods at its Clyde, Ohio,

plant, the capacity of which would then be better utilized. The fact that the 2,000 workers at that facility were not union members would be a strong incentive.

Finally, the value of the land itself cannot be overlooked. Even though the city of Toronto vowed it would not rezone this industrial land in the "near" future, this designation allowed considerable flexibility. For instance, semi-commercial use (i.e., banking, data processing), as found along King Street on the former Massey–Ferguson site, could be compatible with industrial zoning.

Inglis would not permit a competitor to enter the white goods market, nor would Inglis agree to buy replacement parts from outside the corporation. The company planned to relocate all machinery from Strachan Avenue and eventually sell the property. Other Canadian manufacturers were themselves caught up in consolidation efforts and not interested in the Strachan Avenue work force. Foreign investors were not attracted to it either. Even the Spanish worker-owned cooperative, FAGOR, that country's largest appliance manufacturer, could not be enticed to participate.

When the union issued a press release in August 1989, looking for a new partner, the response was dismal. The greatest interest came from real estate and financial interests whose eyes were on a potential fee for selling or leasing lands, or financing either. No firm offer was made by a manufacturer. No companies with serious labour shortages were identified.

The $70,000 Peat Marwick report concluded: "The best opportunity for maintaining the work force in place in potential closure situations resembling the Strachan Avenue case is to obtain input into the closure decision before it is finalized." It was little consolation for 146 Inglis workers over the age of 55, or for the 57 percent with more than 15 years seniority. It was also unrealistic advice for one of the North American unions, which, as a group, almost never enjoyed that level of consultation with employers.

The Last Work Day

No one is ever prepared for the last day. Little can compare to the emotion of watching people who have worked side-by-side for more than twenty years exchange phone numbers. Men and women hugged, laughed, took each others' pho-

The Inglis plant was imposing in its size. The old central prison is seen between two production buildings.

tograph. At 11 a.m. the tow-motor operators drove their fork-lifts in a convoy through the plant. Horns beeping, motors revving, it was a wordless salute to their coworkers of many years.

As the last chassis of the full-size Inglis washer came down the line, someone had the idea to take a black marker and sign this collective creation. Others followed, and perhaps nothing else better reflected the economic contradiction faced by those who cannot hold on to the means of production.

Most of the Inglis workers had something to say on this final day. Dave Parker made no attempt to hide his emotions.

You've probably got friends of your own where you say, 'Well, let's make plans and we'll see each other,' and you may not see them for a year or years or ever again for

that matter. People get caught up in their own lives and in their own jobs again, and you just continue on in life. I would like to think that we would stay close, but once this plant closes down, they'll go get their jobs, and I'll go get my job. Some of the people in this plant, socially, they've seen people every day, probably more so than they've seen their wives and families for 30, 35, 40 years. They're not going to see those people any longer, and it's going to be a social shock to them. I would love to stay here, not because I'd love to work with Inglis, but because I could be around the people I've been with for fourteen years, and I wouldn't have to worry about phoning them once a week or once a month, or seeing them once a year as friends, because I would see them every day.

As the final washer makes its way down the line, it is signed by many of the workers.

Other comments and feelings were captured randomly. In general, outsiders had to be impressed with how Inglis workers were responding to this terrible uprooting. What other choice did they have?

I've been here two years and seven months. Today's the last day. Tomorrow morning, I'll be staying home and thinking about my new career.

Tomorrow is going to be kind of a sad day. Imagine waking up and not coming to work. It's totally different. It's a sad day.

What will I do tomorrow? I have no idea. It hasn't sunk in yet. Maybe in a week or so it'll sink in. I mean, I've been here sixteen years, right. Sixteen years is a long time.

I'm sad because this company is closing down. I will always remember [it] when I want to see my friends. I will always remember [it] when I say why I can't see anybody here. There's a sad story.

First thing I'm going to do is lay down and get a good sleep. I'm tired. And then after that, I don't know. I don't know what I'm going to do after that. Lick my wounds like an old dog. Life must move on. I spent twenty-two years here. I'm going to miss everybody. We have a very close family tie. It's real good and I'm going to miss them. It's not going to be bad today, but tomorrow I think we're going to have the shocks. People are going to feel it then.

I'm coming tomorrow morning to fill out

the form for the unemployment insurance, and after that — after fourteen years working here — I'm looking for a job. I don't know how much luck I'll have to get a job.

The worst part is we got to start over. No matter who you go to work for, you're going to end up working a year, then you only get a week [vacation]. I'm up to three weeks. Another six months, I would have my four weeks. But you got to start over. At the bottom of the line. Go through all the bullshit again. Same ordeal.

I've been here for sixteen years so that's a lot of lunches. My favourite lunch is what I'm eating now. Bologna and hot mustard. And of course, I enjoy the bologna that we spread around this place when we can. There's 600 people here. When I came here 16 years ago, there were 1,000 people worked here. When you think about 600 people being unemployed here, the spin-off will be another 1,000 people. Because there's people that supply us with parts. So it's going to have a rippling effect. And when you consider all the different nationalities and different kinds of people here, we have a pretty wonderful relationship as a group of people. It's a very sad day for me. I'm going to miss the camaraderie and miss a lot of people, and a lot of people we'll probably never see again. It's very, very sad. I wish it wasn't happening, but it is.

Other workers recognized the broader economic context within which they were players in a tragic drama. For a great many people, and not just for those who worked there, it would be hard to imagine the industrial landscape of Toronto without Inglis. There is scarcely a Canadian household that doesn't boast at least one Inglis appliance. There are thousands of Canadians whose aunt, cousin, mother, or brother-in-law worked at Inglis. And yet this plant closed. Anger was often directed at the then prime minister, Brian Mulroney.

A lot of people my age are making decisions they shouldn't have to be making. We were looking forward to our retirement and now the whole world is upset. I worked here 37 years. For 20 years they made no profits. For 17 years, they're making profits and

now they're closing. It's not logical. Big corporations. Thanks, Mr. Mulroney. God bless you, you son-of-a-bitch.

Tomorrow I find another plant to work in and shut it down. It's my hobby. I been in three plants that shut down.

We can laugh and joke, just to keep our strength up because all of us are feeling it inside. My wife is out of work too, because of all of this change — free trade stuff. She used to work downtown at a clothing place and they closed up. They move all their equipment. But what they do is get another factory, make the things there and ship it. That's cheaper. They lay off all the folks. Both of us are out of work.

At noon on this final day, the assembly line stopped. Inglis employees were ushered into an unused section of the plant where coffee and donuts waited. It was appropriate that such a space was found for the last get-together. The power of the union was tied to the physical structure of the plant on Strachan Avenue. Modern factories usually are built on one floor, with few walls, no windows, and a completely open design. The Strachan Avenue plant, by contrast, was full of hidden corners outside of sight lines. Workers could speed-up and stockpile components in order to save up time for union activity. There was always an unobserved storage area where shop stewards could have a word with other workers. This was clearly a factory that belonged to the people who worked there.

Plant manager Ernie Schritt, who had started as a production worker at Inglis, was clearly distressed. He announced that all production goals had been met and bonuses would be paid.

We did get an award for safety and part of that money was used for part of the gift — the memento. It's a little deck of playing cards and it says 'Safety Challenge '89' and there on the face of the card, it's a picture of the plant. It's just a memento. Take it in the right vein.

I hear a lot of talk about the middle-age people are going to have a tough time. It's going to be tough, but at the same time, don't sell yourself short. You people, you know what's happened here. You've done it

Harold Renner and Marg Harrison say goodbye during the final gathering in the plant.

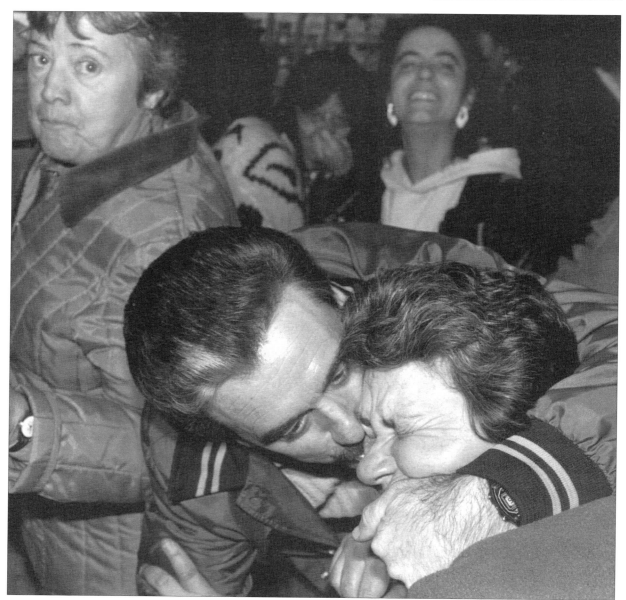

A final goodbye

and you've done such a fantastic job, and you can do the same again in a new start.

Mike Hersh spoke to his union sisters and brothers:

It's very difficult for all of us. This place was much more important than just washing machines, was much more important than just losing a job. We're losing friends. This is a family. We are a family here and I think everybody feels that way. Like a family, we fight. We hate like a family, we love like a family. To tell you the truth, I'm not going to miss the plant. I'm going to miss all of you. I want to say, it was an honour serving you as a unionist.

Leo Gerard was unable to get to the Strachan Avenue plant that day because of pressing commitments. But that didn't stop him from thinking about the events. He knew that what was happening should not have been.

Solidarity sort of pervaded everywhere, and I think it was the sense of solidarity that made the plant work. If there wasn't that sense of solidarity, the place would have just crumbled down and that's why I say that it's an event in Toronto's life that shouldn't be happening. Because with any kind of commitment, anything that went on in the plant could have been even a bigger money-maker. With all the studies, its labour costs in an operation like that are a small percentage of the costs compared to capital investment and raw material. It's the kind of thing that with some legislation and government support — and I don't necessarily mean by way of money, but government support by way of accountability — should never have happened.

What happened to workers at Inglis paralleled the rise and plateau of working-class power in Toronto. Explanations and analysis of this development would go far beyond the bounds of this history. However, as the city divested itself more and more of industry within its borders, the working class also moved into surrounding areas. Neighbourhoods where the lunch bucket was once a common sight now are home to cappucino bars and couples with nannies. It is unlikely that Toronto's working class could in these times bring the city to its knees with a strike.

Finally, the Inglis closure may have to be viewed as part of the natural evolution of business, the rise and decline of an industrial establishment. Workers' jobs are the evident cost of doing business. Who will remember the thousands of workers on Strachan Avenue once the land has been sold and transformed into something other than a factory? Who will acknowledge that this was a place where things were made?

And so, the story of Inglis stands as a lament, not just to one factory, but to what the Canadian economy might have been.

Notes

These notes document the sources consulted in the research for this book. Instead of using note numbers, the authors have provided citations by page number and concluding phrase. The initial page references refer to pages in this book while the words in square brackets correspond to the ends of sentences on those pages. Please note NAC and CTA stand for the National Archives of Canada and the City of Toronto Archives, respectively.

Introduction

Page 9. [work collaboration.] See Susan Meurer, David Sobel, and David Wolfe, "Challenging Technology's Myths: A Report on the Impact of Technological Change in Secondary Manufacturing in Metropolitan Toronto." Labour Council of Metropolitan Toronto, 1987.

Chapter I

Page 16. [1859.] *Guelph Daily Mercury,* 9 October 1886; [the river.] Leo Johnson, *History of Guelph,* Guelph Historical Society, 1977, p. 206; [to Sarnia."] *Guelph Herald,* 22 May 1878.

Page 17. [forging equipment.] City of Toronto Archives, SC 297, Inglis Corporate Collection, box 254, Machine Shop Contracts 1881-1892; [Toronto Reformatory.] *Guelph Herald,* 20 November 1879; [the 1870s.]. 1871 Census of Canada Industrial Schedules, *Globe,* 22 November 1882.

Page 18. [every way"] *Guelph Herald,* 20 November 1879; [would locate.] *Globe,* 22 November 1882; [work elsewhere."] *Toronto World,* 1 October 1882; [Car Foundry.] *Toronto News,* 7 November 1881; [feet long.] City of Toronto Assessment Rolls, 1886.

Page 21. [the rear] Private reminiscence by Clifford Lindsey, n.d., shared with authors; [and Strachan.] E. C. Guillet, *Pioneer Inns and Taverns,* Toronto 1954; City of Toronto Assessment Rolls and correspondence with Toronto Historical Board, 8 May 1992.

Page 22. [throughout the city.] G. Kealey and B. Palmer, *Dreaming of What Might Be.* Toronto: New Hogtown Press, 1987, p. 100; [take in."] G. Kealey, *Toronto Workers Respond to Industrial Capitalism 1897-1892,* Toronto: University of Toronto Press, 1980, p. 71. [an administrator.] *Guelph Herald,* 22 May 1878.

Page 24. [factory inspectors] E. Tucker, "Making the Workplace `Safe' in Capitalism: The Enforcement of Factory Legislation in Nineteenth-Century Ontario," in *Labour/LeTravail,* Spring 1988, p. 45; [were killed.] Ontario Sessional Papers, Factory Inspectors' Reports, 1891, 1901, 1912; [the province.] G. Kealey, "The Honest Working Man," and "Workers' Control: The Experience of Toronto Skilled Workers, 1860-1892," *Labour/LeTravail,* 1976, p. 44.

Page 25 [funereal pillow,"] *Globe,* 6 April 1899; [to work.] *Machinists' Monthly Journal,* vol.19, 1907, p. 763; [was reached.]. *IAM Monthly Journal,* August 1900, p. 444.

Page 26. [deem proper."] *Labour Gazette* III 1902-03,

pp. 375-76. In addition, A.P. Inglis, William's younger brother worked for a number of U.S. steel companies; [was expanded.] "A Survey of John Inglis Co. Limited, and its predecessor, The John Inglis Company Limited, founded 1860," Inglis History Collection, unpublished; [7,000 strikes."] *Toronto World,* July 1903; [nine hours."] as cited in G. Kealey, *Toronto Workers Respond to Industrial Capitalism 1867-1892,* p. 74; [their power.] the insights benefit from P. Bischoff, "Tensions et solidarité: la formation des traditions syndicales chez les mouleurs de Montréal, Hamilton et Toronto, 1851 à 1893," unpublished PhD thesis, Université de Montréal, Department of History; [production buildings.] CTA, Building permits collection, no. 553, 27 May 1904.

Page 27 [a week.] NAC, RG 27, Strike and Lock-out File, 1907, Microfilm T-2684; [open shop."] Ibid.

Page 28. Details about Harry Goudy from a telephone interview with his nephew, Don Goudy, 15 November 1991; details about Inglis workers from the 1880s: City of Toronto Assessment Rolls, 1882-1885, St. George's Ward, *Might's Directories,* 1882-1886, *Iron Moulders International Union Journal,* 1881.

Page 29. [a funeral."] Ibid., p. 999; [will despise."] ibid.; [nearly tripled.] City of Toronto Assessment Rolls, 1909; [they ask.] RG 27, Strike and Lock-out File, 1913, Microfilm T-2690, vol.302, strike no. 82, 9 June 1913; [in,"reserves."] MG27, III, B. 11, vol.91 file Bren guns exhibits. [Toronto brothers.] RG 27, Strike and Lock-out File, 1913, Microfilm T-2690, vol.302, strike no. 82; [industrial unionism] Wayne Roberts,"Toronto Metal Workers and the Second Industrial Revolution," *Labour/Le Travail,* Autumn, 1980 p. 71. Only the moulders did not endorse it; [foundry equipment] NAC, Flavelle papers, MG30 A16, vol. 5, File 47 and NAC, RG 14 D-2 Sessional Papers, Reports of the War Purchasing Commission, vol.137, #149 of 1918.

Page 30. [of Toronto."] NAC MG 30 A 16, No. 64, Fair wages; [unpatriotic action."] ibid.; [causing unrest.] ibid.

Page 31. [and employees . . ."] M. Siemiatycki, "Munitions and Labour Militancy: The 1916 Hamilton Machinists' Strike," in *Labour/Le Travail,* 1978, pp. 131-151 and MG30 A 16, vol.56, Printed material 1915-1916.

Page 32 [be over.] Strike and Lock-out File, vol. 366, p. 766.

Page 33. [great victory.] NAC Flavelle papers, MG 30 A

16, vol.18, File 181; [in 1913.] City of Toronto building permits, and MG27 III B. 11, vol.91 file Bren guns exhibits; [was signed.] *Toronto Star,* 9 November 1918; [Inglis Company."] *Mail & Empire,* 2 May 1919; [strikers' demands."] RG 27 Strike and Lock-out File, 1919, vol.312, p. 184, *Mail and Empire* 3 May 1919; Greg Kealey, "Canadian Labour Revolt," p. 27, in *Labour/Le Travail* vol.13, 1984.

Page 34 [16 June.] Greg Kealey, "Canadian Labour Revolt," p. 28, in *Labour/Le Travail* vol.13 1984; [that summer.] ibid.

Page 35 [a manager] See for example *Powerhouse,* January 1912; [an industrialist.] *Toronto Star*, 9 November 1918.

Page 36. [rising anxiety] MG27 III B. 11, vol. 91 file Bren guns exhibits and letters requesting work NAC, MG27 III B-11 vol. 89; [years, died.] *Powerhouse,* March 1935, p. 92; [himself died.] *Toronto Telegram,* 19 November 1935.

Chapter 2

Page 37. [Bren guns.] These details were revealed during the Bren gun inquiry testimony. See NAC, MG 27 III B11 vol. 11 Bren Gun, production data, Thomas Fisher Rare Book Library, John de Navarre, History of Department of Munitions and Supply. E. Cloutier, *Canada in the Second World War,* Ottawa. 1950, p. 197; 112 NAC, MG 27 III B11 vol.89 Bren Gun, J. L. Ralston.

Page 38. [Allied effort.] NAC MG 27 III B11 vol. 89 Bren Gun, J. L. Ralston; ibid.

Page 39. [to $20,000.] NAC RG 24 vol. 160, exhibit 244; [the Company.] NAC, RG24 vol. 160 exhibit 244.

Page 40 [in Canada.] Report of the Royal Commission on the Bren Machine Gun Contract, Ottawa, 1939, p. 8.; [more weapons] *Evening Telegram,* 10 January 1941; [the time.] *Kitchener Record,* 11 January 1941; [concerned too.] Interview, Robert Bruce, 9 November 1989.

Page 43. [male domains.] See Marjorie Griffin Cohen, "Women's Work," *Markets and Economic Development in Nineteenth-Century Ontario,* Toronto: University of Toronto Press, 1988, Tables 21-25, appendix pp. 167-170. The absence of women at Inglis during WWI may be explained by the continued strength of the Machinists Union at this plant. In addition, while the company made shells, it also made more complex foundry and machining equipment which were installed in other factories. The opportunity for skilled metal work at Inglis was not representative of shell work. This may in turn have strengthened the union's hand over the issue of hiring women; [for them.] see for example CTA, SC297, box 17, "Employment 1942-43"; box from CTA, SC297, box 36 *The Shotgun,* 24 October 1942.

Page 44. [still on"] Interview, Wilbert Finch, 12 May 1989; [rotating.] Interview, Bert Bowler, 10 November 1989.

Page 45. [wasn't exaggerating.] *Globe and Mail,* 19 February 1941. [male help] NAC, RG27 vol. 103 424. 01:280 vol. 1, memorandum dated 5 September 1939.

Page 46. [at present,"], Ibid., memorandum dated 24 October 1939. [female labour.] ibid., memorandum dated 23 November 1939; [seeking work.] ibid, memorandum dated 25 November 1939.

Page 48 [war is.] Interview, Kay Drybrough Bradley, 14 August 1989.

Page 51 [that way.] ibid. [right away.] NAC, RG27 vol. 103 424. 01:280 vol. 2, memorandum dated 28 May 1940; [this company.] NAC, RG27 vol. 103 424. 01:280 vol. 2, memoranda dated 16 July 1940, 28 May 1940.

Page 52. [technician work.]. Ruth Roach Pierson, *They're Still Women After All: The Second World War and Canadian Womenhood,* Toronto: McClelland and Stewart, 1986, p. 71.

Page 53 [very crowded.] Interview, Mary Spratt, 14 April 1989.

Page 55. [wage costs.] NAC, RG27 vol. 103 424. 01:280 vol. 2, memoranda dated 10 May 1941; [Inglis plant], ibid.

Page 57. Box. [every day.] NAC, RG 29 vol.980, File 388-8-60 pt. 5, Survey 17, December 1941; [in them] CTA, SC297, box 17, Employment 1942-43; [correct it.] CTA, SC297, box 17, Employment 1942-43, 5 March 1942; [proper district] Interview, Kay Drybrough Bradley, 14 August 1989; [month alone.] CTA, SC297, box 17, Employment 1942-43; [laughs too.] Interview, Bert Bowler, 10 November 1989. Bowler's impressions underline the concentration of women in a few departments. The overall wartime workforce at Inglis was never more than half female.

Page 60 [the total.] CTA, SC297, box 18, Mobilization and Defense, 1942-43.

Page 61 [rate paid.] CTA, SC297, box 16, Direct Labour, 1943; [an emergency] University of Toronto, Rare Books, J. E. Hahn, *For Action,* self-published, 1954, p. 161-2; [October 1944.] Ruth Roach Pierson, *They're Still Women After All: The Second World War and Canadian Womenhood,* Toronto: McClelland and Stewart, 1986, p. 61.

Page 64. [lead hands.] Interview, Erma Hughes, 25 July 1989.

Page 66 [this firm] NAC, RG27 vol. 103 424. 01:280 vol. 2, letter dated 19 November 1940; [the factory.] NAC, RG27 vol. 103 424. 01:280 vol.2, letter dated 2 December 1940; [and printing.] Based on an analysis of CTA, SC297, box 17, Employment, 1942-43; [her work.] CTA, SC297, box 24, Report — Girl's Club Attendance; [November 1942] CTA, SC297, box 16, letter dated 29 September 1942.

Page 68 [Master Plan] CTA, SC297, box 16; [particularly attractive.] CTA, SC297, box 21, Bert Trestail, 1942-44.

Page 70. [on Saturday.] NAC, RG28A, vol.122 3-C2-1-290, 24 August 1943.

Page 71. Box, CTA, SC297, box 16, memorandum dated 1 December 1943; [these programmes.] Details on this programme are in CTA, SC297, box 19, Music at Work, 1943.

Page 72. [is over...] NAC, RG 27 vol.103, 424:01:280 vol. 2 memorandum dated 7 December 1940; Despite such assurances, the changes to work organization and production technology during the war were not reversed with the Allied victory. These changes had a lasting impact on skilled labour at the point of production, weakening unions on the shop floor as they made significant gains in recognition and bargaining; [Inglis employees.] Interview, Roy and Elizabeth Bragg, 8 August 1989.

Page 73 [both cases] CTA, SC297, box 36; [Blonds!] These attempts at humour appeared in various issues of *The Shotgun,* CTA, SC297, box 36.

Page 74. Box, CTA, SC297, box 36.

Page 75 [bonus system.] CTA, SC297, box 17, Employment 1942-43; [white blouse.] CTA, SC297, box 63, Foreman's Policy Manual; [in 1943.] SC297, box 18, Mobilization and Defence, 1942-43; box, interview, June Pattison Lake, 7 August 1989.

Page 76. [at midnight.] Interview, Roy and Elizabeth Bragg, 8 August 1989; [on us] interview, Bragg.

Page 77. [super job.] ibid.; [steady at.] ibid; [we were.] Interview, Bert Bowler, 10 November 1989; [real character.] Interview, Marion Lindner, 20 September 1991.

Chapter 3

Page 78. [for labourers.] NAC, RG24 vol.160, exhibit 237; [industrial era.] NAC, RG 27 vol.103 424. 01:280, vol.1; [union activity.] NAC, RG 27 vol.103 424. 01:280, vol.1; letter dated 15 July 1939.

Page 79. [application forms.] NAC, MG 27 III B17 vol.90 letters dated 9 and 18 July 1938; [a union] Interview, Jock Carrol, 4 January 1994.

Page 80 [you performed.] Interview, Erma Hughes, 25 July 1989; [secret information] Access/CSIS 1025-9-9047 and numerous interviews; [seriously threatened.] See for example, CTA SC297, box 21 Union Agreement, Re: H. Wilson and R. O'Brien, 1942; [the IAM.] NAC, RG 27 vol.103 424. 01:280, vol.1; letter dated 15 July 1939; [the shopfloor.] NAC, RG 27 vol.103 424. 01:280, vol.1; letter dated 9 August 1939.

Page 83. [own choosing.] Ibid., letter dated 10 July 1939; [Inglis workers] NAC, MG 28 I 268 vol.4, C. H. Millard, Corresp., #4; [essential arms] NAC, RG 24, vol. 6301, HQ 46-73-3 vol.7, "Walter Camm"; [Camm's dismissal.] ibid.; [strictest confidence] ibid.

Page 84 [shown up], Interview, Jock Carrol, 4 January 1994; [encountered opposition] NAC, MG 28, I 268 vol.4; [in Canada] Irving Abella, *Nationalism, Communism and Canadian Labour,* University of Toronto Press, 1973, pp. 56-57; [SWOC's activities] ibid., p. 46; [political discrimination.] ibid., p. 58; [Canadian workers."] NAC, MG 28 I 268, vol.4, file 2; [Steel Workers' Organizing Committee] ibid.

Page 85. [No. 1 was.] NAC RG 27 vol.103 424. 01:280 vol.2, 14 June 1940.

Page 86. ["Unanimous [sic.] Employees,"] Ibid., 10 June 1940; [successful conclusion.] ibid., 25 June 1940.

Page 87 [the war] See for example a father writing to the company for details about the ship his son was serving on, CTA, SC297, box 17, H, Miscellaneous, 1941-43.

[Commercial Division] NAC, MG 28 I-191 vol.10 LL. 235 1943-44; [June 1941] NAC, MG 28 I 268 vol.4, SWOC corresp., #2; [subversive activity] NAC, RG 24, vol.2662 file HQS3680, September 1941; [intelligence officers] Access/CSIS 1025-9-9047.

Page 88. [the people] Interview, Jock Carrol; [Commercial Division] CTA SC297, box 21, Union Agreement CIO, General File, 1942-43, 10 September 1943; [machine shop] interview, Wilbert Finch, 12 May 1989; [similar request] CTA SC297, box 21, Union Agreement CIO, General File, 1942-43, 30 November 1942; [majority membership] ibid., 27 March 1943; [employees involved."] SC297 box 21, [of Labour.] CTA SC297, box 21, Union Agreement CIO, General File, 1942-43; [negotiate with] CTA SC297, box 21 Union Agreement CIO, General File, 1941-43, 19 December 1942.

Page 89. [out freezing] Interview, Eileen Tallman, 3 January 1994.

Page 90. [women employees] SC297, box 21, 28 October 1942; [organize them] interview, Tallman; [any means] interview, Spratt; [holding the bag] SC297 box 21, 9 November 1942; [important activists] interview, Carrol and SC297 box 21, passim.

Page 92. [of accuracy] All quotations, interview, Janet McMurray, Paul Pulk and Ruth Weir, 19 May 1992; [have called] SC297, box 21, Union Agreement Leaflets 1943, *The Production Worker,* 15 April 1943; [IAM] ibid.

Page 94. [their sleeves] Interview, McMurray, Pulk, Weir.

Page 96 [of America] All from informants' reports, SC297, box 21, General File 1942-43; [is true] SC297 box 21, Union Agreement CIO, General File, 1941-43, 1 December 1942.

Page 97. [these activities] SC297 box 21, Union Agreement CIO, General File, 1941-43, 5 January 1943; [never to return] interview, Carrol; [at Inglis] SC297, box 21, Union Agreement, Leaflets, *Inglis Steelworker,* 4 March 1943.

Page 98. [you and me] SC297, box 21, Union Agreement, Leaflets, *Inglis Steelworker,* 18 March 1943; [response too.] Interview, Bragg; [the polls] SC297, box 21, Union Agreement, Leaflets, *Inglis Production Worker,* 12 April 1943.

Page 99 [considerable planning] SC297, box 21, Union Agreement, General File, 1941-43, 29 March 1943; [to vote] SC297 box 21, Union Agreement, General File, 1941-43, 20 April 1943; [be there] interview, Bragg; [very often] interview, Tallman; [their feet] SC297, box 24, Reports, Labour Turnover, 1943; [trade unionist] Interview, McMurray, Pulk, Weir.

Page 100 [What happens then?] SC297, box 21, Union Agreement, Leaflets, 1943, *Inglis Steelworker,* 6 November 1942.

Chapter 4

Page 101. [the war.] *Canadian Women: A History,* Toronto, 1988, p. 306.

Page 102. [this time.] Pierson, p. 215; [much money] and following page, interview, Roy and Elizabeth Bragg,

8 August 1989; [1939-1944."] RG 28A, vol.13, industrial expansion.

Page 105. [wartime demand.] Ibid., p. 49; [in Canada.] ibid., p. 2; [of living.] ibid., p. 5; [invested originally] *Toronto Star*, 4 May 1950; [Products Division.] *Financial Post,* 14 December 1946.

Page 107. [tooling delay...] J. Hahn, *For Action*, self-published, p. 233; [lay offs.] *Globe & Mail,* 25 August 1945; [Inglis organization."] *The Story of Inglis*, n.d., self-published, p. 6.

Page 110 [family use."] ibid., pp. 48-9.

Page 112. [folks home.] Interview, Lynn Williams, 24 October 1989.

Page 113. [short cuts."] Interview, Paul Ryan, 4 May 1989; [up with.] Interview, David Hahn, 30 November 1992; [the States.] Interview, Frank McCuaig, 5 July 1989; [rust away."] Interview, John Fitzpatrick, 26 June 1989.

Page 114. [an attraction."] Interview, Robert Higgins, 27 June 1989; [on Whirlpool], interview, David Hahn.

Page 115. [were retired] Interview, Karen Mills, 24 October 1989; [they did.] ibid.; [own devices.] *Scope*, May 1958, Inglis History Project.

Page 116. [most of it.] Interview, Bonnie Smith, 31 October 1989; [him back.] Interview, Bonnie Smith.

Chapter 5

Page 121. [an understanding.] Interview, Jack Hill, 26 October 1989; [in things.] interview, Bill Townley, 19 April 1989.

Page 122. [the washroom.] Interview, Bert Bowler, 10 November 1989; [about it.] Interview, Mary Spratt, 19 April 1989; [see happening.] interview, Bill Townley.

Page 125. [brought up.] Interview, Paul Ryan.

Page 127. [more comfortable.] Interview, Bill Townley; [got killed] interview, Bert Bowler; [that hole] interview, Syl MacNeil, 19 April 1989; [we said no] Interview, Mary Spratt.

Page 128 [Santa Claus."] Interview, Paul Ryan; [type of thing] interview, Jack Hill; [very much for], ibid.

Page 129. [talk to him.] Box, interview, Jack Hill.

Page 130. [paging system.] Interview, Syl MacNeil; [stay out.] ibid.

Page 131. [about us] Interview, Jack Hill; [take my time.] interview, Bert Bowler.

Page 134. [his fault] Interview, Paul Ryan; [back to work.] interview, Frank McCuaig, 5 July 1989; [as saying] *Globe and Mail,* 26 May 1954.

Page 136. [reasonable control.] Inglis History Project, local union 2900 records, 1959 file, letter dated 19 November 1959; [is represented] interview, Frank McCuaig; [quite well-attended] interview, Jack Hill; [extremely "democratic."] Inglis History Project, union records, File 2, 1959, unsigned, undated ca. 1958.

Page 138. [Always had been.] Interview, Frank McCuaig.

Page 139. [important tool.] Interview, Paul Ryan; [lose the ship.] interview, David Hahn; [of this place] interview, Syl MacNeil.

Page 141. [that way] Interview, Jack Hill; [can't kill it."]

interview, Syl MacNeil; [next day.] interview, John Fitzpatrick; [capital expenditure."] Inglis History Project, Local Union 2900 Records, 1966 File, Statement to Shareholders, 25 February 1966.

Page 142. [hurt them] Interview, Syl MacNeil; [was great] interview, Robert Sim, 20 October 1989.

Page 143. Box, interview, Muriel Monteal, 19 January 1990.

Page 144. [a good time] Ibid; [Friday nights.] interview, Bonnie Smith, 31 October 1989.

Page 146 [U.S. interests] CTA, Inglis History Project, "History of Inglis Limited (formerly John Inglis Co. Limited)," (condensed) unpublished, D.H. Hobbs, 15 February 1980; [strike at all] Interview, John Fitzpatrick; [and Mail.] *Globe and Mail,* 8 July 1974; [wallop them."] ibid.; [negotiation bulletin] CTA, Inglis History Project, union records, file 1974, negotiation bulletin no. 1.

Page 147 Box. [you've gone."] Interview, Robert Sim.

Page 148. [North America.] Interview, Mike Hersh, 9 May 1989; [them out.] ibid.

Page 149. [change it] Interview, Bev Brown, 5 July 1989.

Page 150 [were doing] Interview, Mike Hersh.

Page 151. [against Whirlpool.] Ibid.

Page 152. [suck-holing.] Ibid.

Page 153. [that place] Ibid.

Page 154. [mean everything.] Ibid.; [something terrible."] ibid.; [no limit.] ibid.

Chapter 6

Page 159. [working-class money] Interview, Paul Ryan, 4 May 1989; [ten years],"United Steelworkers of America: Inglis Plant Closure Study" (final draft report), KPMG Peat Marwick, 13 December 1989, p. 7;

Page 160. [decision] Interview, John Utter, 8 May 1991.

Page 162. [difficult period] CTA, Inglis History Project Collection, 1990 File; Interview, Ryan.

Page 165. [do that] interview, Leo Gerard, 6 November 1989.

Page 166. [closure package] Interview, Gerard.

Page 167. [day worked] Inglis History Project, 1990 File, "Closure Agreement."

Page 168. [those attending] ibid.

Page 171. [our local] Interview, Bev Brown, 5 July 1989; [being done] interview, Brown; [a Steelworker] interview, Brown.

Page 172. [is hope] Interview, Peter Chahanian, 3 November 1989; [a farce] interview, Dave Parker, 19 October 1989.

Page 173. [safe ways] Interview, Lynn Williams, 24 October 1989.

Page 174 [local management] nterview, Mike Hersh, 9 May 1989.

Page 179. [in it] Interview, Utter; [is finalized], " United Steelworkers of America: Inglis Plant Closure Study," p. 26.

Page 181-82. All quotations, last day interviews, 29 November 1989.

Page 185. [new start] Inglis History Project Collection, closure ceremony recording, 29 November 1989; [have happened] interview, Gerard.

Credits

Front Matter
Inglis History Project. David Smiley, photographer.

Foreword
Page 5 Inglis History Project. Susan Meurer, photographer

Introduction
Page 8 (top) Inglis History Project. David Smiley, photographer; (bottom) Inglis History Project. David Smiley, photographer; Page 9 Inglis History Project. David Smiley, photographer; Page 10 (top) Inglis History Project. David Smiley, photographer; Page 11 Thomas Fisher Rare Book Library, University of Toronto, *Powerhouse,* 5 July 1919; Page 12 Inglis History Project. David Smiley, photographer; Page 13 Inglis History Project. David Smiley, photographer; Page 14 Inglis History Project. David Smiley, photographer

Chapter 1
Page 15 Archives of Ontario, photography collection, ACC 2719, S12207. Wellington Foundry. Photographer unknown.; Page 16 (top left) With permission, City of Toronto Archives, Toronto Board of Trade, Souvenir Issue 1893; (bottom left) McCord Museum of Canadian History, Notman Photographic Archives, 67, 659-I; (right) National Archives of Canada, J.D. Barnett Papers, MG30 B86, vol.25, Catalogue 5; Page 17 National Library of Canada, *Machinists' Monthly Journal, 1903;* Page 18 City of Toronto Archives, Fire Atlas collection. Reproduced with the permission of Insurers' Advisory Organization (1989) Inc., who are the copyright holders of these maps; Page 19 City of Toronto Archives, SC 297, photo box 22. Photographer unknown; Page 20 City of Toronto Archives, Inglis Corporate collection, SC 297, photo box 28. Photographer unknown; Page 21 Inglis History Project. David Smiley, photographer; Page 22 City of Toronto Archives, SC 297, photo box 22. Photographer unknown; Page 23 City of Toronto Archives, SC 297, photo box 28. Photographer unknown; Page 24 City of Toronto Archives, SC 297, photo box 22. Photographer unknown; Page 25 National Archives of Canada Library, *Machinists' Monthly Journal,* 1900; Page 27 (top) City of Toronto Archives, SC 297, photo box 28. Photographer unknown; (right) *Toronto World,* 23 July 1903; Page 28 Inglis photo album. Courtesy David Hahn; Page 31 City of Toronto Archives, SC 297; Page 32 City of Toronto Archives, Department of Public Works, RG 8 68-56; Page 34 TTC collection, No. 11039. Metro Archives; Page 35 CNE Archives, Bio collection.

Chapter 2
Page 37 Inglis photo album. Courtesy David Hahn; Page 38 City of Toronto Archives, SC 266, *Globe and Mail* collection; Page 39 (top) Inglis History Project; (bottom) City of Toronto Archives, SC297, box 69; Page 41 City of Toronto Archives, SC 266, *Globe and Mail* collection. # 65145; Page 42 City of Toronto Archives, SC297, box 69; Page 43 City of Toronto Archives, SC297, box 36, *The Shotgun,* 24 October 1942; Page 45 City of Toronto Archives, SC297, box 69; Page 46 Courtesy Wilbert Finch; Page 47 (top) City of Toronto Archives, *Globe and Mail* collection #81846-N; (bottom) City of Toronto Archives, SC266, *Globe and Mail* collection. # 86425; Page 48 Courtesy David Hahn; Page 49 (top) City of Toronto Archives, SC297, box 69; (bottom) SC266 *Globe and Mail* collection; Page 50 City of Toronto Archives, SC 297, photo box 21; Page 51 City of Toronto Archives, SC297, photo box 21; Page 52 City of Toronto Archives, SC297, box 69; Page 53 City of Toronto Archives, *Globe and Mail* collection #83328-N,; Page 54 Inglis photo album. Courtesy David Hahn; Page 55 Courtesy Wilbert Finch; Page 56 (top) City of Toronto Archives, SC297, box 69; (bottom) City of Toronto Archives, SC 266, *Globe and Mail* collection, # 71013-S; Page 58 (top) City of Toronto Archives, SC297, photo box 21; (bottom) Inglis History Project; Page 59 City of Toronto Archives, SC 297, photo box 46; Page 60 (top) Inglis History Project; (bottom) Inglis History Project. Susan Meurer, photographer; Page 61 Inglis History Project. Susan Meurer, photographer; Page 62 Inglis History Project. Susan Meurer, photographer; Page 63 City of Toronto Archives, SC266, *Globe and Mail* collection #83302-N; Page 64 City of Toronto Archives, SC 297, box 69; Page 65 (top) National Archives of Canada. PA 169532. Photographer, A. Armstrong. (bottom) City of Toronto Archives, SC297, box 69; Page 67 City of Toronto Archives, *Globe and Mail* collection #S82225-7; Page 68 City of Toronto Archives, SC297, box 69; Page 70 City of Toronto Archives, SC297, box 69; Page 71 Inglis History Project; Page 72 City of Toronto Archives, SC 297, box 69; Page 73 City of Toronto Archives, SC266, *Globe and Mail* collection. # 86748-N; Page 74 City of Toronto Archives, SC 297, photo box 21. Alexandra Studio; Page 75 Courtesy June Pattison; Page 76 Inglis History Project. Susan Meurer, photographer

Chapter 3
Page 78 City of Toronto Archives, SC297, box 21; Page 79 City of Toronto Archives, SC297, box 21; Page 81 City of Toronto Archives, SC297, box 21; Page 82 City of Toronto Archives, SC297, box 21; Page 85 City of Toronto Archives, SC297, box 21; Page 86 Courtesy Ruth McCarthy; Page 89 City of Toronto Archives, SC297, box 21; Page 91 (top) City of Toronto Archives, SC297, box 21; (bottom) City of Toronto Archives, SC297, box 21; Page 92 City of Toronto Archives, SC297, box 21. First appeared in *Manitoba Commonwealth,* circa 1942. Courtesy Harry Gutkin; Page 93 City of Toronto Archives, SC297, box 21; Page 94 City of Toronto Archives, *Globe and Mail* collection; G&M84536; Page 95 City of Toronto Archives, *Globe*

and Mail collection, (top) G&M 84534; (bottom) G&M 84533; Page 96 City of Toronto Archives, *Globe and Mail* collection, G&M 84537; Page 97 City of Toronto Archives, SC297, box 21; Page 98 City of Toronto Archives, SC297, box 21; Page 99 City of Toronto Archives, SC297, box 21; Page 100 Courtesy Eileen Tallman Sufrin.

Chapter 4

Page 101 City of Toronto Archives, SC 297, photo box 24. Photographer, Richard Matthews; Page 103 City of Toronto Archives, SC 297, photo box 24. Photographer, Richard Matthews; Page 104 Inglis History Project; Page 106 Inglis scrapbooks, vol. II. Courtesy David Hahn; Page 107 (top) Inglis scrapbooks, vol. II. Courtesy David Hahn; (bottom) Inglis scrapbooks, vol. II. Courtesy David Hahn; Page 108 (top) Inglis History Project. *The Story of Inglis,* p. 1; (bottom) Inglis History Project. *The Story of Inglis,* p. 48-49; Page 109 City of Toronto Archives, SC 297 box 22; Page 110 Inglis scrapbooks, vol. II. Courtesy David Hahn; Page 111 City of Toronto Archives, SC 297, box 46; Page 112 Inglis History Project. Susan Meurer, photographer; Page 114 City of Toronto Archives, SC 297, box 47; Page 116 Inglis History Project. Susan Meurer, photographer

Chapter 5

Page 117 *Telegram* collection, York University. Photographer, Don Grant; Page 118 Inglis History Project. Photographer unknown; Page 119 Inglis History Project. Photographer Pringle and Booth; Page 120 (top) Inglis History Project. Photographer Peel Photography; (bottom) Inglis History Project. Peel Photography, Brampton; Page 121 Inglis History Project. Susan Meurer, photographer; Page 122 Inglis History Project. Photographer Pringle and Booth; Page 123 (top) Inglis History Project; (bottom) Inglis History Project. David Smiley, photographer; Page 124 Inglis History Project. Photographer, Advertising and Commercial photographers; Page 125 Inglis History Project. Courtesy Stanley Borins; Page 126 Photographer, David Smiley; Page 129 Courtesy Dave Parker; Page 130 *Steel Labor,* August 1950. Courtesy: USWA National Office Library; Page 132 Inglis History Project; Page 133 Inglis History Project. Photographer, Advertising and Commercial photographers; Page 135 (top) Inglis History Project. With permission, Julien Lebourdais, photographer; (bottom) Inglis History Project. Courtesy of Frank McCuaig; Page 137 Inglis History Project. Photographer, Advertising and Commercial photographers; Page 138 City of Toronto Archives, SC 297, box 223; Page 139 Inglis History Project. Local 2900 records, 1961; Page 140 *Steel Labor*, June 1974; Page 143 (left) Inglis History Project. Susan Meurer, photographer; (right) Inglis History Project, David Smiley; Page 144 Inglis History Project. Photographer, Associated photographers; Page 145 Inglis History Project. Local 2900 records, 1964; Page 146 Inglis History Project; Page 147 (top) Inglis History Project. Susan Meurer, photographer; (bottom) Inglis History Project; Page 149 (top) Inglis History Project. Local 2900 records, 1974; (bottom) With permission, Brian Willer, photographer; Pages 150–53 Inglis History Project. Photographer unknown; Page 154 Inglis History Project; Page 155 (top) Inglis History Project; (bottom) Inglis History Project. Nancy Farmer, photographer; Page 156 (right and left) Inglis History Project

Chapter 6

Page 157 Inglis History Project, David Smiley photographer; Page 158 Inglis History Project. David Smiley photographer; Page 160 Inglis History Project. David Smiley, photographer; Page 161 (top) Inglis History Project. David Smiley, photographer; (bottom) Inglis History Project. Susan Meurer, photographer; Page 163 Inglis History Project. Peter MacCallum, photographer; Page 164 (top right) Inglis History Project. Susan Meurer, photographer; (bottom) Inglis History Project. Susan Meurer, photographer; Page 165 Inglis History Project. Susan Meurer, photographer; Page 166 (top) Inglis History Project. David Smiley, photographer; (bottom) Inglis History Project. Courtesy Mike Constable; Page 167 Inglis History Project. Peter MacCallum, photographer; Page 169 (top and bottom) Inglis History Project. David Smiley, photographer; (bottom); Page 170 Inglis History Project. Peter MacCallum, photographer; Page 173 (top) Inglis History Project. David Smiley, photographer; (bottom) Inglis History Project, David Smiley, photographer; Page 175 Inglis History Project. Peter MacCallum, photographer; Page 176 Inglis History Project. David Smiley, photographer; Page 177 Inglis History Project. Peter MacCallum, photographer; Page 178 Inglis History Project. Peter MacCallum, photographer; Page 180 Inglis History Project. Peter MacCallum, photographer; Page 181 Inglis History Project. David Smiley, photographer; Page 183 Inglis History Project. David Smiley, photographer; Page 184 Inglis History Project. David Smiley, photographer